Minds Online

Minds Online

TEACHING EFFECTIVELY WITH TECHNOLOGY

MICHELLE D. MILLER

 Harvard University Press

Cambridge, Massachusetts
London, England

First Harvard University Press paperback edition, 2016
First Printing

Library of Congress Cataloging-in-Publication Data
Miller, Michelle D., 1968–
  Minds online : teaching effectively with technology / Michelle D. Miller.
    pages cm.
  Includes bibliographical references and index.
  ISBN 978-0-674-36824-8 (cloth : alk. paper)
  ISBN 978-0-674-66002-1 (pbk.)
  1. Computer-assisted instruction. 2. Internet in education.
3. Educational technology. 4. Teaching—Computer network
resources. 5. Learning, Psychology of. I. Title.
  LB1028.5.M548 2014
    371.33—dc23   2014006755

For my father,
Thomas Clay Miller, Jr.

Contents

Preface

In 1978, most kids had never seen a computer up close, let alone been allowed to touch one. But stashed away in a back room of my elementary school there was a PLATO terminal, a device designed to present interactive tutorials on mathematics, typing, foreign languages, and the like. We students each got just one hour a week of PLATO time, and for figuring out how to get started or work through the lessons, we were pretty much on our own. Even so, for me, a ten-year-old seriously bogged down in fifth-grade math, this was a novel and utterly engaging experience. I credit it with setting me on a life-long path of curiosity about minds, machines, and learning.

PLATO's 16-by-16 touch-screen grid enabled direct and intuitive communication between user and computer, and it was able to show not just text but also blocky, single-color graphics. It spent each of my one-hour sessions patiently presenting round after round of a pet-store-themed game designed to teach fractions. PLATO was even capable of flashing a little wit, admonishing "Shelly, you have a fish on your finger!" when I failed to drag and drop exactly one-third of my goldfish inventory into a customer's order.

Luck and an unusually well-funded school district made me one of the few people of my generation who experienced cutting-edge instructional technology from the student perspective. Now nearly four decades later, you'd be hard pressed to find an educational institution that doesn't use instructional technology in one form or another. Within higher education, the impact has been especially dramatic. Few issues of publications such as the *Chronicle of Higher Education*, or *Change: The Magazine of Higher Learning*, go by without a new article on teaching and learning with technology, and there are entire scholarly journals and international organizations dedicated to the topic (*EDUCAUSE*, the Sloan Consortium, and the *Journal of Online Learning and Teaching*, to name a few).

Centers supporting online learning are an increasingly common part of university infrastructure, as are specialized learning management systems such as Moodle, Canvas, and Blackboard. Although traditional paper textbooks still dominate the market for primary required course materials, computer-based auxiliaries have multiplied across the disciplines, offering everything from self-testing systems that adapt to the needs of individual learners to animated lab rats in simulated Skinner boxes.

With this explosion of interest in technology came serious inquiry about the most effective practices for online teaching and learning, including the call for a more substantial theoretical rationale for how we design online learning activities and learning environments. This call coincided nicely with the rise of cognitive psychology, a subdiscipline focused on mental processes such as memory, language, and reasoning, which had been around since the 1950s but entered the wider academic and popular consciousness much later.

On the one hand, this new focus on cognition could potentially create the powerful theoretical frameworks and novel insights needed to move forward in the design of new learning technologies. But it also creates a new set of pitfalls stemming from the difficulty of interpreting and applying technical research within cognitive and brain sciences, particularly for nonspecialists. These pitfalls are no reflection on anyone's good intentions or intellectual acumen; rather, they are the unfortunate side effect of the ways in which cognitive researchers conduct and disseminate their work. Cognitive and brain sciences have undergone a phase of rapid development that makes it hard even for those of us within the field to stay on top of current thinking.

Memory research is a case in point. Our understanding of how people remember information has progressed well beyond the "three box" theory focusing on distinct sensory, short-term, and long-term memory components. And yet, you still find scattered references to this concept, including within some contemporary writing about teaching and learning. The last twenty years, in particular, have given rise to a proliferation of new theories and thousands of empirical findings pertaining to memory, making it difficult to impossible to identify and usefully apply the most important concepts. Similarly, neuroscientific work on cognition has gone through a period of remarkable productivity and change. Functional magnetic resonance imaging, for example, has come from its inception as a new technology in the late 1980s to a mainstream method of psychological inquiry. Spirited debates continue about the interpretation and significance of functional imaging studies, even as more and more such studies are produced, further complicating the task of synthesizing what the research might mean for educational applications.

Besides the growing pains wrought by rapid development of the science, jargon and nonintuitive study design also conspire against application of the research. All academic disciplines suffer from opaque terminology to one degree or another, but in cognitive psychology, the problem is particularly acute. "Short-term memory," for example, seems like a straightforward enough term, and most people use it to refer to what they remember from the last few hours or days. Researchers, on the other hand, generally use it to mean *really* recent information, commonly only a few second's worth. Cognitive research studies also depend on a repertoire of study techniques, including recordings of minute time differences (think thousandths of a second) in responses, that bear little resemblance to real-world situations, or are, frankly, highly contrived. This approach is scientifically defensible, given the need for precise control over study conditions, but hard to link to practical application.

Popular and mainstream media are of little help either in decoding major developments in the field, being notoriously prone to zooming in on the most controversial-sounding findings—Men use only half their brains to listen! Political party is neurally hardwired! iPads are doing something to kids' brains!—without tying them in to larger, more important developments in what we know about human cognition.

The challenges to meaningful, useful applications of cognitive research are substantial, but so are the opportunities, especially given the new avenues for teaching with technology. The confluence between rising interest in cognitively based teaching approaches, rapid growth in scientific understanding of cognition, and rapid spread of educational technology is what motivated me to write this book.

This book explains how principles of human cognition can inform the effective use of technology in college teaching. But beyond that, I hope to also convey something that really excites me about contemporary instructional technology: the unprecedented opportunity it affords us to align our teaching with the way the mind works. Here are some of the key ways in which technology can help us optimize the way we teach:

Technology enables frequent, low-stakes *testing*, an activity that powerfully promotes memory for material.

Technology encourages better *spacing* of study over the time course of the class and helps prevent cramming.

Technology facilitates presentation of material in ways that take advantage of learners' *existing knowledge* about a topic.

Technology facilitates presentation of material via *multiple sensory modalities*, which, if done in the right ways, can promote comprehension and memory.

Technology offers new methods for capturing and holding students' *attention*, which is a necessary precursor for memory.

Technology supports frequent, varied *practice* that is a necessary precursor to the development of expertise.

Technology offers new avenues to connect students *socially* and fire them up *emotionally*.

Technology allows us to borrow from the techniques of *gaming* to promote practice, engagement, and motivation.

I believe that technology gives us many advantages over and above traditional, face-to-face classroom techniques, but a clarification is in order. I *don't* believe that instructional technology promotes learning by its mere presence. Nor does it let us evade some of the apparently immutable truths about how we learn—especially the fact that learning requires focused attention, effortful practice, and motivation. Rather, what technology allows us to do is amplify and expand the repertoire of techniques that effective teachers use to elicit the attention, effort, and engagement that are the basis for learning.

This is not a new idea; Arthur Chickering and Steven Ehrmann laid out something much like it in the mid-1990s.[1] They explained how technologies, even basic ones such as e-mail and discussion boards, could be used to advance the practices laid out by Chickering and Zelda Gamson in their seminal 1987 article "Seven Principles for Good Practice in Undergraduate Education."[2] Chickering and Ehrmann point out that the power of instructional technology comes from its alignment with specific aims, such as increasing the meaningful time spent practicing skills or offering frequent feedback—not just by mere presence.

In this book, we will explore the cognitive principles that enable us to create new and better learning experiences with technology, and strategic uses of technology that tie into cognitive principles. The first part of the book focuses on the impact and importance of technology in the contemporary higher education landscape, emphasizing the common principles underlying good teaching in online and face-to-face modalities while addressing some of the major concerns faculty have about the quality of online learning experiences. I'll then discuss in detail each of the three broad areas of cognition that are most relevant to teaching and learning—attention, memory, and thinking—with an eye to how those processes can guide good design of online learning experiences for college students. The next section of the book takes on practical ways to integrate all these strategies into online learning experiences, discussing how to use multimedia effectively and how to apply research-based strategies for getting students motivated to do the work. The final chapter illustrates what all of these different arenas of research—cognitive, multimedia, and motivation—might look like embodied in an actual course, with specific strategies mapped onto each arena and a sample syllabus showing how these strategies might come together in an actual course.

As you may have already noted, I am being fairly loose in my terminology around instructional technology and online learning. This mirrors the breadth of ways in which technology is used in higher education today, as well as the fact that boundaries are breaking down between strictly traditional, face-to-face classroom instruction and online instruction. Boundaries and strict definitions continue to fall apart as more institutions "blend" in-class contact time with structured time spent online, and as more instructors augment their face-to-face classes with activities and assignments conducted online. "Technology," in the context of this book, will refer to tools such as the following, whether in the context of a fully online, "blended," or technology-augmented face-to-face class:

Presenting *content* via computer, for example with illustrated web sites or narrated animations

Learning activities in which students interact with material in a structured way

Exercises such as homework problems

Assessments such as tests and quizzes

Simulations of a process or experience

Demonstrations illustrating how a process takes place

Online social interactions such as online forum discussions

Content creation assignments in which students put together projects such as web sites, podcasts, or wikis

Books like this one run the risk of becoming "cookbooks" containing disjointed collections of assignment ideas built around specific technologies, software applications, and web sites. Such a book would begin to go out of date before it came off the press, and would offer little to guide readers as they evaluated whatever new technologies come down the line in the future. I've therefore grounded the discussion of technology more conceptually. With an idea of *why* certain uses of the technology would be most effective, and knowledge of which types of approaches have proven effective in actual use, you will be empowered to make more powerful design choices and to innovate after today's learning management systems, applications, and gadgets du jour are long gone. This book will give you a new view of what we know about learning, mind, and brain in the context of technology in college courses, enriching your ability to create innovative and effective learning experiences online and off.

Minds Online

Chapter 1

Is Online Learning Here to Stay?

THIS BOOK IS ABOUT how cognitive science can help us shape and refine the ways in which we use technology to promote learning. But before we take on those research-based strategies, let's set the scene for why instructional technology is such a timely concern within higher education. "Chalk doesn't cut it anymore" seems to be the prevailing attitude at many institutions today, and whether you agree or disagree with that sentiment, it's clear that faculty are pressed to incorporate technology when developing their teaching philosophies and pedagogical strategies.

This chapter will explore the different trends, events, and forces for change that led to the explosion of interest in teaching and learning with technology. Notably, few of these factors directly relate to empirical research in how people think, remember, and learn, having more to do with shifts in the economics and organization of higher education. But unscientific or not, these trends provide the context for why we should be investing in the best designs possible for teaching with technology.

In a short space of time, technology in higher education has gone from a smattering of fully online distance-only programs and the self-created web resources of a few motivated individuals, to near ubiquity. Most students graduating from college in the present era will experience at least some part of their education via technology, whether as an enhancement to the traditional, face-to-face approach, fully online courses, or some mix of the two; 31 percent of students report taking at least one fully online class as part of their course-load.[1] Similarly, institutions increasingly expect that faculty will be willing and able to engage in technological approaches to pedagogy, including, at some schools, the expectation that faculty will partici-pate in so-called "alternate delivery" formats.

At my institution, Northern Arizona University, all faculty position advertisements must include interest and/or experience in technol-ogy as a preferred qualification—and as a veteran of numerous fac-ulty searches, I can tell you that it has a measurable impact on whose application rises to the top. This has been true at NAU for over a decade now; our relative isolation in the Four Corners region was one of several reasons we became "early adopters" of online teaching techniques. NAU is located in Flagstaff, Arizona, within Coconino County, the second-largest county within the continental United States; it is over two hours' drive from the nearest large city (Phoe-nix). Tiny communities dot the largely rural geographic region sur-rounding Flagstaff, and their inhabitants depend on NAU's distance education programs to meet their educational needs. NAU also enrolls a substantial proportion of Native American students, who come to NAU from Navajo, Hopi, Hualapai, and other Native Amer-ican nations in the region. These students often face long and treach-erous commutes to our main campus, and thus we've had to get creative about different ways to deliver education remotely. Over the years, we've depended on, for example, "interactive instructional television," dubbed "IITV," a system that used special classrooms equipped with two-way video and audio feed to approximate the in-person classroom experience. Contemporary online learning man-agement systems have largely supplanted things like IITV in our distance delivery efforts, but we still expect that our faculty will be willing to learn and use new technologies as they come along. His-torically, this made us quite cutting-edge compared to most institu-tions, but we are less unusual with every passing year.

A striking example of technology trends in higher education was the explosion of interest in MOOCs (short for "massive open online course"). At its peak in 2012–2013, the MOOC craze dominated news coverage about higher education, generating hundreds of blog posts, articles, and conference presentations by authors scrambling to explain the significance of this new approach to delivering college-level coursework. There is no one defining form or technique that makes an online course a MOOC, but typically these courses involve (1) collections of online multimedia source material such as video lectures, (2) online assignments and tests, and (3) mechanisms for students to discuss course material and comment on each other's work. Interaction with the course instructor is generally limited or absent, as by definition these courses are designed to accommodate thousands of students at once; any feedback that students do get is largely provided by auto-grading or by peers within the course.[2] For a time, MOOCs were at the forefront of media coverage about higher education, spurred by the creation in 2012 of Udacity.com, a for-profit online education company, and the entry of a number of high-profile institutions into partnerships with other for-profit on-line course companies such as Coursera. Udacity's philosophy and approach sprang from the experiences of its founder, Sebastian Thrun, a Stanford computer scientist who had experimented with putting coursework online and inviting anyone, worldwide, to join in work-ing through it.

When Thrun addressed the Sloan International Conference on Online Learning in the fall of 2012, he presented the MOOC concept as a truly revolutionary way to engage millions of people worldwide in high-quality, low-cost educational experiences, helping kick off an explosion of interest among both traditional universities and for-profit online education companies.[3] Some educational leaders cau-tioned that MOOCs were still largely experimental and lacking in truly innovative pedagogy; one pundit, former University of Massa-chusetts president Jack Wilson, even compared the typical MOOC style to the "writing hand" films that dominated educational tech-nology in the 1970s.[4] Numerous others pointed to the alarmingly low completion rates—usually in the single digits—of the vast ma-jority of MOOCs, questioning whether these really deserved to be seen as effective at all. As the revered academic leader and researcher William Bowen put it, "As far as I am aware, right now there is no compelling evidence as to how well MOOCs can produce good learning outcomes for 18-to-22-year-olds of various backgrounds studying on mainline campuses—and this is an enormous gap in our knowledge" (p. 60).[5]

Despite the skepticism, institutions scrambled to jump onto what they perceived as a major trend. Harvard invested $30 million in MOOCs, despite significant faculty skepticism about the value of these online offerings; San Jose State University, similarly, pressured instructors to adopt MOOCs as part of their courses, only to provoke a very public pushback from a wide swath of their faculty.[6]

Other MOOC initiatives around the country—including those at American University, Amherst, and Duke—began to experience similar backlash, with institutions announcing that they would pull back from or suspend efforts to blend MOOC content into the curriculum.[7] The MOOC craze-and-crash dynamic even made it into the legislative realm: In California, State Senator Darrell Steinberg introduced a bill that would have drastically expanded acceptance of MOOCs for credit within the state university system. However, just a short time after creating it, Steinberg put the bill on hold pending review of other developments in public university online courses.[8] For-profit MOOCs suffered a number of further PR setbacks at around the same time. Udacity opted to cancel a high-visibility mathematics course with 20,000 participating students due to poor quality, and similarly, Coursera shut down a 40,000-student course because of catastrophic technical and design failures.[9]

Where do MOOCs currently stand as a force for reenvisioning the role of technology in higher education? In a widely cited 2013 article, professor Richard Wellen argued that MOOCs should be considered a bona fide "disruptive" force, despite their decidedly poor completion rates and often-weak pedagogy. [10] In Wellen's view, MOOCs are important as an *economic* force, not an educational one, given that they represent a form of "unbundling" the components of a university education. It's clear that in other industries (commercial music comes to mind), unbundling has been profoundly transformative, making some facets obsolete and fundamentally changing how consumers select and purchase the product. Wellen predicts that in higher education, MOOCs could push middle- and lower-tier institutions to focus solely on teaching, cutting out other activities like research that are, in a sense, subsidized by the relatively convenient and low-cost degrees the institutions provide to students.

Market forces could also accentuate a growing "star system" for faculty, expanding compensation and opportunity for the few who provide top-level content for MOOCs while relegating other faculty to low-compensation, low-autonomy positions. On the one hand, "consumers" of education might financially benefit from the ability to purchase unbundled academic "commodities" such as course content, while opting out of other pricey features of university life such as athletics, residence life, or student support services. On the other hand, such a MOOC-ified future would likely feature homogenized course content and fewer contributions of universities to the wider social good, among other possible negative impacts. Although Wellen's dystopian vision is arguably somewhat extreme, it's still plausible enough to suggest that we academics need to keep an eye on MOOCs and their potential to profoundly change our professional lives, entirely apart from the question of whether MOOCs are a good way to learn.

But this picture of MOOCs as a tidal wave of disruption gets more complicated when you consider the results of a recent large-scale survey conducted by the Babson Research Group, a major player in the national assessment of online teaching and learning.[11] According to lead researcher Jeff Seaman, the study sample of over 2,500 chief academic officers at institutions of higher education in the United States revealed deep ambivalence about MOOCs. Most institutions don't currently offer MOOCs, and about half called themselves "undecided" as to whether they would offer any in the future. Substantial proportions of respondents cited concerns about both the sustainability of MOOCs—i.e., whether they would take up too many resources to build and run—and their quality. The survey also contradicted the often-related vision of globally connected students engaged in collaborative learning across cultures and geography, with most respondents stating that most of their MOOC students hailed from the same geographic regions as their face-to-face students.

As for the potential *value* of MOOCs, opinions were eye-opening: zero respondents stated that "generating income" was the primary benefit, but many—over 50 percent—cited the ability to learn more about how to build bigger, more effective forms of "traditional" on-line courses. In other words, MOOCs could be useful testing grounds for new instructional techniques. And although institutions don't see MOOCs as income providers, they do see them as good public relations—a way to draw potential students into the standard credit-bearing courses that do add to the bottom line. This is especially tempting for smaller, more obscure institutions, for whom MOOCs can essentially serve as a relatively low-cost form of advertising.

There's one other view of the value of MOOCs—particularly relevant to the purpose of this book—that's currently percolating to the top of the discussion. The content of MOOCs is often highly modular, meaning that it can be pieced out topic by topic; this modular quality, coupled with open access, can make them ideal building blocks to complement rather than replace traditional courses. Coursera CEO Daphne Koller is one advocate of this view, envisioning a future in which MOOCs are an essential part of "blended learning" approaches, where students master basic concepts online, then spend face-to-face class time practicing, discussing, and actively engaging with the material.[12] In this formulation, MOOCs aren't a replacement for more personalized instruction, but a form of course content selected by the instructor to accomplish specific aims of the class. The president of the not-for-profit learning venture EdX, Anant Agarwal, points out that this blended approach has already taken off at his home institution, MIT, where half of all students currently use EdX materials in a blended-learning fashion.[13]

Time will tell whether MOOCs fundamentally transform education as we know it, disappear like an overnight fad gone stale, or something in between. But if nothing else, MOOCs were a major wake-up call for faculty and administrators who hadn't yet fully engaged with technology and teaching. Perhaps that is one reason why MOOC-mania took off the way it did, reflecting not people's reaction to MOOCs per se, but rather to educational technology in general. And although it's possible that MOOCs themselves may have peaked and crashed, educational technology decidedly has not.

So with MOOCs as a case in point, what is driving the trend toward technology in higher education? Some of the major forces pushing it forward are as follows.

Factor 1: Economics

This factor is often cited cynically by faculty and enthusiastically by administrators, particularly in financially squeezed public institutions. Faculty commentators have raised alarms over what they see as the drive to replace highly skilled, tenure-track faculty with less-skilled, non-tenure-track instructors whose job it is to merely supervise the delivery of prefabricated online content.[14]

Judging from the business model of the University of Phoenix and similar for-profit institutions, there is some basis for this claim. While the specific arrangements vary, these institutions tend to favor highly standardized content and little leeway for individual instructors. Technological delivery of material facilitates this standardized approach, but isn't one and the same with it; it's possible, after all, for institutions such as the University of Phoenix to maintain the standardized approach for traditional face-to-face courses as well.

Administrators, meanwhile, are learning that technological delivery does not automatically equal cost savings. Among specialists in this area, the economics of educational technology are controversial; it is notoriously difficult to pin down the cost of *any* component of higher education, let alone costs specifically associated with instructional technology.[15] In fact, earlier in the history of information technology in higher education, the more hotly debated question was whether technologies would end up *increasing* costs.[16] Indeed, one of the most extreme efforts to automate course delivery—Carnegie Mellon's "Open Learning Initiative"—has yielded a limited suite of courses that run essentially without instructors, but cost between $500,000 and $1 million apiece to develop.[17] That's hardly a practical solution for administrators looking for short term-savings. It's also worth noting that the University of Phoenix model doesn't reduce staffing costs as drastically as you might assume. Their student-faculty ratio is actually fairly low, at around fifteen students per faculty member, so even at "piecework" wages, the investment in instructional staff is still substantial.[18]

Part of the ambiguity around costs results from the many distinct sub-forms technological delivery can take. There are courses that run entirely online, which are sometimes (but not always) a part of fully online degree programs. These are distinct from blended courses in which some proportion of the traditional amount of in-person class time is replaced by online activities, such as virtual laboratory exercises or online discussions. Other courses keep all the face-to-face time but augment or enhance it with an online component that students participate in outside of class. Lastly, there is the MOOC variant described above, characterized by large size, open enrollment, and low levels of interaction, feedback, and supervision from the instructor.

In spite of these many remaining questions, it was not long before some institutions began to claim significant financial gains from some forms of technological delivery, primarily fully online and blended formats. In 2011, for example, the *Chronicle of Higher Education* reported that Southern New Hampshire University escaped dire financial straits by offering numerous online courses. As the story reported, these online courses ended up becoming the "economic engine" subsidizing the rest of the institution's offerings.[19]

Some blended-learning courses have produced measurable cost savings through mechanisms such as reduced faculty time spent preparing and delivering lectures and reduced cost for classroom facilities. Enhancing classes with technology can also provide financial benefits of a sort, if you consider reduced failure and retake rates a cost savings—with the caveat that this strategy only works if technology is used in ways that actually *do* produce better student outcomes.

Regardless of the actual impact any given technology project may have on costs, examples such as these continue to drive perceptions among administrators and faculty that doing things online is less costly than traditional approaches, or even potentially profitable.

Factor 2: Student Demand

There is much hype about the "wired" generation of students now entering college.[20] However, the idea that the present generation of traditional-age college students is both overwhelmingly dependent on and extremely comfortable with technology is probably a significant oversimplification.[21] Faculty who teach computer skills courses, for example, often bemoan the fact that their students *think* they know programs like Word or Excel inside and out, but in fact have little command of the extended features of those programs.[22]

These cautions aside, today's students do typically enter college with the expectation that technology will play some role. There are several strands to this expectation, especially with respect to perceived *flexibility* of learning with technology—something that students cite as one or even *the* top reason to choose online learning options. The attraction of flexibility is particularly strong for constraints on where and when students complete their coursework.[23] As the home page for *Online Learning Mag* pitches it: "Online education allows you to earn a degree on your own time. If you need to provide for your family or even just keep afloat financially yourself, you can keep a full-time job and earn your online degree in your off time."[24] Technology may also increase flexibility in how students approach their assigned work; online discussion forums, for example, allow students to reflect on and revise comments to the class, unlike the rapid-fire responses favored by traditional in-class discussion. Lastly, student demand for technology may grow out of a general social expectation of rapid communication, frequent feedback, and continual access to help and support—after all, this generation of traditional-age students grew up with systems such as *Homework Now* (www.homeworknow.com), where they could access assignments around the clock and message a teacher with one click.

Today's students may expect and—to a certain extent—feel comfortable with technology in educational settings, but they also have a very low tolerance for technology that works poorly, is difficult to navigate, or is superfluous to the class. In other words, student demand for technology is high, but student *standards* for smoothly functioning, educationally worthwhile technology are even higher. Fortunately, many technology-related complaints can be headed off via practices such as checking content ahead of time with an institutional e-learning center, something that can uncover any technical glitches before a class goes live. It also makes sense to actively manage student expectations around reasonable instructor response times for e-mails, discussion posts, and the like.[25]

Factor 3: Increased Focus on Measurable Evidence of Learning and Student Success

This factor stems from the perception that technology-enhanced teaching produces better outcomes, coupled with a new emphasis on tangible assessment of learning. We will return to this idea in Chapter 2 and throughout the book as we consider empirical evidence for the effectiveness of online and technology-enhanced teaching methods and specific techniques that take advantage of how human cognitive systems work. For now, though, the key point is that institutions are demanding evidence that our teaching approaches are paying off—and are willing to explore all kinds of nontraditional tools for making this happen.

This heightened focus on assessment is accentuated by the fact that, increasingly, less-elite schools are deemphasizing the goal of raising the quantity and qualifications of the students they admit. Instead, they are concentrating on the *success* of those admitted students, measured by how many students pass the classes that count toward degrees. At my home institution, for example, the state legislature recently overhauled the university funding system so that more money is granted based on how many students complete degrees, and less funding comes from the sheer number of students we admit. This "performance funding" concept, which is becoming more widespread throughout the country, naturally puts pressure on administrations to find new ways to meet students where they are, academically speaking, and turn them into successful students.

At the same time, there is a widespread disenchantment with the ability of traditional teaching methods to produce these measurably improved outcomes. The traditional lecture—derided as the "Velveeta of teaching methods"[26]—receives special scorn from educational reformers, who single it out as one of the most ineffective things you can do in a classroom. PowerPoint, the modern lecturer's weapon of choice, attracts criticism for everything from its marked propensity to create boredom[27] to its supposed ability to corrupt our very thought processes.[28] The failings of lecture may be oversold,[29] especially in light of the fact that it survives in so many cultural forms such as the wildly popular TED (Technology, Entertainment, Design) talk format (www.ted.com). Broad condemnation of lecture also tends to miss the fact that its effectiveness depends on how well and appropriately it is used—and in this sense, lecture is not unlike any other teaching method, technological or not.

Time will tell what, if any, long-term impact this current round of criticism will have on the dominance of lecture as a teaching method, but if nothing else, the criticism shows that there is a strong interest in developing effective alternatives. Some alternatives, such as in-class peer learning groups, do not depend on technology, but many others do—such as the blended learning techniques described earlier, or collaborative learning activities that take place online.

Factor 4: Availability of New Technologies

In a prescient 1991 article, physicist and teaching innovator Eric Mazur described how educationally relevant technologies of the day— easy-to-use databases such as Hypercard, simple animation programs, laptop computers—were becoming widely accessible to teachers and students.[30] And as Mazur predicted decades ago, ubiquitous access to personal computers, databases, and rich media is now a reality.

Take sound editing technology. When I was working on speech perception research in the early 1990s, I needed an expensive professional editing software package (Macromedia's SoundEdit), a special microphone, and a high-end personal computer with a substantial amount of RAM added to the standard hardware—all just to be able to do rudimentary recording and rearranging of my media files. This specialized technology would have been completely prohibitive had I not had support for equipment purchases as part of a federally funded research grant. Today, amateur audio editors can use GarageBand, a completely self-contained music and audio application included in the iLife software suite for $79—with speed and capabilities far exceeding the pricey, hard-to-master programs like SoundEdit that were the standard just a few years before.

This easy availability, plus the existence of information technology infrastructure in virtually every institution of higher education, has removed the barriers to entry that a few years ago would have kept many institutions from pursuing new ways to use technology. Furthermore, individual instructors no longer need special skills or substantial institutional support in order to try technology. In sum, one reason that interest in technology is exploding is that it is easier and cheaper than ever before.

Factor 5: Curiosity and the Drive to Innovate

Faculty as a group have an intrinsic interest in creating new ways to spark students' passion for learning. A certain amount of the faculty discourse on technology in education criticizes the impact of technology on academia, with for-profit, fully online programs being an especially popular target. However, thriving blogs such as *Wired Campus* (http://chronicle.com/blogs/wiredcampus/) at the *Chronicle of Higher Education*, and *Technology and Learning* at *Inside Higher Ed* (http://www.insidehighered.com/blogs/technology-and-learning), demonstrate that interest in technology is not just something imposed on faculty by profit-driven outsiders.

Indeed, some of the most influential voices advocating educational technology have been faculty leaders, including highly esteemed figures such as Nobel laureate Carl Wieman.[31] Furthermore, some of the most interesting applications of technology have been developed not by corporations, but rather by teachers. The iClicker classroom response system (http://www.iclicker.com/) and the Coglab psychology simulation software are just two examples. Faculty have also been pioneers in the use of what Steven Ehrmann calls "worldware"—software that wasn't designed for education but is repurposed for that use.[32] YouTube video clips, virtual interactions in Second Life, even e-mail itself—these tools are enhancing education for students around the world purely through the interest and innovation of individual faculty.

All of these themes—financial pressures, student interest, focus on student success, innovation—tie into another highly influential trend, the *course redesign* movement. Course redesign, as conceived by Carol Twigg of the National Center for Academic Transformation (NCAT; www.thencat.org), is both a set of techniques and a philosophy for rethinking the organization, delivery, and pedagogy of college courses. The central goal of course redesign is to increase learning and success while simultaneously controlling or reducing costs. NCAT is the organization most associated with the course redesign movement, but there are other groups with similar approaches, such as the Next Generation Learning Challenge project (http://nextgenlearning.org) and the Red Balloons Project (http://www.aascu.org/programs/RedBalloonProject/). Course redesign has had a substantial impact on higher education across the country; NCAT reports on its web site that it has sponsored fifty-five major course redesigns nationally, many as part of large-scale, state-funded grant programs.

Course redesign places particular emphasis on foundational courses, i.e., the introductory-level classes that are (not always, but often) large, unchallenging, and dominated by lecture. This type of design tends to elicit passivity and disengagement on the part of students, leading to low levels of successful course completion. Besides the fact that they are often ripe for new approaches, foundational courses are also a natural focus of redesign because their large enrollments make them costly to deliver. Lastly, because foundational courses are prerequisites for advanced coursework, failing these courses sets students up for delayed degree progression and poor performance in courses later down the line.

Improving the educational impact of a course while simultaneously making it cheaper to deliver is a tall order, and so course redesign offers specific techniques for revamping courses. These techniques tie back into the alternative, technologically enhanced formats discussed earlier in the chapter. NCAT's "standard" templates for redesign include the following:

Fully online model. Course designers devise ways to achieve all of a course's objectives with activities completed via a learning management system or similar online means, without any traditional, face-to-face class meetings. Savings come from the ability to reuse online materials for subsequent iterations of the course and from not needing to spend instructor time and institutional resources (classroom facilities, etc.) on scheduled class meetings.

Replacement model. Similar to what they would do in the "blended" or "hybrid" approach, course designers take some proportion of face-to-face class time and reallocate it to structured out-of-class activities, which are usually done online. Savings work similarly as they do for fully online courses, but could be less, depending on how much class time is replaced. Increasing section sizes may also be feasible under this model, providing another source for cost savings.

Supplemental model. Course designers enhance and add to what students do in the traditional course with structured out-of-class activities (again, usually online), looking to elicit productive student effort and promote mastery of learning objectives that are particularly challenging. As with the replacement model, supplemental course redesign can reduce costs by allowing section sizes to go up without creating a net loss in quality or student success. Improving student success can, in theory, be another mechanism for cost savings, by reducing the number of seats needed for students retaking the course after prior unsuccessful attempts. However, this is something of a matter of opinion, as not all organizations see reduced retake rates as "legitimate" savings.

Buffet model. Course designers set up multiple alternative pathways through a course, using technology to assign students to pathways (based on student preference or performance on pretests) and to manage the logistics of multiple ways of completing a course. For example, students might complete individual assignments *or* participate in group work *or* complete work under the supervision of a teaching assistant, depending on which approach works best for them. Cost savings would work similarly as for the supplemental model.

Emporium model. Emporium courses have a face-to-face component, but one that bears little resemblance to traditional class time. Students complete structured work, delivered online through a learning management or publisher-supplied homework system, but do so in a supervised environment with as-needed help provided by on-site staff. This model, popular for redesigns of foundational math courses, has its most famous example in Virginia Tech's Math Emporium (http://www.emporium.vt.edu/). This large, custom-built facility is situated inside a remodeled retail space near campus. Cost savings come from the ability to accommodate more students with fewer instructional staff.[33]

Course redesign is not just about reshuffling seat time and assignments. Regardless of how those aspects of the course are changed, there are a few overarching best practices that guide choices about the design of the new course. These include emphasizing active learning (and the flip side, deemphasizing traditional lecture) while reconceptualizing progress through the course as mastery of objectives, rather than as a predetermined chunk of class time spent on each topic. Successful redesigns also foreground student time and effort coupled with abundant feedback. Lastly, a redesigned course should be structured as one coordinated effort across all sections (the "redesign the whole course" principle), with systems in place that keep individual sections from drifting away from the agreed-upon design and objectives of the course.

NCAT requires all of its projects to assess the impact of redesign on learning and success, and some have produced impressive evidence of improved outcomes. Some prominent examples are as follows. At Virginia Tech, going to the emporium model resulted in significant improvements to course pass rates.[34] A similar initiative at the University of Idaho also resulted in significantly improved pass rates and improved course grades for precalculus.[35] Granted, grades do not equal learning, but as the project leaders point out in their report, the Idaho redesign used comparable tests and assignments before and after the redesign, making these assessments a reasonable reflection of what students actually learned. Carnegie Mellon's supplemental-style redesign of an introductory statistics course resulted in a 22.8 percent increase in scores on a concept exam,[36] and the University of Tennessee–Knoxville's replacement redesign of Intermediate Spanish produced significant improvements in oral proficiency measures.[37] Even critical-thinking skills can be targeted in a redesign: Florida Gulf Coast University found significant improvements in essays scored specifically for critical thinking, as well as improvements in content knowledge exam scores.[38] Also encouraging for the course redesign concept are patterns of *which* students tend to benefit most, in terms of improved grades and pass rates: among NCAT redesign teams that tracked student demographics, several reported that redesign-associated improvements were significantly greater for minority and other underserved student groups.[39]

The course redesign philosophy critically depends on technology, not as a panacea or end unto itself, but rather as the means to make its ambitious goals feasible. As with the "lever" philosophy discussed earlier, the idea is that technology opens up ways to engage students outside traditional class time and in ways that are more effective than the traditional lecture.

At NAU, we followed the redesign philosophy when we restructured our Introduction to Psychology course as part of an NCAT-led, state-funded grant program back in 2007–2009.[40] We in the department had grappled with this course for years, seeing grades stay disappointingly low while students—and administrators—clamored for additional seats in the course. An unacceptable number of students earned Ds and Fs in the course, even as we asked pitifully little of them: optional (and usually sparse) attendance at primarily lecture-based classes, a few multiple-choice tests, reading the textbook on their own (this was also essentially optional and, from what students told us, done sporadically or not done at all). Some instructors added online homework, online discussions, or other enhancements, but these enhancements were inconsistent from section to section and semester to semester. The lack of consistency was not surprising, given that instructors had to set up these activities with little assistance, thus adding to the already heavy load of constantly preparing lectures and managing the e-mail generated by 100–150 students per section.

Our supplemental-model redesign changed a number of things about the class, but our main focus was on asking more of students while building in efficiencies that would allow us to manage that additional coursework. A dedicated coordinator—whose duties were counted as part of his or her faculty workload—set up and maintained one common "course shell" within the university's learning management system that all sections would use. Within this shell, students completed activities that complemented and reinforced the reading and class time expected of them.

We imported a publisher's test bank and set up timed, low-stakes chapter quizzes with randomly sampled items for each attempt. In a twist that we learned from NCAT veterans John Broida of the University of Southern Maine and Gordon Hodge of the University of New Mexico, we allowed—or rather exhorted—students to take each quiz multiple times, counting only the highest grade they earned out of all the attempts. These quizzes were due before the topic was covered in class, thus ensuring students were better prepared and supporting a more participatory in-class experience. We further promoted participation—and effectively required attendance—by using an in-class student response system (also known as "clickers") capable of recording, aggregating, and displaying answers to questions embedded in presentation slides.

Aiming to take advantage of the wealth of interactive psychology resources already available on the web, we created a set of "online exploration" assignments tied to course material. Each assignment directed students to a specific web site and told them what to do there, emphasizing what they were supposed to find, do, learn, or otherwise glean from what they saw. For the neuropsychology topic, e.g., we sent them to the online Harvard Brain Atlas (http://www.med.harvard.edu/aanlib/home.html) with instructions to describe in their own words particular structures and landmarks within the brain, then to contrast these brain images taken from healthy individuals with those associated with different disease processes.

Students earned credit for the assignment by going back to the course shell and answering short-answer questions reflecting what they saw and did during the online exploration part of the activity. Using the Rubric tool in our learning management system, we set up detailed grading guidelines that emphasized the student's first-person experience of the site, rather than fine-grained factual information; this in turn enabled our graduate assistants to mark hundreds of answers in a relatively short time.

This redesign expanded how many students we could accommodate, cut the cost of delivery by about 30 percent, and significantly increased the proportion of students successfully completing the course.[41] Crucially, without having technology at our disposal, we never could have realized the innovations we created in this redesign project. This was especially true for the repeatable reading quizzes— a technique that was highly useful for improving in-class discussion and exam scores—and for the web exploration assignments. If we had tried to replicate either of these in traditional, paper-based format, the photocopying alone would have been prohibitive, not to mention the logistics of collecting and returning thousands of paper documents. By using the technology that was readily available to us, we were able to do things that we *knew* were beneficial to students, but had never managed to consistently carry out before.

This brings us back to trends pushing institutions toward instructional technology: cost savings, emphasis on student success, and all the other factors discussed earlier in this chapter. The course redesign movement is but one high-profile manifestation of these trends. Given the continued momentum of course redesign and related concepts, it is clear that technology in higher education is in fact here to stay—and that learning to use it well is a worthwhile investment for individuals and institutions.

Chapter 2

Online Learning: Does It Work?

Is THE TREND toward more technology in teaching is a *good* trend? Does technology degrade or improve learning—or have no real effect at all? In fairness, we should acknowledge that for most of the history of formal higher education, we haven't asked for empirical evidence of the effectiveness of traditional teaching techniques. In that sense, we're holding technologically aided teaching to a higher standard when we ask whether it really does produce the desired results of intellectual mastery, self-awareness, self-management abilities, critical-thinking ability, and all the other goals of a college education.

Even though we have only recently begun to systematically assess traditional college teaching, it makes sense to ask what students get out of fully online and technologically enhanced coursework. This is particularly true given an odd quirk of how faculty in higher education tend to view the effectiveness of online teaching. According to Jeff Seaman, one of the lead researchers in charge of generating the most comprehensive national analyses of online education, the proportion of faculty who believe in the value and legitimacy of online education is relatively low—in the realm of 30 percent—and holding steady, even as the proportion of faculty actively involved in online education exceeds that number and is rising.[1] This means that many of the very same individuals who deliver online learning believe that it's an inferior form of education.

Clearly, there is deep-seated ambivalence among faculty about online teaching and learning, and for faculty to be maximally effective online, this ambivalence has to be addressed. This chapter will weigh the evidence that online teaching is effective, first taking into account how it differs from traditional teaching, as well as some underlying similarities. It will then take on some of the concerns about the integrity of online learning, in particular the risks of cheating and of superficial engagement with course material.

In some fundamental ways, good teaching is the same in any modality. Here are some of the common hallmarks of quality shared by online and traditional teaching:

An Emphasis on Student Effort as the Basis for Success

As Chickering and Ehrmann put it, "time plus energy equals learning."[2] This formula is a bit simplistic, but it highlights the value that academics traditionally place on working hard to achieve success. Unfortunately, there is a growing disconnect between this traditional academic value and how contemporary college students approach learning. Time-use studies indicate that the average number of hours spent by college students on schoolwork has been in steady decline for several decades now and is currently at a record low of twenty-seven hours per week.[3] The widely discussed 2011 book *Academically Adrift* further argued that of the time students do invest, disturbingly little is spent on intellectually demanding work such as writing and critical reading.[4]

As the discussion around student investment continues to develop, there may be a national trend toward deliberately eliciting more effort, and better-quality effort, from college students. Online learning is well situated to take advantage of this trend. Chickering and Ehrmann point out that online learning can encourage increased study time, given the 24/7 access to learning activities.[5] Online activities can also provide more opportunities for effortful practice than are feasible within the confines of face-to-face class meetings, as we touched on in the Preface and will return to in Chapter 4.

Making Students Feel Connected

Two of Chickering and Gamson's principles—encouraging student-faculty contact and encouraging cooperation—both tie into this theme of interpersonal connectedness. Many other writers on teaching and learning have noted the power of social connections in traditional face-to-face learning environments, suggesting that instructors promote connectedness through icebreaker activities, individual office hour meetings, and group work. Online course designers also need to consider the social side of the course. As online teaching expert Judith Boettcher reminds us, "we learn as social beings in a social context," and thus students are acutely sensitive to the presence (or absence) of their instructor and classmates in the online environment.[6] Looking back on the debate over MOOCs, this has been one of the sharpest criticisms of online mega-courses—the impersonal nature of a learning environment where thousands of students may be left to learn mainly on their own.

Frequent, Rapid, Informative Feedback

This traditional "best practice" is widely cited as one of the things instructors should spend as much time and thought on as possible.[7] Teaching experts Eric Mazur and Carl Wieman have been passionate advocates of providing a more dynamic, feedback-rich experience in traditional lecture classes.[8] Similarly, rapid feedback is a key feature of the best online learning experiences.[9] There are myriad ways to accomplish this online, including peer feedback, auto-graded quizzes, and branching lessons that present varying content based on student input.

Taking Students' Current Knowledge and Understanding into Account

This point is emphasized the most among teaching experts who favor cognitively based theories of learning. John Bransford, author of the classic guide *How People Learn: Brain, Mind, Experience, and School*, foregrounds the role of preexisting knowledge as one of the most important factors teachers should keep in mind when designing learning activities; he advises that the best outcomes happen when teachers first determine what students know, then set about building on that existing foundation.[10] Similarly, researcher Susan Ambrose lists prior knowledge as a major guiding principle for teaching and learning, pointing out that prior knowledge can actively conflict with and thus delay new learning.[11] Teaching lower-division psychology provides a perfect example of this problem. Although they may be unaware of the scientific discipline of psychology, students have been inquiring about human behavior their whole lives, and come to the subject with well-developed—although often incorrect—ideas about why people do what they do. Teaching scientific psychology, therefore, isn't just a matter of feeding students new information, but rather, altering their existing knowledge about human behavior and fitting new ideas into that existing structure.

In the online context, instructors can take prior experience and knowledge into account using techniques for customizing course content or presentation. One method is adaptive testing, a way of presenting test questions whereby the system gradually eliminates items from the test set based on what the student has already correctly answered. For example, if a student has already correctly identified "time on task" as one of Chickering and Gamson's seven principles, the balance of questions will shift to other principles, until all have been correctly answered. This approach is one way in which online instructors can implement the broader "best practice" principle of identifying what learners know, then customizing the course based on that knowledge.[12]

In sum, there is a lot of overlap between the principles of good online teaching and good face-to-face teaching, a position also endorsed by the American Distance Education Consortium (www.adec .edu). Table 2.1 shows this overlap as it appears in "best practices" lists drawn from traditionally oriented and online-oriented teaching resources.

These example "best practices" lists diverge on a few points, but there are several notable recurring themes, which in turn echo the

Table 2.1

Chart of principles for optimal college teaching excerpted from four "best practices" frameworks. Note the high degree of overlap among the different frameworks with respect to the six general principles shown in the chart: peer-to-peer interaction, active student engagement in learning, emphasis on practice and student effort, personalization to the individual student, variety, and emphasis on higher thought processes, i.e., going beyond mere memorization.

| | TRADITIONAL FACE-TO-FACE TEACHING | | SPECIFICALLY ONLINE TEACHING | |
	CHICKERING AND GAMSON	AMBROSE	BOETTCHER	AMERICAN DISTANCE EDUCATION CONSORTIUM
Peer–to–Peer Interaction	Good practice encourages cooperation among students		Create a supportive online course community	Allows group collaboration and cooperative learning
Active Student Engagement in Learning	Good practice encourages active learning	To become self-directed learners, students must learn to monitor and adjust their approaches to learning		Promotes active learning Encourages active participation, knowledge construction
Emphasis on Practice and Student Effort	Good practice emphasizes time on task Good practice communicates high expectations	Goal-directed practice coupled with targeted feedback enhances the quality of students' learning	Share a set of very clear expectations for your students and for yourself as to (1) how you will communicate and (2) how much time students should be working on the course each week	
Personalization to the Individual Student		Students' prior knowledge can help or hinder learning Students' current level of development interacts with the social, emotional, and intellectual climate of the course to impact learning		Is learner-centered Fosters meaning-making, discourse

continued on next page

continued from previous page

Variety	Good practice respects diverse talents and ways of learning		Use a variety of large group, small group, and individual work experiences Use both synchronous and asynchronous activities	Provides multiple levels of interaction
Emphasis on Higher Thought Processes		To develop mastery, students must acquire component skills, practice integrating them, and know when to apply what they have learned	Prepare discussion posts that invite questions, discussions, reflections, and responses	Based on higher-level thinking skills—analysis, synthesis, and evaluation Focuses on real world, problem solving

Column 1: *Seven Principles for Good Practice in Undergraduate Education*, by Arthur Chickering and Zelda Gamson

Column 2: *How Learning Works: Seven Research-Based Principles for Smart Teaching*, by Susan Ambrose

Column 3: *A Quick Guide for New Online Faculty*, by J. V. Boettcher (revised 2011 and available at http://www.designingforlearning.info/services/writing/ecoach/tenbest.html)

Column 4: Characteristics of quality web-based teaching and learning from the American Distance Education Consortium, http://www.adec.edu/admin/papers/distance-teaching _principles.html.

points listed earlier in the chapter. They emphasize the role of students as active agents in their own learning and the importance of social interaction between students and between student and instructor. They also suggest that course designs enable good communication between students and instructor, and allow for variety and personalization. Lastly, they remind us to focus on higher-order thinking and skill building, not just assimilation of facts. What these lists tell us is that, broadly speaking, good teaching is good teaching, regardless of technology.

For another perspective on principles of good teaching, consider the techniques used by computer-game designers, who, after all, make their living creating irresistibly motivating virtual experiences. Education researcher Michele Dickey draws intriguing parallels between the qualities of engaging learning environments and "addict-ing" computer games, pointing out just how much these two seem-ingly disparate realms overlap in terms of their essential features.[13] In her analysis, games and engaged learning both offer focused goals, in which standards for performance are clear, and you get lots of rapid feedback about how you're doing in relation to those goals. Tasks and activities are challenging, but—crucially—there is pro-tection from initial failure, so that you get lots of chances to meet those challenges. You operate in an atmosphere of social interactiv-ity, which offers you solidarity with others and affirmation of your successes. And lastly, you have autonomy and a good deal of free choice over what you do and how you do it.

Later in this book (Chapter 8), we will return to the connection between games and learning and consider how to maximize moti-vation using "gamification" principles. But for now, the take-away message is that there is significant potential for online learning to borrow some of the power that drives games to be so compelling. Encouragingly, this power can be realized through a fairly acces-sible set of general principles enumerated by Dickey. Note that the qualities Dickey cites aren't superficial features we might as-sociate with computer games, such as music, cute characters, or colorful animation. Rather, they involve deeper aspects of how the game environment works, such as feedback, collaboration, and user autonomy.

The fact that game design principles flow so easily into principles of compelling teaching is another reason to believe that traditional face-to-face and online teaching have deeply rooted similarities. That said, there are some salient differences between the two, mainly with respect to the logistics of setting up learning experiences in virtual space. Here are some important factors that differentiate teaching online from the traditional approach:

Timing and Synchronization of Coursework

Instructional designers use the terms "synchronous" and "asynchro-nous" to distinguish learning activities that students have to do at a specified time versus at any time of the student's choosing. The asynchronous model is popular for online coursework, allowing students to finish their work within flexible time windows without being yoked to classmates. Face-to-face coursework, by contrast, tends to favor the synchronous approach, with many of the learning activities taking place during scheduled times in which students are working (or attending lecture) together. Much has been written about the ideal balance of one versus the other in online learning.[14] This issue is one that online instructors need to ponder carefully when they set up their courses, as the introduction of real-time, synchronous activities such as scheduled chat-room discussions comes at the cost of students' flexibility to complete coursework anytime, anywhere—which is, after all, one of the main reasons students choose online learning in the first place.

Student Preparedness to Use the Technology

As noted in Chapter 1, just because students are in their teens or twenties does not mean that they use technology as naturally as they breathe air. Many college students, even traditional-age ones, lack the technical skills needed to do online learning activities— and the fact that they can capably navigate Facebook, Instagram, or Reddit does not mean that they can effortlessly master instructional technology. When I teach, I routinely have to help students with basic tasks such as setting up accounts on third-party web sites or using Track Changes for multiple drafts in Microsoft Word. On-line instructors, as well as those who rely on technology to enhance face-to-face classes, need to teach not just their subject material but also computer skills—without needlessly rehashing those basic skills for students who are technically fluent.

To deal with this issue, it helps to see technical skills as domain specific, not one single ability that students either have or don't have, and scaffold each new technology separately. It's true that some individuals seem to gravitate toward technology of all kinds, picking up new applications and techniques relatively quickly; certainly a basic understanding of how computers and the Internet work is also helpful in a wide variety of technical tasks. However, most students will need help when they are learning the ins and outs of a new technology, be it a learning management system, student response system device, or third-party web site. Incorporating targeted modules into course content about how to use the major technologies is a good practice for fully online courses as well as those that have a heavy technology focus. In NAU's Introduction to Psychology course, for example, we hit on the idea of creating narrated mini-videos that illustrated how to use the online tracking system for signing up for required research studies. Students could watch the videos as many times as needed as they figured out how to set up and access their accounts, which we found much more effective than a rapid-fire, onetime demonstration in the face-to-face class meeting.

Similarly, many institutions have their own "how-to" modules for commonly used features of their learning management system, which faculty can link to in their own course content. Having well-designed modules that show exactly how to use the technology is half the battle, but it's also important to *require* that this content be mastered, much as you would for any other major concepts within the course. This can be accomplished by assigning students to answer test questions on the technology (perhaps as part of a syllabus quiz), or by making the different features part of assignments early in the course (for example, assigning students to access and post on a discussion board, or show proof that they have set up an account on a third-party web site they will need later in the course).

Heavy Reliance on Text

Although online course content ideally incorporates at least some multimedia, for the most part learning online means learning through the written word. As one educator put it, "E-learning requires the student to read course material, post written responses, and interact with fellow students though threaded online text-based discussions. . . . One common element of E-learning is that the primary instructional method is reading text."[15] Online courses *can* be designed with an emphasis on alternating text with other forms of delivery, such as animated narration or Skype conversations, but it is difficult to get around the need for a great deal of written communication. This contrasts with the typical face-to-face course in which lecture, audiovisual demonstrations, and spoken discussion are a major part of the learning activities.

Students who aren't strong readers, or who just prefer non-text modalities, are at particular risk of falling behind in a text-heavy environment. Unfortunately, we don't have many solutions for these less-proficient readers. Minding the reading level of material, keeping it to the level of a newspaper or lower, is one basic strategy.[16] When using synchronous, fast-paced activities like real-time chatting, it's also important to weigh any potential benefits against potential difficulties for slower readers.[17] Building in lots of those aforementioned alternate forms—narration, audio, and video—can also give a boost to less-proficient readers.

Increased Need to Explain the Course Structure and Requirements

This factor might fade as more students get experience with online coursework and as online-course designers begin to converge on commonly accepted conventions for course structure. In the meantime, though, students often come to online coursework with a less-developed sense of how things work than they would for a traditional course. Traditional courses superficially resemble high school classes, in that they are organized around set times and places for meeting, textbooks, and schedules of deadlines—so even students with little or no college experience can fall back on this familiar script to figure out what to do next. Just showing up for class can assure these less-experienced students that they will probably get by. But how do you "just show up" for an online class? In an online class (or the online parts of a blended or combination online/traditional class), it may not be clear where to start, how to spend one's study time, or when the work is due. Good design, of course, offsets the problem of orienting students to the layout of the assignments—but even in a well-designed online course, students as well as teachers have to work harder to establish a basic understanding of how the course will work.

Social Distance—Especially for Fully Online Courses

Social distance is the flip side of the "social presence" concept first articulated in the early days of telecommunications.[18] It has to do with the exchange of social cues and the feeling that one is authentically interacting with another person in the virtual environment. Creating social presence is another thing that online instructors need to pay special attention to, for example by encouraging students to offer personal information, eliciting supportive communications between students, and using communication tools that transmit facial expressions and vocal tone. Going the extra mile to do this doesn't just make the class more pleasant, but is also an important predictor of success in the course.[19]

The social feedback instructors get from students is also radically altered in an online environment. In a traditional classroom setting, students' faces give you an instant read on confusion, disengagement, and other important problems. Students stop by before or after class to clear up muddy points or talk in-depth about topics that caught their interest, and the give-and-take of an interactive lecture gives you a good grasp of students' level of understanding, at least for the ones who speak up. Online, these interactions are usually heavily time-delayed and mediated by text, particularly e-mail and discussion posts—two communication formats that have a well-known propensity to misrepresent emotional tone. To compensate, online instructors need to make formal inquiries to students about how the class is going, as well as keep a close eye on data such as frequency of log-in, late assignments, and assessment scores so that they can form an accurate picture of how students are faring.

The Potential for Technical Problems to Disrupt or Completely Derail the Course

Even when students have the skills and support needed to navigate online-learning activities, the technology may simply fail to work. Ask any online-teaching veteran and you will hear tales of vanishing assignments, system-wide outages at the worst possible times, and other assorted war stories. University infrastructures have evolved to provide much more technical support than in the "old days" of online education, and makers of educational technologies have done a lot to eliminate bugs and crashes. But at the same time, advances in what we can do with technology—running programs on mobile devices, streaming audio and video, linking third-party software to our main learning management systems—mean more opportunities for failure of critical course components. Even that most basic driver of technology, reliable electricity, isn't a given in many parts of the world—a sobering thought given the push to extend online learning globally.

The stakes are high for getting the technology to work, as technology problems are one of the main qualms that students have about getting involved in online learning.[20] To head off potential disaster, online instructors have to expend extra effort by pretesting their materials for any glitches, making contingency plans for outages, and cultivating excellent working relationships with their institutions' IT support units.

These factors differentiating online and traditional face-to-face teaching tend to have a logistical or practical flavor to them, rather than pointing to deep qualitative differences in what we can accomplish with the two different approaches. And it isn't as though the face-to-face classroom is free of logistical challenges—those coveted well-illuminated, perfectly temperature-controlled lecture halls with flexible seating arrangements don't come easily either. We simply may not notice these types of challenges as much, given that they are usually the more familiar to us.

The parallels in good teaching across different approaches and technologies can help us feel more confident that the online option doesn't automatically limit our power to teach well. But do these parallels translate into measurable evidence of effectiveness for online teaching, compared to the traditional face-to-face alternative? A number of large-scale empirical research projects have taken aim at that question, and in general, the answer is yes.

The most ambitious among these empirical studies is a widely cited paper published by the U.S. Department of Education, which combined the results from multiple studies in order to assess overall trends in the data.[21] The result of this multi-study meta-analysis was clear: online delivery produced a statistically significant, small-to-moderate-size *advantage* for learning. The USDE researchers set stringent criteria for the studies they included, keeping only those with rigorous experimental designs directly contrasting online and traditional course delivery, substantial use of the Internet to deliver instruction in the online-learning condition, and statistical controls for differences in prior ability between online and traditional versions of the course. Studies also had to have empirical measures of student learning, not just subjective student or instructor perceptions of effectiveness. Notably, *blended* course designs—i.e., courses that combine online and face-to-face components—produced particularly good outcomes, compared to fully online and completely face-to-face courses.

In their interpretation, the authors explained that the different delivery formats were not identical in terms of the quality and amount of work given, time on task, and other important features. Thus, it may not be the online factor per se that explains why online and blended learning came out ahead. But given that the relevant question for instructors is whether online learning *can* be as effective as traditional—not whether there is something special about computer-mediated learning—these findings offer powerful evidence that online learning can be good for students.

Another meta-analysis investigated how the difference in course grades earned in face-to-face versus online courses changed over the nineteen-year span between 1990 and 2009.[22] Similar to what the USDE researchers found, students earned significantly better grades in online courses overall. Additionally, the study revealed that the online advantage shrank in the mid-1990s and grew again fairly rapidly after 2000—perhaps because in the mid-nineties, there was a fad for so-called "online learning" experiences that consisted of merely converting traditional textbook materials to CDs and mailing those out to students. The researchers pointed out that the resurgence of the online advantage in the 2000s coincides with the rise of more-interactive, more-powerful tools embedded in commonly available learning management systems. This all provides further evidence that—particularly with optimal use of the tools available—online teaching can produce better rates of course completion.

What about student learning, independent of grades? Learning and grades are notoriously difficult to separate in any practical way, despite being two very distinct concepts. It's not surprising, therefore, that the research literature contains few large-scale, precisely controlled comparisons of learning across different class formats. One exception is a 2012 study of lower-division statistics courses in which researchers compared learning—defined as scores on a nationally standardized test of statistical literacy and scores on common final exams—across traditionally taught, 100 percent face-to-face statistics courses and those that employed an online system to deliver part of the instruction.[23] Students in this nationwide study were randomly assigned to participate in one or the other of the class formats, offsetting any systematic differences in the types of students who tend to choose blended versus face-to-face courses. The results were clear: student learning was virtually identical across the two formats. Students reported liking the blended courses a little less, and also reported spending less time on blended courses, but both groups learned about the same amount of the core course material.

Some caveats about this study are in order. It comprises one rarefied segment of online learning given that it used just one very well-designed and highly regarded system for the online component (Carnegie Mellon's Open Learning Initiative statistics courseware). And it had a very narrow focus—one course within one discipline. Even so, this study does a good job of showing that under tightly controlled conditions, well-designed online learning activities can produce learning gains comparable to those achieved with face-to-face instruction.

These studies—with their heavy if not exclusive focus on student grades—offer important evidence in favor of the online format. But they also conjure up one of the most contentious issues connected to online teaching and learning: the question of cheating. Who are the people earning the superior grades associated with online coursework—our students, or others enticed to do the work? How did these people complete the work—with or without aids that we wouldn't allow in our face-to-face classes? Collaborating illicitly, or working independently? These questions have dogged online learning for years, and may never be completely put to rest.[24] However, despite all this uncertainty, it is possible to draw some reasonable conclusions about the likely preponderance of cheating in online coursework, and to find ways to design online learning experiences that reduce the risk of cheating.

Without specialized technological aids or elaborate arrangements for in-person proctoring, it may indeed be impossible to verify that a given assignment was completed as directed by a given student. Research on academic dishonesty has focused far more on the traditional classroom than on online coursework.[25] Even so, there is enough relevant work to get a sense of the problem. Based on some theories of why students cheat, we would predict more cheating online because of perceived anonymity and the sense of distance between faculty and students. And according to survey research (as well as typical faculty opinion pieces on the subject), faculty believe that cheating is more common online.[26] Faculty were further sensitized by the high-profile "Shadow Scholar" story that unfolded over 2010–2012, in which disillusioned academic Dave Tomar admitted to selling his services to legions of cheating students for over a decade. Granted, the majority of Tomar's fraudulent work was submitted in traditional face-to-face courses, but he also admitted to taking on a substantial amount of online work, such as required discussion posts.[27] In any case, academic dishonesty is an emotionally fraught and anger-provoking subject for faculty (just view the hundreds of online comments on stories such as the ones on Tomar to get a sense of *how* fraught), and the addition of the online dimension only heightens faculty anger and sense that things are out of control.

Some advocates of online learning retort that cheating is also rampant in face-to-face courses, which is hardly comforting, but makes the online format look a little better by comparison. Advocates also rightly assert that standards for traditional courses rarely meet the stringent criteria needed to satisfy critics of online learning—that if in fact the issue were fully addressed for online courses, they would end up significantly more secure than their traditional counterparts.[28] And as for the distance and anonymity arguments, it may be the case that online interaction is not necessarily any more alienating than being one among hundreds or thousands of other students in a large face-to-face course—a situation that is quite common at many institutions. It's even conceivable that online courses could be *less* conducive to cheating because of factors such as smaller class sizes and increased interactivity.[29]

Consistent with these theoretical ideas, empirical studies of cheating behavior largely provide a reassuring picture, one in which online learning is *not* plagued with rampant dishonesty. Cheating is secretive behavior, so it's not the easiest thing in the world to study its actual incidence. But it's not impossible—researchers have devised a number of techniques that allow them to make reasonable estimates despite the secrecy and stigma around the subject. The simplest is anonymous self-report, i.e., surveying students as to whether they have committed different forms of academic dishonesty. This approach likely underestimates the actual incidence, given that—even anonymously—people are somewhat loath to admit engaging in behaviors that society disapproves of. However, unless there is some reason why traditional and online students are different with respect to falsifying self-reports, survey responses are still informative as to the relative commonness of cheating in the different class formats. There are other ways to get at the question, such as comparing average grades on proctored versus unproctored exams, or as one research group did, surreptitiously photocopying exams before returning them to students for self-grading, then comparing the self-reported grades to the actual grades.[30]

A particularly clever way to estimate cheating is the "randomized response" method, which promotes honest reporting via an extra layer of anonymity.[31] In a randomized response survey, students get one of two survey questions, one of which targets the behavior of interest (e.g., "have you ever cheated on an exam in this class?") and one of which asks an innocuous, irrelevant question (e.g, "do you prefer vanilla ice cream to chocolate ice cream?") for which the experimenters know the likelihood of different responses. No one knows who got which question, making it completely untraceable who answered "yes" to the target behavior. Researchers then untangle how many people probably said yes to the target question by assessing the difference between the predicted proportion of "yes" responses to the irrelevant question and the actual proportion they got. For example, if they know ahead of time that 25 percent of people say they prefer vanilla ice cream, but in their survey 50 percent said yes to the "vanilla ice cream or cheating" question, then in all likelihood, around 25 percent cheated.

Using techniques such as these to get at the data, the preponderance of studies report equivalent or even *reduced* rates of cheating for online compared to face-to-face students.[32] In particular, an often-cited study using the randomized response technique found no greater incidence of cheating in online courses.[33] But a minority of studies do show greater incidences of cheating in online courses.[34] Other studies focusing not on actual incidence, but rather perceptions, suggest that students *believe* that cheating is more common online.[35] Given that students have far more exposure and experience to actual incidences of online cheating than do faculty members, this finding is particularly disturbing.

On balance, the research suggests that some concern is warranted, but it's probably not the case that cheating is everywhere—or that the problem would go away if all coursework were transplanted back to the face-to-face setting. It's up to the instructors and institution to decide how they want to balance concerns for academic integrity against other factors, such as expense, instructor time, and flexibility.

It's also important to look at academic honesty not just in terms of catching cheaters, but also in terms of prevention—and indeed, as part of the course's overall plan for promoting student learning. James Lang's book *Cheating Lessons* makes the compelling argument that academic integrity is best addressed by creating classroom environments that support engaged learning.[36] Drawing on behavioral science as well as pedagogical research, Lang observes that cheating is heavily influenced by situational factors. It is most common in the presence of four key characteristics of the learning environment: emphasis on performance, as opposed to mastery; high stakes; external or extrinsic motivations, such as money or grades; and low expectations of success. In other words, we would predict that students would be highly prone to cheat on a test or assignment when a great deal is riding on the outcome, when students mainly care about performing to earn some external reward, and when they don't believe they have a good shot at succeeding through legitimate effort.

Fortunately, these factors are within the instructor's power to influence, through course design and how requirements are communicated to students. Low-stakes, frequent assessments, as an alternative to the traditional system of having just a couple of major exams or papers per semester, are a particularly good deterrent. Having less riding on any one test or assignment makes the risk of being caught less attractive and makes it more complicated to bring in an accomplice, given that such collusion would have to be done over and over throughout the semester. Having frequent opportunities to succeed also tends to improve students' sense that they have the power to do well through their own effort, a theme we will revisit in Chapter 8. Online tools are particularly useful in courses with a small-stakes/frequent assessment design, making this feature relatively easy to set up and execute compared to purely traditional tools such as in-class pencil-and-paper exams.[37] And as Lang argues, this is one anti-cheating technique that is also good for promoting learning—something we will consider in detail later in this book.

Several other prevention techniques follow Lang's concept and also lend themselves well to online learning. These include designing courses to include a wider array of types of assignments and assessments, including open-ended ones, to get a broader picture of how each individual student is performing across the semester and offer opportunities to note any drastic changes to style that would indicate possible dishonesty.[38] Lang also emphasizes the value of creating specific and/or personalized types of assignments, rather than recycling the same "generic" ones semester to semester, because generic topics make it too tempting (and easy) for students to purchase standard-issue papers on the Internet. According to this reasoning, it's better to assign students to, say, craft a speech to their local city council or write a memo to a hypothetical employer, compared to having them write a standard "compare and contrast" essay.

Another relatively low-cost strategy for preventing cheating in the first place is to make academic dishonesty standards explicit to students.[39] This goes beyond simply putting a policy online or making general announcements such as "cheating will not be tolerated."

It is a near-certainty that students understand less about academic dishonesty than their instructors assume, and furthermore, there are likely to be substantial discrepancies between student and faculty definitions of which specific behaviors constitute cheating. To address this, you can teach the cheating policy the same way you would any other important concept within the course—i.e., giving students clear explanatory materials, pushing them to meaningfully engage with those materials, and holding them accountable for proving that they have mastered them. Requiring that students complete an academic honesty module early in the semester—your institution may have one readily available via the library or e-learning center—is a good practice, and is another technique that works particularly well online. Beyond teaching students what cheating is, the literature on online course design also offers quite a few "best practices" lists and suggestions for discouraging cheating; Baron and Crooks (2005)[40] and Krsak (2007)[41] are two good examples.

Other integrity tools tend to fall more under the category of policing, and less under Lang's concept of preventing dishonesty via learner-centered course design. Nevertheless, these can be a good complement to one's overall plan for promoting integrity within the course. Some to consider include the following:

- Commercial plagiarism detection tools such as Turnitin, SafeAssign, or PlagiarismDetect.[42] The precise way these programs work is proprietary, but in general, they compare coursework to massive databases of student papers, web pages, scholarly journal articles, and other materials that students might be tempted to plagiarize.

- Remote proctoring. Some universities provide remote testing centers, or they require students to travel to campus for proctored testing at university centers. Failing that, there are other creative proctoring solutions, such as allowing a commanding officer, clergy person, or even fire station personnel to serve as a designated proctor.[43]

- High-tech commercial solutions. The development of for-profit test security systems is in full swing, with services that can use facial recognition software, remotely lock down forbidden web sites, monitor students via web cameras, and more. Technology even exists to identify users through their unique patterns of typing.[44] Kryterion and ProctorU are two examples of these types of proprietary systems, and more companies will probably crop up in the coming years as more institutions compete to offer high-integrity online programs. Given the price and complexity of such systems, instructors would have to collaborate with their institution to use them, but if security is a high concern, it is good to know that options are out there.

Let's turn now to a more elusive issue: whether online learning unwittingly encourages minimal, superficial student effort, or what some of my colleagues disparagingly call "just pushing buttons." If students are doing their coursework at home—or at the coffee shop, gym, or who knows where—can we be sure that they are intellectually engaging with material as they would in a face-to-face classroom?

One way to tackle this question is via Bloom's taxonomy, a framework for assessing the intellectual complexity of student learning activities that ranks these cognitive processes from the most routine to the most sophisticated.[45] The taxonomy was significantly revised in 2001[46] to incorporate an added dimension of the type of knowledge students are incorporating into their learning processes, but like the original, the newer version emphasizes the progression from least to most sophisticated intellectual activities. The spectrum of cognitive processes is as follows:[47]

- Remembering
- Understanding
- Applying
- Analyzing
- Evaluating
- Creating

For instructors, the taxonomy provides a practical tool for identifying the different cognitive processes we want students to engage in. It also offers a means for researchers to directly compare intellectual engagement within face-to-face and online courses. One such study found that in the online version of a course (upper-division histology), student questions were weighted more toward the sophisticated end of the scale taxonomy, compared to the face-to-face course, and furthermore, online students performed better on the assessment of content mastery.[48] The researchers pointed out, in particular, the favorable comparison with respect to faculty-student interactions, noting that these personal exchanges were virtually absent in the traditional lecture-style version of the course. Similarly, a study of online discussion postings in a teacher education course found that student posts significantly improved in terms of Bloom's taxonomy over the course of the semester, and that students also improved on a quantitative measure of critical thinking.[49]

These findings suggest that, broadly speaking, it is possible for online learning environments to elicit intellectual engagement across the spectrum of cognitive processes, from least to most sophisticated. Future research may pinpoint more of the differences in what cognitive processes are foregrounded specifically in online learning. If current trends are any indication, much of this research will focus on online discussion groups, particularly how they can build the thinking skills that make up the top of Bloom's hierarchy. Of all possible online learning activities, discussion seems an unlikely candidate for building the more intellectually hefty skills; as the researchers Xin and Feenberg put it, "Online discussion is paradoxical. It consists in a flow of relatively disorganized improvisational exchanges that somehow achieve highly goal-directed, rational course agendas" (p. 2).[50] Yet, they argue, intellectual engagement is at the heart of a well-run online discussion, as it requires activities such as reasoning from examples, defining terms and concepts, and other central aspects of critical thinking. In Chapter 6, we'll return to the issue of how to best promote learning using online discussions, but for now, they serve as one clear example of how we can promote and document student intellectual growth using online methods.

There is one further practical caveat about intellectual engagement in online learning activities—something that comes back to the time-and-effort factor cited by so many experts on quality undergraduate education. More so than in the traditional classroom, students can seriously underestimate how much time and effort is required to succeed in online learning. Part of this problem may have to do with the much-vaunted "flexibility" of online coursework. If the idea is that online learning fits in between family time, paid work, travel, child care, and everything else in life, it likely ends up an afterthought tacked on after all those other life activities are addressed. And as we all know, exhausted, distracted, time-pressed students are unlikely to achieve stellar intellectual gains in *any* instructional format. Some experts argue that online learning's tendency to become a "third shift"—i.e., something tackled after work and family duties are done—places a particular burden on female students, given their greater responsibility, on average, for the "second shift" of family work.[51] Furthermore, in face-to-face teaching, you can ensure that some bare minimum of time is devoted to classwork (by policing attendance), and you can schedule classes when students are likely to be fresh (i.e., not in the middle of the night). Neither of these basic strategies for ensuring maximal engagement is easy to do online.

Like many other quality issues, the third-shift problem can be addressed through forethought and savvy design choices. One good place to start is with a heavy dose of socialization at the beginning of the course about your expectations for student time commitment. Simply exhorting students that they will have to work hard and put in time has limited impact, but at least you can get your expectations out into the open early. Following through on your stated expectations, by having some small-stakes work due early in the semester, is another good practice for getting students into the right mindset. Beyond laying out your expectations and following through on them, you can consider scheduling some synchronous-style work if you are concerned that students are just squeezing in little bits of work at odd hours. This approach has costs (such as potentially disadvantaging slower readers, as mentioned previously) and may be perceived as user-unfriendly by students, but it's a clear way to exert more control over the pacing and timing of work.

You can also exploit the student usage data that's tracked within your learning management system to get a better picture of the time students spend on various components of your class. Those data can then help you refine and shape your online learning practices. For example, I was surprised to learn that my online Introduction to Psychology students were routinely going into discussion forums as their "first stop" upon logging in to the course, and once they were there, they were spending much more time than I originally antici-pated. I used that information to better understand the role that dis-cussions played in building the social cohesion and "fun" factor of the course, and as an informal red flag for students who weren't as invested in the course. In another online class (Cognitive Psychol-ogy), research collaborators and I found that the number of discus-sion posts students made were the number one predictor of their overall course grade, even though these made up only a tiny fraction of course points.[52] Based on this information, I built in more choices of discussion topics and began contacting students who weren't par-ticipating early on. The online environment presents many such op-portunities to get to know your students' work patterns better and spot ways that they can improve—all of which further reinforces the quality of the online learning experience.

So is the trend toward online teaching and learning positive or negative? In other words, is online teaching *quality* teaching? Hall-marks of quality—student effort, frequent and high-quality interac-tion, active learning, and so forth—appear to be quite similar across modalities. Empirical research on outcomes tends to favor online learning, with some studies even turning up substantial advantages, particularly for designs where online and face-to-face components complement one another. More research is needed on outcomes that emphasize thinking skills—such as those that constitute the top of Bloom's taxonomy—over grades, but there are some encouraging re-sults here too. Lastly, empirical evidence suggests that the much-publicized concerns about cheating on online coursework may be substantially overblown. With all this in mind, it makes sense to con-clude that quality online learning experiences are possible—and turn our attention back to maximizing that quality.

Chapter 3

The Psychology of Computing

So FAR, WE'VE ESTABLISHED that technology in higher education is here to stay, and considered whether high-quality educational experiences are possible online. But what about the human side? How do human beings interact with computers and with one another via computers? If we are going to contribute, via our teaching, to the further expansion of computing into everyday life, we should ask ourselves what the likely impacts are on how we think, reason, and communicate with others. In other words, how do computers change us?

Psychologists have barely begun to put together coherent theoretical frameworks for how ubiquitous computing changes human thought.[1] This hasn't stopped the popular media from putting out numerous ominous-sounding claims about supposed effects of technology on our minds and brains. Some amount to a "moral panic," that is, a wave of overreaction to social change fueled by the self-interests of people who build careers by perpetuating and magnifying the issue.[2]

Decades ago, American society went through another technological upheaval that people thought would fundamentally reengineer human interaction, cognitive abilities, and public discourse.[3] What was this disruptive technology? Radio. Much like the Internet in contemporary times, this technological wonder sparked tremendous optimism about its potential to expand minds, bring the world to people isolated by geography and circumstances, and unite people as never before. A "national radio college" was even proposed to Calvin Coolidge's administration as a way of propagating a system of distance education throughout the United States and perhaps even the world.[4]

But there were also significant concerns—that citizens would become illiterate, critical-thinking abilities would decline, and personal relationships would fall apart. Scholars got into the act, pumping out book after book analyzing and criticizing the impacts of radio. [5] Some worried that this new, easy source of information would make libraries and newspapers, and perhaps even reading itself, obsolete.[6] The potential impacts on children aroused particular alarm. As one concerned researcher wrote in 1936: "This new invader of the privacy of the home has brought many a disturbing influence in its wake. Parents have become aware of a puzzling change in the behavior patterns of their children. They are bewildered by a host of new problems, and find themselves unprepared, frightened, resentful, helpless. They cannot lock out this intruder because it has gained an invincible hold of their children." [7] Substitute "the Internet" or "smart phones" as the new invader and this quote could pass for something written today.

Radio didn't create a global, information-driven utopia, but neither did it cause total social or psychological collapse. The same is likely true for computers. Other potential consequences, though, are more difficult to assess. Do brain scans *really* reveal that heavy technology use rewires the brain? Does interacting online *really* bring out the worst in our social natures? Is it true that students who grew up with technology—so-called digital natives—are fundamentally, even neurologically, different from previous generations? And, as author Nicholas Carr memorably asked—is Google making us stupid?[8]

Nobody wants to risk making their students stupid by sending them onto the Internet, so before we inject even more technology into students' lives, it's reasonable to ask about the psychological impacts. Many of these impacts—such as the way computers affect interpersonal communication—are also directly relevant to the ways in which we set up and manage online learning experiences. Unfortunately, the atmosphere of moral panic around the topic, combined with the absence of a good theoretical framework, has set up a situation where hyperbole and misinformation thrive. With that in mind, let's consider some of the major myths about the psychology of computing—and then, what the facts mean for our teaching.

Myths, Facts, and Consequences

Myth: Today's computing and mobile communication technologies are able to "rewire" the brain at a neural level, fundamentally transforming our ability to think.

THE CLAIM: The rapid spread of computing into every corner of life represents a drastic change in lifestyle for many of us, and so pundits—and a few academic researchers as well—have begun to ask whether we can be neurally altered by constant interaction with computers. The underlying idea seems to be that interacting with information via computers is such a uniquely powerful experience that it rearranges our very neural structure—changing us irrevocably and perhaps even blocking us from interacting with information as we did in the pre-computing era, i.e., through books, paper, and face-to-face conversation. Particularly damaging, this line of reasoning goes, are the technologies that encourage brief, superficial engagement with people and ideas—Google searching and Twitter being prime offenders.

These worries about computing and the brain coalesced in a 2010 bestseller by journalist Nicholas Carr titled *The Shallows: What the Internet Is Doing to Our Brains.*[9] Carr traces the history of technologies for gathering and transmitting information, from an early "writing ball" that Friedrich Nietzsche used to type out his later works to the search engines Carr relies on for his own book research. He declares the Internet to be the most powerful "mind-altering technology" mankind has ever known, rivaled perhaps only by the invention of books. Reading on the Internet is fundamentally different from reading paper-based text, according to Carr; among other things, brain scanning studies show that Internet browsing produces neurally distinct patterns of activation, and those changes persist after only short periods of "exposure" to the web.

THE REALITY: Pundits have a point about the massive inroads technology has made into the lives of people in industrialized society, and indeed, some of these technologies have reached a level of sophistication that falls somewhere between astonishing and creepy. Search engines anticipate what we're going to type before we type it, Amazon suggests the perfect title based on our past history and the preferences of millions of other users, and Google Maps may just have a picture of our home for all the world to see.

And as a species, we can't get enough of it. Particularly with the advent of incredibly powerful mobile devices such as tablets and smart phones, many people compute constantly, day in and day out. In my undergraduate course Mind, Brain, and Technology, the students and I kick off the semester by drawing up a one-day "technology diary" chronicling the electronic devices we use throughout a typical day. According to these diaries, the majority of class members (myself included) habitually use our smart phones to go online before we even get out of bed in the morning. This pattern echoes a recent survey in which 81 percent of respondents said they kept their smart phones switched on all night long, and around 40 percent said they started using their phones right after waking up.[10]

What's less clear is the actual neurological impact—if any—associated with this mass usage of technology. One problem has to do with the breadth of the concept of neural "rewiring." Technically speaking, computing experience does alter our brains at a neural level, but so does just about anything else that we remember. As cognitive scientist Steven Pinker points out, "Yes, every time we learn a fact or skill the wiring of the brain changes; it's not as if the information is stored in the pancreas. But the existence of neural plasticity does not mean the brain is a blob of clay pounded into shape by experience."[11] Computing has no more special power to transform mind and brain than do other compelling life experiences, Pinker observes—and given that the rise of computing has coincided with an explosion in worldwide intellectual and scientific discovery, it seems unlikely that any transformation has resulted in a net intellectual loss. Just as critics warned against the intellect-destroying dangers of television at the same time as IQs were rising, and others cautioned about the ills of violent video games while crime plummeted, antitechnology arguments like these are fundamentally inconsistent with social trends.

There are other reasons to take "rewiring" claims with a grain of salt. There is remarkably little peer-reviewed research to support claims about how Internet use affects the brain's ability to process information. According to one such claim, we read online text in a superficial, "F-shaped" pattern of eye movements, which alters our processing of that information compared to what we would do with a paper-based text.[12] But the data that were actually gathered for this non-peer-reviewed study had to do with patterns of eye movements, not brain activity; they also fail to illuminate what such a difference in eye movements might mean for understanding or remembering the content.

In another study cited by Carr, neuroscientists used functional brain imaging to contrast patterns of neural activity in people with limited prior exposure to web browsing before and after they were exposed to this new (to them) way of taking in information.[13] Sure enough, web browsing did produce measurable differences compared to a simulated book reading experience; it produced activation in a wider range of brain areas, particularly those in frontal regions having to do with decision making and judgment. These differences between reading and browsing persisted in the cyber-naïve volunteers over time, providing physiological evidence for neural change specifically associated with online activity.

The problem, however, is in figuring out what these changes mean. On the one hand, does the wider activation contribute to "techno-brain burnout," as implied in a *Scientific American* article ("Meet your iBrain") that talked about this research study?[14] Or do they simply point to the fact that web browsing is "novel and mentally stimulating," as hypothesized in another article about the same study?[15] It's also unclear whether these findings are generalizable across different demographics and situations. Importantly, the volunteers for the study were all middle-aged to older adults, ranging in age from fifty-five to seventy-eight. Focusing on older people made practical sense given that the researchers specifically needed to find volunteers with limited prior online experience, but this limitation restricts the study's applicability to young people—who happen to be the ones we're usually talking about when we discuss the dangers of constantly being online. It's also unclear whether the changes in brain function associated with web browsing impact activities *other* than web browsing in any meaningful way.

In sum, there is good reason to doubt that computing causes global physiological changes in the brain, or that any such changes detract from our cognitive abilities. But what about the related issue of multitasking—something that tends to go hand in hand with ready access to lots of Internet-enabled devices? Computers, tablets, and smart phones ostensibly do many of the same things as their traditional counterparts—books, paper, wristwatches, pencils, day planners—but unlike them, they can do a lot of *other* things at the same time. This presents the typical user with an astounding array of distractions. And many users opt right into these distraction opportunities, simultaneously cuing up e-mail, games, instant messaging, web searches, shopping, and video, just to name a few.

What are the cognitive implications of multitasking abetted by technology? This question breaks down into two parts: first, what short-term effects on performance result from doing multiple things at once, and second, what long-term changes might occur as a result of habitual multitasking. The first question is easy—study after study in the field of attention research shows that with only a few exceptions, doing tasks concurrently detracts from performance, even when we subjectively feel confident that we can do both at once. One of the highest-profile, and most dangerous, examples is driving while carrying on a cell phone conversation. Many people feel quite confident that they can competently do both at once, but the evidence is clear that cell conversations drain cognitive resources away from driving, substantially impairing reaction time and other measures of performance.[16]

Multitasking is also a threat to performance in academic settings. Generally speaking, academic achievement decreases as with increased multitasking—including texting, instant messaging, and going on social media—either during class or while doing out-of-class assignments.[17] There is some indication that students can capably multitask under limited circumstances; one study found no decrements in memory for a studied text passage when a short instant-message type conversation was carried on at the same time, although this only held up when students controlled the pacing of the material.[18] Especially worrisome is the finding that students who multitask on laptops during class not only score worse on a test over the presented material, but also cause students *around* them to do more poorly.[19] As we will explore in more detail in Chapter 4, attention is a limited resource, and anything that drains attention away from the task at hand is virtually guaranteed to reduce learning.

What about the second question—whether habitual multitasking causes long-term changes in cognitive functioning? The best information we have to date comes from a line of research on the cognitive and neurological characteristics of "chronic media multitaskers."[20] Study participants filled out a survey querying how many hours they typically spent using different communications technologies—everything from TV to music audio to instant messaging—and how often they used more than one at the same time. From these two measures, the authors calculated an overall multitasking score, which they correlated to scores on a suite of working memory and attention tasks. Heavy multitaskers performed significantly worse, especially for tasks requiring them to focus on one stimulus while ignoring other stimuli.

This is a concerning finding, but as the study authors themselves caution, this correlation doesn't mean that multitasking *caused* changes to cognitive abilities. Rather, it could be that individuals who find it harder to focus in the first place are drawn toward using lots of different technologies at once. It could also be the case that worse performance on this particular set of tests—which favored the ability to focus in the face of distraction—is balanced out on other tasks that favor the ability to take in a little information from a lot of inputs at once.[21] In other words, the pattern of performance associated with habitual multitasking might simply be different, not worse.

WHAT THIS MEANS FOR TEACHING: We don't need to worry that creating a fully online class, or one heavily infused with technology, will contribute to mental decline. It's questionable even whether habitually multitasking with technology causes long-term alterations to the brain or decrements in mental functioning. However, multitasking across different devices, applications, and so forth does appear to hurt performance across a variety of activities, including comprehending and remembering class content. Students may insist that they juggle these things so naturally that they are exempt from this principle, but their subjective feeling of confidence is deceiving; people typically have poor awareness of their attentional limitations, and extensive experience with multitasking doesn't usually make us any better at it.[22]

For example, consider how damaging techno-multitasking could be in a blended course. Blended designs usually feature major amounts of independent, online coursework combined with shorter-than-normal periods of in-class time. For this setup to work, students have to master a certain amount of the material before coming to class and remain attentive and engaged while they are there. Because class time is so limited in blended designs—even more so than in a typical lecture-based class—not a moment can be wasted. Creating a specific policy on the use of different devices in class—and following through on enforcing it—is well justified by what we know about the power of multitasking to undermine learning both in the multitaskers and others around them.

It's harder to deter students from dysfunctional multitasking when they're doing online work on their own, but explicitly teaching them about attentional limitations and multitasking may help. In Chapter 4, I offer more ideas for doing so in online environments, but this can also be done in the face-to-face setting (e.g., during class time in a blended course). One in-class demonstration[23] of the hazards of multitasking goes like this: You instruct students to complete a simple task—tapping one another on the shoulder sequentially, so that you tap your neighbor as soon as someone taps you. You start the demonstration by tapping the first student at the front of the class, so that the "tap" winds its way through the whole class. Have the students do it first while they are devoting full attention to the activity, and time how long it takes for the tap to relay all the way to the end. This gives you a rough idea of students' reaction time under relatively undistracted conditions. Then, repeat the exercise while giving the students the option to pull out a cell phone and start texting. You'll find—amid much giggling about being told to text during class—that the time to transmit the tap slows down radically, showing that even an incredibly simple action can be thrown off by carrying on a text conversation at the same time.

Myth: Students today are part of a "digital native" generation whose experience with computing makes them fundamentally different from older cohorts.

THE CLAIM: The term "digital native" was coined by Marc Prensky to describe individuals who have grown up in the era of ubiquitous computing and Internet, as opposed to "digital immigrants" who adopted these technologies later in life.[24] The exact metaphor that underlies the digital nativism concept varies across different authors, but in general it casts technology use as analogous to language learning. In this idea, using technology, if done from childhood, can be like speaking one's native tongue—effortless, fluent, and woven throughout one's cognitive processes. But if it's adopted as an adult, it's only mastered slowly, painfully, and imperfectly. Like second-language learners who never quite lose their accents, digital immigrants struggle to master the technology that their younger, native counterparts handle with ease. And much like native speakers, digital natives take what they've grown up with for granted, never imagining how they would function without it. In fact, they may not even view things like social networking or smart phones as "technology," but rather just as a part of the landscape of normal life.[25]

It follows that growing up with technology creates a cognitive generation gap. According to the numerous different descriptions of this gap, digital natives think in a holistic, nonlinear way compared to their seniors: "Individuals raised with the computer deal with information differently compared to previous cohorts. . . . A linear thought process is much less common than . . . the ability to piece information together from multiple sources" (pp. 2.4–2.5).[26] And thus digital natives and older people learn differently, with the digital natives emphasizing visual-spatial processing over text, preferring learning by doing, and favoring ultra-rapid response times combined with rapid attentional shifting.[27] These preferences may even be neurally hardwired, as some authors claim: "While the brains of today's digital natives are wiring up for rapid-fire cyber searches, however, the neural circuits that control the more traditional learning methods are neglected and gradually diminished. The pathways for human interaction and communication weaken as customary one-on-one people skills atrophy" (p. 49).[28]

The digital native concept has major implications for the role of technology in college teaching. For one thing, it suggests that, much as digital immigrants struggle *with* technology, digital natives struggle *without* it. Taken to the extreme, this interpretation would mean that teaching without technology is akin to asking students to function in an unfamiliar language environment, thus setting them up for failure. It follows that older instructors must "translate" old-style materials into digital form, for no other reason than to make them accessible to younger generations.

THE REALITY: The idea that the generations are wired differently for technology is appealing, but probably wrong. Consider one opinion I heard stated in a discussion of technology in modern life: "I'm from a big, traditional Italian family, and I don't like how technology is always interfering with family life. We'll be having a get together, and everyone is looking down, playing with their phones. . . . Put it down and pay attention to the people who are actually here, right in front of you!" Try to picture the individual who said this. Is it someone your own age? Older? A grandmother, perhaps? In fact, this critic of technology is twenty-two-year-old Hillary Cacioppo, a college senior. She said this in context of an in-class exercise I put on to demonstrate the breadth of attitudes toward technology, in which students lined up along an imaginary continuum from "love technology" to "hate technology." Part of a substantial number who situated themselves at the "hate" end, Hillary was not alone in articulating what she found intrusive about mobile phones and similar technology. Today's students may have grown up with technology, but that doesn't make them mindless advocates for it.

A growing chorus of skeptics are putting tough questions to the digital nativism concept. Researcher Mark Bullen has been a particularly vocal critic of the supposedly unique qualities of Internet-generation students, stating that "it is too easy to look at statistics on use and make all sorts of inferences but what good research has shown is that using a computer, tablet or smart phone for one task doesn't necessarily translate to others, doesn't make the user a *sophisticated* user of the technology and doesn't necessarily have any impact on other skills and traits."[29] Bullen also criticizes the research basis for digital nativism, which he describes as heavily reliant on anecdotal reports and other nonscientific approaches.[30]

Survey results from today's traditional-age college students reveal a more goal-directed, or "context sensitive" approach to technology than the digital nativism narrative would suggest.[31] Students tend to choose specific technologies as means to accomplish particular goals—e.g., communicating with professors or sharing files with classmates—rather than viewing technology as part of the very fabric of life. Furthermore, their computing skills can be surprisingly limited; although younger students tend to draw on a wider array of technologies to communicate with one another, they are no more likely than their older counterparts to feel especially digitally literate.[32] And despite everyday use of various applications and search technologies, they may have very superficial conceptual understanding of these tools.[33] Nor are they especially likely to enjoy using technology, or to want to use it pervasively through their social and educational lives.[34] Some research even suggests that, on average, *older* students tend to be more competent with technology in educational settings.[35]

WHAT THIS MEANS FOR TEACHING: There's little reason to believe that ubiquitous computing has transformed the younger generation of students into tech-savvy, tech-dependent individuals who think in ways that are distinct from those of their older counterparts. But what's the harm in acting as if the nativism idea is true? First, its underlying metaphor, that of the native tongue, is deeply misleading; it underestimates the capacity of older individuals to adopt and effectively use technology, and suggests a wider and more permanent gap in generations than actually exists. This faulty metaphor can lead to mindlessly adopting technology merely for its own sake, when instead we ought to be selective and goal-focused in using technology to teach.

Second, the metaphor could discourage us from offering the real and needed technical guidance that students—even young students—need in order to succeed in technologically enhanced classes. As teachers, we need to ensure that *all* students, regardless of age, learn the technologies we ask them to use in our courses. As described in Chapter 2, this is one of the major distinguishing characteristics of online teaching and learning—students often need to learn how to use the technology at the same time that they are mastering course content. Knowledge about one system or tool often fails to transfer to another, further underscoring the need for explicit technology teaching, even in the case of the most cell-phone-addicted "digital native" students.

Myth: Computing—especially social networking à la Facebook—destroys real-life social relationships.

THE CLAIM: Facebook's explosion into the public consciousness in the late aughts triggered new rounds of questions about the impact of technology on our lives and minds.[36] Some critics argue that sites like Facebook destroy, or at least deemphasize, real-world social relationships. Even among enthusiasts, "social media diets" are an increasingly popular method for weaning oneself off this allegedly addictive form of computing.[37] Others wonder whether social media—with its emphasis on self-congratulatory posts and self-portraits—can lead to unhealthy self-centeredness, or even full-blown narcissism.

THE REALITY: The appearance of rich, multimedia online social spaces is indeed a major development in how most people incorporate technology into daily life. Facebook is the most obvious example of such a social space, but it is not the first or only one, having developed alongside other, less successful systems such as Myspace and Friendster. It also coexists with an array of other specialized online social worlds that use discussion boards, profiles, and more to link people with common interests.[38]

Questions about the interpersonal impacts of social networking are important for online instructors, as plenty of us are now incorporating social media in one form or another into our teaching. To address them, we should first back up and consider the impact of the Internet at large on social life and social relationships, something that researchers have considered since the Internet first left the confines of the academy and entered mainstream life. In general, research put to rest early fears that the Internet would lead to a society of disconnected, depressed shut-ins.[39] Much worldwide e-mail use serves to build social relationships in one way or another, and over the long run, time spent with family and friends does *not* decrease as Internet use increases.[40] Furthermore, online relationships can and do develop into real-world friendships—a possibility heightened by the peculiar finding that people who meet first on the

Internet actually tend to like each other *more* than those who first meet face to face.[41]

Critics can perhaps be excused from some of their initial alarmism about the effect of Internet on the social fabric, given that the rise of television did indeed produce devastating effects on community life, such as the "bowling alone" phenomenon famously documented by sociologist Robert Putnam. But, for whatever combination of reasons, the Internet does not share television's propensity to steal time from real people. Perhaps this reflects our hyper-social nature as a species—given the technology and the choice of how we spend our time, we're largely opting to use new technologies to add to our social repertoire, rather than substituting the nonsocial for the social.

The Internet in general doesn't erode social relationships, but social networking in particular may have some worrisome social and psychological impacts. Narcissism has actually been associated with Facebook use, albeit in limited ways. There's a positive correlation between scores on psychological tests of narcissism and the overall number of Facebook friends, as well as intercorrelations between a person's narcissistic traits, the overall level of Facebook activity, and the self-promoting nature of content posted.[42] All these findings suggest that, unfortunately, Facebook may highlight the self-aggrandizement and self-importance associated with narcissistic tendencies. The ability to exert near-total control over one's self-presentation, coupled with the ability to amass hundreds or even thousands of "friends," may make Facebook a particularly attractive platform for narcissists.[43] Similarly, narcissistic traits of entitlement and exhibitionism are associated with antisocial behaviors specific to Facebook, such as reacting angrily to negative comments or being hostile when other people don't respond to your posts right away.[44] It is important to note that research does *not* suggest that merely going on Facebook will turn someone into a narcissist, but the association between characteristic Facebook activities—posting, friending, commenting—and narcissistic traits does paint an unflattering psychological picture of what many users are doing while they are there.

College teachers will also be shocked—shocked!—to learn that in college students, increased overall Facebook use is associated with lower academic performance. One study of undergraduate business school students showed that higher self-reports of using online social media correlated with poorer grades, and that students who rated themselves as highly distractible were particularly likely to report both heavy use of social media and poor academic performance.[45] Poor academic performance is also, unsurprisingly, associated with use of Facebook during class meetings.[46]

Overall, Facebook does not seem to have the power to transform people's personalities. But it does offer a brightly lit stage on which people play out their existing personality traits, sometimes in amplified form. Heavy Facebook users are made up not just of narcissists, but also of socially skilled extroverts: "people people" who enjoy socializing and are adept at social interactions in general.[47] Further research into what attracts people to Facebook reveals distinct uses connected to different goals and needs. Primarily, they use it when they feel disconnected with others, and usage does seem to satisfy connectedness needs.[48] Put another way, people like to go on Facebook when they feel lonely, then back off when the loneliness abates. And people can, under the right circumstances, gain an authentic boost to social connectedness from this unique online form of social interaction.

WHAT THIS MEANS FOR TEACHING: Computing is not necessarily an asocial or antisocial activity, and online communication has the power to complement rather than compete with "real" social interaction. Social media, however, is a special case. Given what we know about it right now, instructors shouldn't take lightly the decision to encourage—or even require—something like Facebook in their courses. Students who are shy or socially awkward in the face-to-face classroom are likely to be the same way on social media, and students with tendencies to be grandiose or self-centered will likely exhibit those tendencies to a heightened degree in the Facebook environment. And unfortunately, "Facebook wars"—those prolonged negative exchanges prompted by perceived slights, snarky comments, and other miscellaneous faux pas—have a distinct tendency to spread rapidly and produce collateral damage. It's as if the same massive interconnectedness that makes social networks a so irresistible also draws people—with amazing speed and efficiency—into interpersonal conflict.

But if we don't use social media, aren't we missing out on the opportunity to reach today's young students in their preferred medium? The public perception seems to be that all young people are enthusiastic, willing Facebook addicts, but the truth is much more nuanced. As one study of college students revealed, not all people in this young demographic love social media.[49] Importantly, young people show a strong tendency to segregate their "work" and "nonwork" social media time, preferring to use social media for non-school-related activities only.[50] Some traditional-age college students avoid social media altogether, citing concerns about what future employers may discover about them, privacy or personal safety issues. Others simply dislike spending their time that way. So before incorporating social media into their teaching, instructors need to consider how they will accommodate these legitimate concerns—for example, by providing alternatives or using a medium other than Facebook to provide a social networking experience. And they will need to plan to spend a lot of time orchestrating and supervising the experience, so that the negative aspects of social media (narcissism, conflict) don't take over.

It's also crucial to set up class materials in ways that aren't open to the Facebook world at large, and that don't require students (or you!) to open up their entire profiles to the whole class. The details of Facebook's privacy mechanisms are constantly changing, but in general, they offer ways to set up groups where students can interact without "friending" one another. Closed groups, for example, are invitation-only, and although the general public can see the closed group's existence, only members can see the content. Groups for Schools is another useful feature that enables you to restrict membership of your group to people associated with your school and allows you to share content with students without forcing them to share personal profiles with one another.[51] As more instructors weigh the benefits and drawbacks of Facebook, there are starting to be more guides to best practices to educational uses of social media—and given that there are so many potential drawbacks, these are well worth consulting.[52]

All three of these ideas about how computers change us—that computers rewire our brains, digital natives are different, and computers harm social life—can be categorized as myths, or at best, myths containing a grain of truth. There's one other major impact of computing, though, that is no myth at all: the way in which communicating via computer radically alters how a message comes across. This is a major consideration for instructors, given that online learning activities almost always require students to communicate with one another and with us via some type of technology.

Technology-mediated communication is a fact of contemporary life, particularly for academics, for whom e-mail has taken over as the preferred means of workplace communication. E-mail alternatives such as text messaging and computer-based instant messaging have both taken off in work and social contexts, combining the text-based, asynchronous format of e-mail with the immediacy of the telephone. And virtual "bulletin boards" are the preferred medium for public and semipublic discussion of every topic from hot political issues to the best way to manage your cat's diabetes.

E-mail and discussion posts are currently the primary means by which students in online courses communicate with instructors and with other students, but there are other means as well. Students may also communicate and collaborate via "wikis," the form of collaborative online writing made famous by Wikipedia. Free online tools such as Wikispaces.com allow instructors to set up class-specific areas for students to create pages about class topics, edit and add to one another's work (with all changes tracked by time, date, and author), and comment on the work via discussion boards. For example, students in my graduate Teaching Practicum course used Wikispaces to create pages about different teaching guidelines and techniques (Chickering and Gamson's principles, advice on public speaking, active learning ideas, etc.) and to comment on what they found particularly useful about one another's pages. Besides e-mail, discussions, and wikis, there also are less text-heavy, more immediate communication formats including Internet-based video phone technology (e.g., Skype) and synchronous chatting (in which written messages appear in real time in a scrolling, online conversation rather than being posted and responded to after a delay).

What do we know about how all these different modalities change communication, especially in learning environments? For one, they offer some advantages over messy, real-time face-to-face discourse. E-mail and discussion board posts are lean and uncomplicated, offering little in between the verbatim text and the reader that might change the interpretation. Online written communication is also less swayed by characteristics like gender, race, age, and attractiveness that can bias us when talking face to face.[53] E-mail and discussion postings have also been lauded for their ability to promote more thoughtful discourse—owing to their asynchronous, time-delayed nature—and provide a feeling of protection from the sometimes-intimidating social setting of the classroom or faculty office hour.[54]

But there are major downsides as well. Online written communication strips away most of the nonverbal cues that help us identify tone, intent, and the emotional state of the speaker. E-mail in particular is notorious for producing misinterpretations of emotion, something that e-mail users tend to learn the hard way sooner or later. Perhaps we ought to know better, but we can't seem to keep ourselves from trying to interpret emotions in e-mail or text messages, or from trying to get them across to our intended readers.[55] Common as they are, emoticons are only moderately effective at fine-tuning a written message. They are necessary but not sufficient to effectively communicate qualities such as sarcasm; overall, the literal written message tends to override emoticons.[56] Even worse, people tend to underestimate the positive emotion and overestimate the negative emotion in e-mail messages; this *negative bias* means that even an objectively neutral message can easily be interpreted as critical or hostile.[57]

The limitations of online communication may lead to emotional misunderstandings, but there's another problem: Some of the perceived malice in online communications isn't misinterpretation at all, but rather, exactly what the writer intended. People can be incredibly *mean* online—why? Unfortunately, some people have personality types and communication styles that predispose them to becoming online bullies.[58] And even those who aren't prone to bullying can be pushed toward it by the feeling of anonymity associated with being online. Disinhibition—i.e., the relaxing of our usual impulse control systems—is heightened by social environments in which we feel less identifiable as individuals.[59] It's associated with doing things we normally wouldn't, including hostile behavior such as flaming, and also increased self-disclosure.[60] A riot is the perfect example of a deindividuated environment, enabling individuals to be swept up in the anonymity of a crowd and thus predisposing them to do things they would never dream of in their normal lives.

So is online communication a virtual riot? Anonymity could be responsible for some, but not all, of the excess self-disclosure and verbal abuse associated with disinhibited online communication.[61] Much of online communication today—and most of class-related online communication—is not really anonymous, given that at the very least one usually entrusts a service provider with personal information when setting up an account. Furthermore, what seems to be more important than actual anonymity is perceived visual anonymity. Being visually obscured has powerful effects on what we say online. Just including a video link in a synchronous online discussion, for example, significantly decreases the amount of self-disclosure people put forth.[62] Eye contact is a particularly important aspect of visual communication; introducing eye contact reduces disinhibited, hostile behavior even more than does identifying participants by name.[63] Even fake visual representations can have big impacts on online comportment. In one study of an educational simulation, students were assigned young, attractive avatars (cartoons used to stand in for one's picture online) and allowed to use made-up online names. This setup seemed to encourage students to make inappropriate comments to each other ("hey babe," and so forth), despite the fact that the exercise was clearly intended to be educational.[64]

The balance between private and public self-awareness also affects online disinhibition.[65] In a typical online situation, one is intensely focused on personal awareness and interior experience, and less focused on one's role in relation to other people or to society at large. Similarly, the online environment tends to make us feel unusually "in control." We can answer a post right away, or put it off till later; we can post a picture of our choice, or none at all. Even if we're on a live video feed, we can pick the background and angle. This exaggerated feeling of personal control can lead us to focus more on self than we normally would, encouraging us to shed our normal social inhibitions.

Text-based communication, emotional tone, disinhibition—online communication is a real minefield. So how do we as teachers manage online communication, both to promote learning and keep the class atmosphere from devolving into the online equivalent of smashed windows and burning cars? First, online instructors themselves need to be adept at editing messages so as not to come across as hostile or hectoring in the online environment. Emoticons might help, but can't be relied upon to prevent misinterpretation. Similarly, we can explicitly educate students about the pitfalls of online written communication, explaining the negative bias, issues around sarcasm and the like, and modeling good ways to get message and tone across in a collegial fashion. Bear in mind that students are prone to disclose more and be less restrained than they would in the face-to-face classroom setting, and in contrast to face-to-face interactions, what they disclose is permanently out there, and can be copied and spread over the whole Internet. Depending on what you are teaching, a certain amount of sharing and informality may be desirable, but it can easily cross a line: thoughtful candor is good, "hey babe!" is not. Tell students explicitly not to share more than they feel comfortable sharing—and give parameters about what's not OK to share, even for those less-inhibited students who feel comfortable sharing pretty much everything.

Also consider introducing some visual aspect to students' online profiles—if not a full-blown video feed, then at least a profile
picture—to take the edge off the visual anonymity that can contribute to over-sharing and verbal cruelty. Lastly, it's important to
take a hard line on any communications that resemble flaming, i.e.,
name-calling, put-downs, and similar abuse. Online bullying may
be common, but fortunately, the research suggests that it can be
strongly moderated by all kinds of environmental factors, from enhancing visibility to introducing consequences.

Concluding Thoughts on the Psychology of Computing

Returning to the overarching question of this chapter, what can
we conclude about how computing changes us? Clearly, technology
changes the quality of our communications, necessitating more
careful handling of matters such as tone and emotional nuance but
also paving the way for more thoughtful, deeper forms of discourse
compared to face-to-face conversation. Social media represent a
powerful and transforming influence on interpersonal interactions,
although they don't have the ability to transform our personalities.
Communication impacts aside, there is little reason to believe that
computing in and of itself produces fundamental neural and cognitive changes, nor do younger students *have* to be taught with technology because they have been neurally programmed to need it.

The tools available to us reinforce certain cognitive skills while
deemphasizing others, and the availability of technology no doubt
causes us to approach intellectual tasks differently from how we
otherwise would. But this selective reinforcement is nothing new.
As cognitive psychologist Raymond Nickerson observes, people
have been creating technology to expand their cognitive capabilities
for millennia, and the range of these cognitive enhancers properly
includes everything from the alphabet to slide rules to Google. Technology impacts thought, yes, but the influence is hardly a simplistic
one: "The relationship between technology and cognition is one of
dependency that goes both ways. There would be little in the way
of technology in the absence of cognition. And cognition would be
greatly handicapped if all its technological aids were suddenly to

disappear. Technology is a product of cognition, and its production is a cyclic, self-perpetuating process. Cognition invents technology, the technology invented amplifies the ability of cognition to invent additional technology that amplifies further the ability of cognition . . . and so it goes" (p. 25).[66] The tools we use can and do change us. But when we use these tools mindfully, we can remain in control of those changes, shaping them to benefit our students.

Chapter 4

Attention

FOR THE FIRST DECADE I worked at NAU, I ran an interactive exhibit at an annual event called the Flagstaff Festival of Science. Wedged in among the robotics demonstrations, the insect zoo, and microscope slides covered in pond water, my booth was something I envisioned as a way to promote the public image of psychology—especially cognitive psychology—as a "real" empirical science. But firing up people's interest in a field focused on invisible mental processes can be challenge—especially when you're competing with the physics students one booth over who are building rockets out of soda bottles.

To turn mental processes into something concrete and—hopefully—exciting, I fell back on demonstrating one of cognitive psychology's most surefire cognitive effects. I printed up a supply of stickers covered in an array of color words that were themselves printed in different colors: *red yellow black orange red blue purple yellow*, and so on. The order of the words isn't important, but crucially, the ink color is deliberately mismatched to the words, so that *red* is printed in any color other than red, *yellow* is printed in anything other than yellow, and the same for all the other colors. I passed out the stickers to visitors and asked them to read the words out loud, which is easy enough. Then, I asked them to try doing the task just a bit differently: saying the *name* of the ink colors, instead of reading the printed words. Almost without exception, when people look at the printed word *red* and try to say *yellow* (or whatever color the ink happens to be), it derails them—something that provides an immediate, unmistakable experience of how important attention is to performing even simple cognitive tasks.

My booth visitors were experiencing a very well-known phenomenon called the Stroop effect.[1] To demonstrate it for yourself, you can simply type off a few lines of color words in your word processor (being sure to mismatch the words and their colors); you can also find good-quality online Stroop demonstrations at http://faculty.washington.edu/chudler/java/ready.html or http://www.math.unt.edu/~tam/SelfTests/StroopEffects.html. This effect—discussed in more detail later in this chapter—illustrates quite dramatically the central role of attention in our cognitive processes. When attention is grabbed by the wrong thing—in this case, the meaning of the written words—other cognitive processes can grind to a halt.

I chose attention to start off our in-depth discussion of cognition and online learning because it is the foundation supporting many of the processes involved in learning. The more research psychologists do, the more we realize that we can't separate cognition from the mechanisms we use to allocate our cognitive resources. And so, to build processes such as memory, critical thinking, and so on we instructors need to consider how attention interacts with the design of our learning activities. Fortunately, online learning tools offer a number of ways to optimize the way we use students' attentional resources during teaching and learning.

How Attention Works

Attention is the complex and somewhat mysterious process of allocating limited cognitive resources across myriad competing demands. It is intimately tied up with consciousness, perception, and memory, involving multiple regions and structures within the brain that direct our thought processes from one millisecond to the next. So what does it mean to pay attention? It is surprisingly difficult to define in precise terms, despite our intuitive sense of what attention looks and feels like. However, this difficulty hasn't stopped psychologists and neuropsychologists from pursuing numerous productive lines of research into the topic. We may not know exactly what attention *is*, but we know a lot about how it *works*.

From the research to date, we can piece together a general idea of what happens in the mind and brain when we are engaging attention. Information comes in from the senses and undergoes some degree of preconscious analysis, in which information that is critically important to survival or that relates to present goals is passed on for further processing. This selection is carried out by mechanisms in the brain that constantly balance selecting information from particular regions in space (i.e., where we are visually focusing from moment to moment), information that relates to our present priorities and goals, and information that is important to survival regardless of our present goals.

Much of the work of sifting through and selecting information takes place in a set of interconnected brain regions known as the frontoparietal attention network.[2] Within this network, sensory information—things we see, hear, and feel—is coordinated with our present intentions and goals and turned into mental representations of things in the world. As an end result, cognitive processes are "biased" toward information that is consistent with goals or otherwise highly relevant—meaning that goal-relevant, prioritized stimuli get processed ahead of other things.

Say that you are preparing some materials for the day's class. As you scan your bookshelves looking for a particular volume, brain regions within the frontoparietal attention network ramp up processing of visual information falling in the spatial areas you're concentrating on as your eyes fixate on one book after another. These regions do the same thing for information whose meaning fits with the topic you're thinking of, so that any relevant words and phrases you run across pop right into your conscious awareness. Suddenly, a voice emanates from the hallway, urgently shouting "Watch out!" The sharp onset of the auditory stimulus, coupled with the survival-relevant meaning of the words, triggers the brain to override what you were focusing on previously, automatically switching the priority to what's going on in the hall. In this way, your attentional mechanisms are selectively ushering into consciousness the most relevant and important things going on at any given moment, taking into account both your immediate goals and overarching survival goals.

From the research, we can extract a set of key facts about attention that are particularly relevant to our role as teachers and designers of online learning experiences. The first key fact is that attention is limited. There are a number of metaphors we can use to conceptualize our limitations; you can liken attention to a camera that can take in a great deal but only hold a small part in sharp focus at a time, or to a bank account that can be divvied up but can't dip below zero. We have a considerable amount of voluntary control over how we allocate attention, but this voluntary control is far from absolute—it can be disrupted, both by external things going on around us and by our own internal thought processes. Sensory stimuli that are sudden and intense—like the shout in the above example—trigger an involuntary shift of attention known as the orienting response, in which we shift our eyes and sometimes even our body posture toward the attention-grabbing stimulus.

Other factors can create involuntary attentional interference as well. The Stroop effect demonstrated earlier in this chapter results from the conflict between a process—word reading—that is practiced to the point where it can't be suppressed and another task, naming the ink colors. Emotional factors can also create Stroop-like interference effects. People with spider phobia, for example, trip over color naming for spider-associated words like "legs," "hairy," and "web."[3] Besides illustrating the problems that happen with divided attention, the Stroop effect also underscores our attentional limitations, showing how even a simple cognitive task—describing colors—can be derailed by competing demands.

At first, that key point—attention is limited—sounds obvious, given that we all know that we can't handle infinitely many tasks at once. Yet, the limitations are stricter than most of us realize. A stark demonstration of just how narrow our focus can be came from a celebrated discovery in attention research, the *inattentional blindness* effect documented by the researchers Arien Mack and Irving Rock.[4] To produce the effect, researchers asked volunteers to inspect a visual display containing two crossed lines, purportedly to judge which of the two lines (horizontal or vertical) was longer. The real question, though, was whether the participants would notice something else—a shape, group of moving shapes, even a written word—plainly visible next to the lines they were inspecting. First, participants would see one or more "noncritical" trials, without an unexpected feature. Then, without warning, they would see a "critical" trial, with the unexpected feature shown quite obviously in the display. Mack and Rock discovered that on a substantial number of these critical trials, participants completely failed to notice that there was anything else there, presumably because the participants were concentrating so hard on figuring out which of the two lines was longer.

The inattentional blindness effect illustrates a broader truth about human perception and attention, that looking and seeing are two different things—and that we are remarkably prone to missing stimuli when our attention is directed elsewhere.[5] This phenomenon doesn't just occur during exotic laboratory tasks; a number of researchers theorize that it can happen in real-world situations requiring divided attention, even high-stakes tasks in which people are presumably highly motivated and attentive. Experienced airline pilots performing simulated landings, for example, have been shown to (virtually) collide with aircraft unexpectedly present on the runway, possibly because they get too engrossed in other aspects of the landing task to notice important but unexpected stimuli.

This leads to another main point about our limitations: the disconnect between our actual and perceived capacity. To illustrate, people generally endorse the idea that cell phones detract from driving, and yet at the same time overwhelmingly claim that they themselves are capable of driving safely while on the phone.

In their book *The Invisible Gorilla: And Other Ways Our Intuitions Deceive Us*, attention researchers Christopher Chabris and Daniel Simon characterize this disconnect as a fundamental limitation of human thought. We have a vivid subjective experience of the things we pay attention to, but we erroneously extend this subjective impression to everything else we didn't pay attention to. And we assume that anything that's unusual or visually striking will grab our attention, when this simply isn't true.[6] In sum, we are terrible judges of what we will and won't be able to handle with respect to our own

attentional processes, which can in turn cause us to habitually overload ourselves.

But isn't it true that *some* people have extra capacity to juggle,
either by way of special cognitive endowments, intelligence, or the
right kind of personality? Similarly, couldn't extensive occupa-
tional experience—as an emergency first responder, say, or police
detective—expand people's attentional abilities so that practically
nothing would get by them? While this possibility can't be ruled
out for every individual, everywhere, it's implausible that people can
undergo generalized, across-the-board expansion of attentional abilities due to experience or talent. It's a seductive assumption, though;
Chabris and Simon relate that they get a steady stream of inquiries
from readers who are simply convinced of some variation of the idea
that the world is made up of distinct categories of people (popular
variations include women, smart people, detail-oriented people)
who can multitask better than anyone else. The majority of the research, however, demonstrates that situational factors—particularly
the cognitive demands the person is trying to juggle at once—are
far more powerful in determining performance, compared to individual factors. When it comes to our limitations, we are essentially
all in the same boat, regardless of our gender, IQ, personality, or
anything else—and assuming otherwise just makes the illusion of
attention worse, given our predilection for categorizing ourselves
as exceptional. Attention deficit hyperactivity disorder (ADHD) is a
special case of individual differences that we will return to later in
this chapter, but suffice it to say that ADHD status in and of itself
doesn't change the central fact that most of us miss far more than
we realize.

Although it can't meaningfully be expanded, capacity can be altered by another factor: practice, which can lead to a state of seemingly effortless processing termed *automaticity*. In a classic study
from 1976, researchers trained a pair of research participants to
write down words to dictation while simultaneously reading short
stories. This dual reading and writing task took nearly thirty hours
of practice to learn, but through this process, participants mastered
the ability to accurately copy down words while fully comprehending the stories, averaging upward of reading 350 words per minute

and writing 40 words per story.[7] Chabris and Simon allude to this practice factor in their discussion of individual differences in attention, pointing out that while expertise in an arena doesn't expand the capacity to multitask, it can reduce the demands of well-practiced parts of the task so as to give the appearance of increased capacity. They caution, though, that even practiced professionals can rapidly get overloaded as soon as the task gets into territory that is outside their expertise or that depends on their noticing unexpected stimuli (as in inattentional blindness). In other words, it's not that the "bank account" of attention grows, but rather it's the costs that shrink— leading to improved performance, even with multiple demands, in well-practiced individuals.

Thus far, we've reviewed these key facts about attention: it shifts both voluntarily and involuntarily; it's limited, although demands can change drastically as a function of practice; and we have surprisingly little intuitive awareness of when our limitations are exceeded. One further issue to consider is how interrelated attention is with other cognitive processes. Conscious awareness is one such process. Although it may fall to philosophers to ultimately define what it means to be conscious of something, attentional processes play a major role in determining what enters our consciousness.[8]

Attention is also highly intertwined with visual processing. Attentional processes guide how we visually explore the environment, and furthermore, are necessary to ensure the subjective experience of "seeing" something. This is dramatically illustrated by what can happen when brain injury disrupts the connections between attention and vision, resulting in phenomena such as "hemineglect" and "blindsight." In hemineglect, individuals can *see* stimuli in an affected area—typically one side or the other of the visual field—but fail to respond to those stimuli unless prompted. Blindsight is a similar phenomenon in which individuals report no conscious experience of sight in the affected area of the visual field, but show evidence that they are processing visual stimuli on an unconscious level. One blindsight patient learned to correctly point to visual targets within a blind spot he had developed as the result of a brain injury, although he never developed a conscious awareness of sight in that area.[9] Even our ability to perceive the passage of time has an attentional component. Paradoxically, people with better ability to focus their attention are *worse* at monitoring the passage of time while they engage in another task, perhaps because noticing time is itself a form of distraction.[10]

Memory, though, is the most intriguing meeting point between attention and the rest of cognition. Without getting too deeply into the details of how memory works—topics we will tackle in Chapter 5—it's clear that we remember very little in the absence of focused attention. Researchers have probed this question using a variety of methods, but most famously with the so-called "shadowing" task. Shadowing involves putting a pair of headphones on a participant and playing two separate streams of speech, such as narrative text or digit strings, into each ear. The participant is asked to verbally repeat back what is played into one ear, while ignoring the other. Using this technique, researchers can probe comprehension and memory for unattended material.

Participants in shadowing tasks generally handle this divided-attention task well, but in general, they remember little of what they heard on the unattended channel.[11] I do an in-class demonstration of the shadowing procedure by having a volunteer come to the front of the class and asking him or her to shadow a news article being read out loud by another student. At the same time, I sit on the opposite side and read a different article, which they are instructed to ignore. Almost without exception, students can recall practically nothing from the article (mine) that they were ignoring. But they are not simply blocking out the unattended material—rather, they are applying some degree of cognitive processing at an unconscious level. We know this because certain words will almost always get through on the unattended channel. Most notably, saying someone's name grabs their attention, a phenomenon termed the "cocktail party effect."[12] More subtly, the meaning of words on the unattended channel can influence the interpretation of ambiguous words on the attended channel, so that, for example, people are more likely to interpret the word "bank" to mean "riverbank" if river-associated words are being played on the unattended channel.[13] In sum, we do process material at some level even when ignoring it, but little or none of it makes it to memory.

This appears to be true in the visual modality as well as the auditory modality. For example, conversing on a cell phone substantially reduces memory for things seen during the driving simulation, even things that were right within the field of vision.[14] Another striking demonstration of this memory-attention connection is the *change blindness* phenomenon discovered by the researchers Ronald Rensink and J. K. O'Regan.[15] In this effect, the viewer examines a photograph in which some reasonably large element, such as a building or land feature, is changed across alternating versions of the picture. Most people notice the change right away, which they may chalk up to their memory of what they saw in the first version of the picture. However, briefly interrupting the viewer's attentional focus—usually accomplished by introducing a blank screen that "flickers" between versions for a fraction of a second—often results in failure to notice the change. Change blindness is hard to believe until you experience it for yourself, and it's best viewed dynamically, with the flicker interrupting photos at a regular rate. It is worth checking out one of the many freely available online demonstrations of change blindness, such as this one: http://www2.psych .ubc.ca/~rensink/flicker/download/. And as with other attentional limitations, we have poor self-awareness; people wildly overestimate their own immunity from experiencing change blindness, predicting that they will be able to spot far more of these changes than they actually do.[16]

Rensink and O'Regan interpreted change blindness as evidence that we construct very little in the way of a detailed, lasting memory representation of the world around us. Part of the reason for this is that we don't pay focused attention to that much of what we see, relying instead on continuing visual exploration of the scene in order to maintain awareness of it.

When we do pay focused attention to an object or person within a scene, the typical results are very different. Elements that link in some way to the theme or meaning of the picture are much less subject to change blindness, perhaps because they attract focused attention and thereby trigger the formation of a memory.[17] Subsequent researchers have offered somewhat different interpretations of the change blindness effect,[18] but even taking recent reinterpre-

tations into account, the point stands that attention heavily influences what we remember, and without it, we remember precious
little.

Working memory, it turns out, is also increasingly seen as intertwined with attentional processes—so much so that some experts
even see working memory and attention as one and the same.[19] So
what is the precise nature of the interrelationship? Researchers are
still working on the details, but one main idea is that attention directs what is going to be held in working memory—i.e., information that is critical to accomplishing one's goals at the moment—
and keeps that information readily available. In one version of the
theory, working memory consists of items in long-term memory
that are held in a highly activated or available state, and within that
set of activated items, there is a subset that is the focus of attention.[20] Thus, working memory and attention are constantly playing
off one another, selecting relevant information and keeping a small
amount of that information in "ready" state. We'll return to the issue of working-memory theories in Chapter 5, but for our purposes
here, suffice it to say that you can't meaningfully talk about working
memory without referencing attention.

Support for this view of attention and working memory comes,
in part, from studies of individual differences in working-memory
ability.[21] It turns out that working memory is an arena of cognitive
functioning where there is significant variation among individuals,
and researchers have turned up a number of surprising and informative connections between an individual's ability to pay attention,
his or her working-memory capacity, and the ability to effectively
carry out a diverse range of cognitive tasks. This individual-differences
work portrays attention as the capacity to pick out and maintain
task-relevant information while holding irrelevant information at
bay. When this capacity is strong, needed information can be accessed quickly and efficiently, without "contamination" from irrelevant information. This usually results in quicker and better task
completion, but reduces the ability to respond to task-irrelevant
information. We can see, then, just how it comes to be that this
one process—attention—reaches across so many different realms of
mental life.

These realms definitely include learning and academic achievement. In primary and secondary school students, there is a substantial relationship between selective attention abilities and the development of core academic skills, particularly reading. Mathematics ability, as well, seems to be related to the ability to filter out irrelevant or no-longer-relevant information, with math anxiety as a surprising correlate. Although math anxiety is clearly an emotional phenomenon, its impact on math performance is mediated by attention and working memory.[22] In math-anxious students, situations such as timed math tests tend to trigger a flood of irrelevant thoughts—"I hate math," "I'm going to be embarrassed," and so forth—that drain off attentional resources. This attentional drain compromises the ability to maintain task-relevant information in working memory, thus triggering the very difficulty completing math problems that the student was dreading all along. For these students, doing math feels something like what the rest of us would experience if we tried to do math calculations while simultaneously reciting the alphabet backward—a recipe for frustration and poor performance.

When Attention Works Differently

Let's now turn to what cognitive science tells us about people with disorders of attention, most notably attention deficit hyperactivity disorder (ADHD). Given the popular media hype about ADHD diagnoses—and alleged overdiagnoses—this question is one where we have to be particularly careful to focus on the science. Is ADHD something that actually impacts cognition in meaningful ways? Or is it, as some say, essentially one big diagnostic hoax? Depending on whom you listen to, such a hoax is abetted by either overambitious parents desperate to boost the achievements of their mediocre offspring, or conversely, lazy parents seeking to drug their high-spirited kids into submission. Another twist on this popular culture idea— one that is particularly germane to the topic of this book—is that computing itself causes ADHD, perhaps through the hyperstimulation of gaming, visual imagery, and unlimited access to information. With more students coming to us with legally mandated accommodations—which also apply to online work—this is an issue that all instructors need to consider.

Psychology research contradicts the "mass diagnostic hoax" idea, suggesting instead that ADHD is a bona fide clinical phenomenon. ADHD diagnosis is associated with distinct patterns of brain structure and function, documented across numerous studies using brain imaging technology.[23] As you'd expect, these differences between ADHD and non-ADHD individuals tend to involve brain areas associated with attention, but may also include areas involved with rewarding and reinforcing behavior. This jibes with research findings that cognitively, people with ADHD score lower on tests of certain aspects of working memory and selective attention.[24] ADHD also appears to have a strong genetic component, and it isn't limited to Western, affluent, high-tech cultures,[25] two findings that contradict the popular idea of ADHD as merely a side effect of growing up in the American cultural context.

Surprisingly enough for a disorder with "hyperactivity" in the name, stimulants—e.g., methlyphenidate, which also goes by the brand names Ritalin and Metadate—are the commonest type of drug therapy for ADHD. However, this seeming contradiction becomes clearer when you consider that one thing these medications do is increase activity in brain areas associated with selective attention.[26]

Millions of individuals are indeed diagnosed with ADHD, but this may reflect factors other than a massive diagnostic fad. First, it is important to realize that the best estimates of the prevalence of ADHD in the population are about 3–7 percent, hardly what you would call epidemic levels.[27] There is also a question about whether ADHD may be *under*diagnosed. As early as the 1980s, diagnosticians were beginning to suggest that behavioral issues chalked up to family dysfunction, emotional difficulty, or even vision problems might actually be due to ADHD.[28] In other words, it's not that millions of people have suddenly developed ADHD, but rather that there's an influx of people who might previously have been diagnosed with other disorders, or simply never properly diagnosed at all.[29] Indeed, increases in the number of prescriptions written for stimulant ADHD medications disproportionately include underserved and underdiagnosed populations.[30] Taken together, these facts go against the idea that ADHD diagnosis is simply a fashionable way to excuse individual differences in personality, ability, or motivation.

What does this tell us about teaching college students with ADHD? First, we can roughly estimate that, if your class is fairly representative of the U.S. population, about one in twenty of your students is likely to have ADHD—not a whopping number, but enough to crop up with some regularity. Some will have the benefit of ADHD drug therapy, and others won't, especially if they fall into historically underserved groups such as women and people without access to adequate health care. Generalizing very broadly, students with ADHD will likely show more extreme versions of the attentional limitations that non-ADHD people experience, such as being even more likely not to catch important information when they are juggling multiple demands. Screening out irrelevant information— such as directions for a previous task, extraneous thoughts, and so on—will also be particularly challenging for an ADHD person. It follows from this that, although ADHD does represent real and substantive differences in brain and cognition, the measures we take to help *all* students manage attentional demands will help ADHD students even more. In other words, we don't need to design different learning environments for ADHD and non-ADHD groups— good design is just particularly beneficial for students with attention problems.

What Attention Means for Online Learning

How do we improve the chances that our materials will be attended to, and thus remembered? Several strategies emerge from what we know about attention as well as from empirical evidence on online learning.

STRATEGY 1: ASK STUDENTS TO RESPOND

It's unusual for us to stay focused on something that we are just passively observing. Attention almost inevitably wanders in the absence of "targets," meaning stimuli we have to act on. Similarly, as we saw in the first section of this chapter, attention is all about matching resources to goals—and the problem, in a learning situation, is that long-term goals (wanting a good grade, to achieve a degree, etc.) don't suffice to direct attention in the short term. But something like needing to answer a question or formulate an opinion *can* create a short-term goal that directs our resources.

Given this, it makes sense to elicit responses from students as often as we can. In a face-to-face classroom, experienced teachers intuitively accomplish this by asking for discussion, calling on students, using student response systems, and interspersing a variety of interactive activities—think-pair-share discussions, minute papers, demonstrations—into lecture. Like these experienced face-to-face teachers, online teachers and designers need to always be thinking about how they will keep students focused, using the tools available in the online environment.

Some forms of learning activities naturally lend themselves to a great deal of active give–and–take, for example, simulations and games. Synchronous activities, such as scheduled chats, also demand a certain level of focus because of the time pressure. Other materials, such as blocks of text presented asynchronously, are a recipe for inattention. Oftentimes, we do need students to read stretches of written material online, and this is a reasonable expectation—but there are ways to balance reading with active responding so that students are less tempted to mindlessly click through. One technique is to weave in active response questions throughout the text, for example by presenting students with a question at the end of a page's worth of material. These can be closed-ended multiple-choice type questions that simply check for understanding; optionally, you could set the pages not to advance until the student chooses the correct answer. This isn't the only option, though—any question style can be used to ask students for opinions, reflections, personal examples, or what points they are unclear on.

Interspersing questions also works particularly well for online lectures. Even when you present information with media such as video or narrated slides, attention often flags—and learning suffers. In one study directly targeting this issue, college students viewing video lectures of introductory statistics concepts reported less mind wandering and remembered more information when the lecture was broken into segments with brief quiz questions in between. This performance advantage held up over time, so that students in the interspersed-quiz condition did better on the post-lecture cumulative test. And although the frequent quiz breaks kept students more attentive, they did not seem to tip them over into anxiety; students who did the interspersed quizzes actually reported *less* anxiety about the cumulative test.[31]

Granted, this approach—asking for multiple short, low-stakes responses throughout presentation of text material—can generate an excessive amount of material to grade. Short of sticking only to auto-graded multiple-choice questions, there are other creative ways around this issue. For example, you could select a certain number of open-ended responses to post on a weekly discussion board, and grade the rest for completion only—the incentive for thoughtful responses being that any given answer might go up for public viewing. Alternatively, you can use fill-in-the-blank questions strategically, by first auto-grading responses in which the student used the correct wording that you specified in advance, then going back over just the *incorrect* responses in order to spot any acceptable answers that didn't match the wording you specified in the auto-grading scheme. You can also spot-grade randomly selected short-answer questions. Figure 4.1 illustrates how these last two grading systems would work.

Other techniques for introducing more student responses might be available, depending on your learning management system. Moodle offers a function within Lessons—its term for learning activities—by which student responses determine what material is presented and in what order. This "branching" arrangement can be as simple as presenting more details on material that the student missed in a multiple-choice question, or as complex as creating a "story line" that varies based on student choices. Here's an example: Students in a clinical psychology course could read case studies of individuals with different sets of symptoms. For each case study, students would choose a diagnosis and a course of treatment; these choices would lead them to different outcomes for the patient. Students could then start over and make different choices, resulting once again in different outcomes—an interactive, attention-grabbing

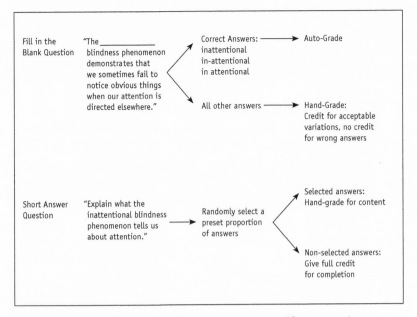

Figure 4.1. Options for mass-grading quiz questions without resorting to multiple-choice format. Two formats are shown: fill-in-the-blank and short-answer, along with an example question. For fill-in-the-blank questions, correct answers can be auto-graded, and all incorrect answers reviewed and marked correct if they are acceptable variations. For short-answer questions, a proportion can be randomly selected for detailed grading, and all other good-faith efforts at complete answers given full credit.

way of illustrating the relationships among different symptoms, diagnoses, and therapies in clinical psychology.

STRATEGY 2: TAKE ADVANTAGE OF AUTOMATICITY

Recall that attentional demands decrease with practice, up to the point where we can seemingly complete a task without needing to pay attention at all—a state termed *automaticity*. When a process becomes automatic, more cognitive resources are left over for other things. In teaching and learning, this can take the form of students' being able to bring more high-level thinking skills to a task once they have mastered the necessary foundational knowledge and lower-level skills. Students learning to write in standard American Psychological Association format, for example, can focus more on the conceptual side of their papers once they are well practiced at citing sources and creating the right section headings. Automaticity probably can't be achieved for cognitive processes requiring you to put information together in new ways or apply original analytical thought,[32] but for routine tasks it's often achievable.

One thing that gets in the way of automaticity is the pronounced tendency of teachers and students alike to underestimate the amount of focused practice needed to get to this stage. It's easy to end up settling for one- or two-shot activities when many more opportunities for application and practice are really necessary. Nor are endless, repetitive drills ideal for engaging students—and in the case of traditional homework, the lag between submission and grading doesn't offer the rapid feedback that is a central part of effective practice.

Fortunately, this is an area where online learning really shines. With auto-grading, the ability to create unlimited permutations of problems, and the ability to give immediate feedback, we can require our students to engage in more practice than ever before. We can also shift our mindset about practice problems from summative assessment—i.e., using them to judge student achievement—to mastery, meaning that we push students to achieve at least a minimal level of competence before proceeding to the next level. Online learning lends itself to mastery learning in particular because it enables individual tracking of each student's progress through the material, routing them back through parts they need to continue working on, or putting more advanced students ahead in the material—something that is nearly impossible to do in a face-to-face setting with more than just a few students. This "mastery learning" mindset ties back into the automaticity concept because it puts us in a better position to ensure that students have gotten the basics down, freeing up capacity to take on the next step in the material.

My colleague Elizabeth Brauer and I used this approach to improve performance in one of her electrical engineering courses, Introduction to Linear Circuit Analysis. A highly experienced and observant teacher, Elizabeth told me that for years, she had noticed that students stumbled over a couple of the basic principles they would need to apply over and over when working with circuits, such as Ohm's Law. Generally, they understood these basic principles just fine, but took too long applying them—as if they needed to consciously review with every new problem. "If you have to look up Ohm's Law every time you work on a circuit," Elizabeth told me, "you aren't going to last long as an electrical engineer."

We settled on automaticity as a guiding principle for what we wanted to do to enhance student learning, adding a required on-line component to the face-to-face structure of the class. The online component we envisioned would have some similarities to online homework, in that it would use the university's existing learning management system (Blackboard Vista) to present a sequence of problems, each time using a random-number generator so that problems would be different across students and across attempts.

But we included several distinctly nontraditional features as well, features explicitly built to use the capacities of online work to increase automaticity. First, the attempts were *unlimited*, with students encouraged to make as many attempts as possible. Second, the attempts were *timed*. We upended the usual exhortation to students to work through problems slowly and carefully, instead telling them that we wanted them to work toward speed as well as accuracy. The speed factor figured into the grading for the assignment like this: If they beat the time goal we set in advance, we added a ten-point time bonus to the score. For each minute over the goal, we took away one point. Table 4.1 shows several typical sequences of student scores for one of the modules, illustrating how time went down and scores went up over multiple attempts.[33]

When we brought in these timed, repeatable modules, scores on the associated exams went up significantly; on an end-of-semester survey we administered, most students agreed that the modules helped them understand material presented in class, helped them practice skills needed to do well on exams, and overall were a useful part of the class.[34] Note that there wasn't anything particularly complex about the technology we used for the modules—the innovation was more about changing the incentives and expectations around homework, as well as fully exploiting the capabilities of the learning management system we were using. And because students worked on these modules largely independently, they didn't displace

Table 4.1

Three examples of student scores and time spent across multiple attempts—Ohm's Law assignment.

STUDENT	ATTEMPT AND DATE	SCORE	TIME
A	1. June 11, 2010, 12:50 AM	55.8	00:20:12
	2. June 11, 2010, 10:41 AM	66	00:14:01
	3. June 11, 2010, 11:05 AM	90	00:10:29
B	1. June 7, 2010, 6:43 PM	68.4	00:36:27
	2. June 7, 2010, 7:02 PM	75.6	00:12:02
C	1. June 7, 2010, 4:46 PM	51.6	00:50:05
	2. June 7, 2010, 5:10 PM	87.6	00:14:50

covering more conceptually sophisticated material during class meetings.

In summary, when we are designing online learning activities, we can take advantage of automaticity like this: (1) identify the lower-level skills that are automatic in experts, but not in our novice students, (2) find ways that technology can allow us to create practice opportunities and feedback for those lower-level skills, and (3) set up incentives for completion that stress speed and mastery, not just finishing an arbitrary, preset number of problems. The concept of automaticity also helps us remember that reinforcing lower-level skills complements the development of higher-level skills, rather than displacing them.

STRATEGY 3: ASSESS COGNITIVE LOAD

The cognitive load theory (CLT) focuses on how learners allocate working memory and attention resources during learning, particularly the ways in which instructional designs can unwittingly impose additional resource costs on learners.[35] Since its inception, CLT has branched out into a number of subparts to the theory, but for practical purposes, its most important aspect has to do with identifying three distinct demands on cognitive resources during learning: *intrinsic* cognitive load, *germane* cognitive load, and *extraneous* cognitive load.

Intrinsic cognitive load refers to the cognitive demands that are inherent to what you are learning—such as the working memory you need in order to juggle the different pieces of information you've been given during a learning activity. *Extraneous cognitive load* refers to the cognitive demands of navigating instructions and the information to be learned—that is, dealing with the instructional procedures and materials themselves. Lastly, *germane cognitive load* refers to the working-memory resources needed to acquire new information.[36]

According to CLT researchers, there isn't much that can be done about intrinsic and germane load—they are a fixed function of the complexity of what you're teaching, and can't be compressed without harming the amount of learning. It's the extrinsic load that we *can* do something about, and thus numerous studies have focused on how to reduce the resources drained off by cognitive processes not related directly to learning. Examples include trying to figure out what parts of a labeled diagram go together,[37] how to use the chat function in a learning management system,[38] or how to turn in one's assignment online.[39] Or as one researcher defined it, "extraneous load is imposed by the material but could have been avoided with a different design" (p. 108).[40] According to the CLT framework, when less cognitive power is taken up by extraneous load, more is left over for intrinsic and germane load—resulting in better ability to handle complex material and better learning overall.

As a system for creating precise explanations for where resources go during learning, CLT is far from perfect. The distinction among the three types of cognitive load can be fuzzy, and cognitive load is difficult to measure with precision. Many studies simply ask study participants to rate, after the fact, how mentally taxing they found different parts of the learning process—an obviously imprecise way of getting at the moment-to-moment fluctuations in resource allocations that CLT focuses on.[41] It's also unrealistic to try to reduce all extraneous load to zero, and in actual learning situations, students may make up for cognitive overload with common strategies such as jotting down notes.[42]

Despite these problems, CLT does fit with the major principles outlined earlier in this chapter, especially the part about strict capacity limitations and the division of resources as a critical precursor to memory. Furthermore, it provides some good general guidelines for making learning environments that are less distracting and thus more productive. Cognitive load researchers have pointed out, for example, that when we ask students to integrate information drawn from separate sources—such as how-to instructions located in one place and the task itself located somewhere else—students have to spend resources switching their focus from one to the other.

CLT tells us that instructions, labels, and key facts needed to complete a task should be readily visible in the same place where students are using the information to do the task. Students learn more from diagrams when explanatory labels are incorporated right into the diagram itself, or better yet, when the students themselves use drag-and-drop to position labels within the diagram.[43] CLT also suggests that it's good practice to separate out technological skills from content wherever possible. For example, one study of high school students using spreadsheets to learn mathematical concepts found that students did better when they learned spreadsheet skills first, then tackled the mathematics content, compared to trying to master both at once.[44]

In an online or blended course, this could take the form of assigning an introductory set of exercises just targeting important tools within the learning management system. As an example, my colleague Michael Rader set up a detailed module in the online Introduction to Psychology course we developed together.[45] Students had to do this preliminary module before attempting any of the other assignments; among other things, the assignment required them to use the Blackboard e-mail function to send the instructor a message containing the phone number for student technical support, use the discussion tool to post one message and one reply in the "Getting to Know You" forum, and use the online course calendar to answer a question about an important due date in the course. From a cognitive-load standpoint, this module paid off in more cognitive resources available for concentrating on course concepts, and fewer cognitive resources spent on figuring out how to use Blackboard Learn.

STRATEGY 4: DISCOURAGE DIVIDED ATTENTION
Recall that the other surefire way to sabotage a cognitive process is to combine it with another attention-grabbing activity. Because Internet-enabled devices offer so many more capabilities than just

access to one's learning management system or e-book, online learning is always going to be particularly vulnerable to dysfunctional behaviors such as alternating instant messaging, e-mail, videos, and social networking with the learning activity at hand. This behavior is hard enough to police in the face-to-face classroom, let alone in the typical online environment, but there are a few techniques we can try.

The more smoothly learning activities work, the less temptation there will be to get sidetracked on something else; any delays, frustrations, or points where students have to wait for instructions present a window of opportunity for distraction. But this often isn't something we have control over as instructors, given that we usually have to work within the limitations of our school's chosen learning management system. We can, however, make fast-paced, gap-free operation a priority if we are selecting a free-standing online learning product, such as a textbook auxiliary.

Putting in synchronous elements—where students log on and work, often collaboratively, at a prescheduled time—is another possible way to discourage dysfunctional multitasking. Introducing time limits could work in similar way. There are significant costs associated with both of these approaches, however, as students typically find synchronous work less convenient. Many also find strict time limits unduly stressful, leading to the need to make accommodations where appropriate. Also note that when technical issues cause students to run out of time, this creates an issue for you, the instructor, as you have to decide whether to give the student another attempt. Depending on the nature of the learning activity, synchronous and timed work may be worth the hassle, but not always.

Besides setting up the learning environment to be reasonably fast-paced and seamless, we can take a different tack altogether and inform students directly about why divided attention is harmful to learning, costs them time, and means more effort in the long run. Recall from earlier in this chapter that we are remarkably poor judges of how much we can pay attention to at once; this means that there is a lot of room for improvement in what students understand about their own attentional systems. A brief informational module at the beginning of the course can help enlighten students about their limitations, emphasizing that research shows that seemingly harmless multitasking almost inevitably means worse performance.

Even better, dynamic demonstrations of change blindness and inattentional blindness are widely available online. One YouTube video that I like to show in class, titled "The Amazing Color Changing Card Trick," purports to show a rather mundane card trick in which red-backed cards turn into blue-backed cards. Then, the video rewinds and shows all of the *real* changes that took place unnoticed while students were intently focusing on the cards: the shirt color of both actors, the background, and tablecloth all completely change in front of the audience's eyes.[46] Due to focusing exclusively on the deck of cards, almost everyone misses these changes.

I have presented variations on this informational module to undergraduates in different fields on and off for years; it can be an engaging way to help students handle the inherently distracting online environment in which they do so much of their coursework.[47] Candidly, there still needs to be empirical testing of whether these one-shot modules have a long-term impact on how students manage their own attentional processes during learning. However, they are relatively easy to present, given the wealth of freely available demonstrations and nontechnical overviews of effects such as change blindness and inattentional blindness.

I'll add one more potential strategy that ties into attention, with the caution that it depends on a psychological phenomenon that is still under investigation. Researchers have found that interacting with nature—e.g., taking a short walk on a nature path—restores the ability to focus attention, more so than an equivalent break without a nature component, such as walking through an urban environment.[48] Even more surprising, *pictures* of nature can also produce improvement to attention, and there is some preliminary evidence that this effect translates over into a digital environment.[49] Whether this phenomenon is due to our evolutionary history, inherently calming characteristics of natural scenes, or some other factor is still unclear. However, including nature scenes as graphics in online materials is a low-risk, easy intervention that—in theory—could produce a small boost to students' ability to focus.

In sum, attention is the foundation for all the cognitive processes we want to promote as instructors, especially memory. And within the human cognitive system, attention is a precious, limited resource. In the online environment, it's easy for students to mentally check out, and when they do, your painstakingly prepared learning experiences have little impact. So as designers of learning experiences, we should also think of ourselves as stewards of students' limited stores of attention. We do this by educating them about multitasking and divided attention, and by pushing them to put in the practice time needed to make routine skills automatic. We make our presentation of materials as seamless and timely as possible, and minimize the attention drain of extraneous load, making sure that students don't have to constantly switch back and forth between instructions, illustrations, text, and so on. And we keep them engaged by asking questions—about their understanding of what's been presented, their opinions, and personal examples. Optimizing your learning experiences for attention is the first step toward optimizing it for memory and higher thought processes.

Chapter 5

Memory

BUILDING STUDENTS' MEMORY for course material is not the sole aim of teaching, but it matters. Memory is central to the cognitive side of teaching and learning; it is the mechanism by which our teaching literally changes students' minds and brains. It's fashionable among educators to disparage "mere memorization" as opposed to the sophisticated reasoning skills we hope to foster, but this is a false dichotomy. Focusing on memory doesn't need to detract from higher-order thought processes. You can't make solid arguments, invent new applications, or apply critical thinking without a foundation of information in memory.

As James Lang wrote, "When a student in my survey course on British literature asks me about the Irish potato famine, she should expect me to expound upon the role that the British government played in exacerbating that 'natural' disaster, but she should also expect me to know—without my having to stop class and Google it—that the first potato crop failed in 1845, and that crop failures continued for the next half-dozen years. Likewise, if I expect my students to understand the complex historical and literary relationship between Ireland and England, I want them to know roughly where the famine falls in the historical timeline of that relationship. . . . So memory matters, even for those of us teaching the most complex cognitive skills we can imagine."[1] Lang observes that this complementary relationship extends beyond the classroom and into high-stakes real-world situations. Emergency room doctors interpreting test results, lawyers in the heat of questioning, salespeople interacting with customers—all of these are examples of situations where memory is crucial for fast, effective performance.

To design memorable learning experiences, it helps to have a theoretical understanding of how memory works. But this is easier said than done. Memory theorists disagree, especially with respect to so-called *immediate memory*, the catchall term for concepts including short-term memory, working memory, and sensory memory. Memory research is at a point where many previously accepted truths—for example, that short-term memory is a separate system, or that we hold seven things (plus or minus one) in memory at a time—are being called into question. This is good for the vitality of the field, but it is a challenge for those of us who want to use memory theory to guide our teaching. Perhaps because of the ongoing theoretical debates, and perhaps because of the increasing technical complexity of contemporary memory theories, the newer conceptions of memory don't tend to make it into teaching guides.

Understanding memory is also hard because in some ways it goes against our intuitions. For example, many of us have a strong sense that we are most likely to remember things we have seen many times over. Look at the preferred study strategies of many of our students, who spend hours paging through textbooks, highlighters in hand, hoping to create lasting memories via mass exposure. It's also an implicit assumption of the traditional concept of college instruction, where educational impact is measured by "seat time" spent viewing lectures that, as often as not, merely rehash those same heavily highlighted textbooks.

The folk idea that memories are built out of repeated exposure can be dispatched with a simple demonstration. Try it now. Take a piece of scratch paper and, from memory, sketch out something that you've seen thousands of times in your life: the front and back of a penny.

You can't do it, can you? A quick look at the real thing will verify that your memory of a penny, represented by the drawing you made, is strikingly inaccurate. I've run this demonstration with hundreds of students and workshop participants over the years. Not once has anyone completed it without making at least one major error. Showing

Lincoln facing to the left (right is correct) and misplacing text (E Pluribus Unum, LIBERTY, etc.) are two common ones, but there are other entertaining variations, such as the array of jaunty hats my students have bestowed on Lincoln (he's actually bareheaded).

This demonstration replicates a classic study in which researchers asked participants to sketch a penny from memory, and found atrocious performance.[2] The researchers ran the procedure again as a multiple-choice test, this time asking people to select the correct alternative from an array of plausible variations—but participants did only a little better than random chance. Researchers tried probing memory for a highly familiar *auditory* stimulus as well, quizzing people on something they had heard over and over for weeks: the new call numbers for a BBC radio station, announced repeatedly on channels that most people heard day in and day out. Once again, participants seemed to remember practically nothing.

So what does the penny-memory effect tell us about mass exposure and memory? One reason why we don't remember things like the details of pennies is that we process these common stimuli in a passive, inattentive way.[3] Recall from Chapter 4 that focused attention is essential for forming memories. Without this focused attention, we can look at a penny ten times—or a hundred, or a thousand—and fail to form a lasting representation in memory.

Furthermore, the low priority we give to pennies—or similarly, the fact that pennies don't really relate to important goals—also impedes memory. We don't really *need* to rely on detailed memory representations of pennies to get by in daily life, nor do we get emotionally invested in little things like this—and thus, a detailed memory isn't worth spending scarce cognitive resources on. The penny effect presents some important lessons for course design: never rely on exposure to build memory, but rather, strive for active, attentive engagement that ties to goals.

Other findings from applied and basic memory research offer further ideas for optimizing online teaching and learning. In fact, it's particularly important for online teachers to know about memory theory because technological tools open up ways to take advantage of memory principles in ways we never could before. As we'll explore later in this chapter, there are a number of techniques—such as frequent testing, multiple small-stakes assignments, and customizing material for individual students—that tap into memory principles, but are impractical or impossible to carry out in the traditional face-to-face classroom. By using these, we have the potential to not only match but well exceed the face-to-face learning experience. Doing so effectively requires both a general understanding of memory theory and a selective focus on the aspects of the field that are most germane for our teaching. In the rest of this chapter, we'll toggle between those two sides of memory research—theoretical and applied—to come up with the most innovative ways to tap into our students' memory processes.

Memory Theory

OLDER THEORIES OF MEMORY

Modern theories break memory down into three main parts: *encoding*, meaning the process of turning information into some kind of lasting memory representation; *storage*, meaning maintaining memory representations for some period of time; and *retrieval*, meaning accessing stored representations, usually so that they can be used to accomplish a task or serve a goal. These terms are still current today, and they provide a useful framework for describing all the different facets of what it means to remember something.

Historically, one of the most important theories of how encoding, storage, and retrieval work was the so-called multi-store or "modal model."[4] This is the theory that describes memory as an assembly line of sorts, with three distinct work stations. Information that comes in through our eyes and ears makes its first stop in a component called *sensory memory*, which holds a great deal of information, but only for a few seconds at best. The next stop is *short-term memory*, which holds a small amount of information in a highly available state. The contents of short-term memory also tend to disappear within seconds, but they can be held a while longer through *rehearsal* (saying something to yourself over and over). Lastly, information—particularly information that has been rehearsed—can make its way over to *long-term memory*. In order for you to use the information later, you have to retrieve it from long-term memory and put it back into short-term memory for the duration of the task.

The theory has intuitive appeal, and it explained laboratory findings that were considered highly important at the time, such as the
fact that we are more likely to remember the last few items in a list.
But it wasn't long before researchers began picking apart its central
assumptions—and today, virtually nobody who specializes in memory theory believes that the modal model is literally true. We now
know, for example, that rehearsal is not the most important reason
why we store some things in long-term memory, and not others.[5]
The model also glosses over many important distinctions in memory,
such as the fact that meaningful information is more memorable.

CONTEMPORARY THEORIES

You can still pick up echoes of the modal model in contemporary
memory research, but much has changed since then. Unfortunately,
none of this new research has produced a universally accepted memory theory that's intuitive, inclusive of the research findings to date,
and simple enough to fit nicely on a page. So although you can no
longer place your confidence in teaching techniques based on the
three-component modal model, there's no one simple alternative you
can base everything on. But even with that in mind, we can still glean
a number of key theoretical ideas from the contemporary memory
literature—ideas that can directly inform our instructional designs.

Working memory and the multi-store concept. The closest thing we
have to a replacement for the modal model is the working-memory
concept created by researcher Alan Baddeley in the 1970s and expli-
cated by many researchers since.[6] Working-memory theory superficially resembles the modal model, in that there are separate specialized components that handle immediate memory. Like the modal
model's short-term memory component, aspects of working memory are also very limited with respect to how much they can hold
and for how long.

However, in contrast to the modal model, immediate memory
isn't just one all-purpose holding tank, but rather a system of sub-
components geared to handling specialized information, including
(but probably not limited to) word sounds and visual-spatial information. Furthermore, immediate memory systems aren't mere buf-

fers for information, but can also perform operations—such as the rearranging we'd do if we were mentally alphabetizing a list of to-be-remembered words. Lastly, these multiple specialized components are all orchestrated by another mechanism called the *central executive*. Researchers are still hotly debating exactly how to define and measure central executive functions, but there is some general agreement that they are closely linked with attention.

Besides this attentional link, another important principle that comes out of the working-memory theory is that the capacity of each of these specialized subsystems is limited, yet independent. This means that maintaining verbal information won't interfere much with maintaining some other kind of information, such as a visual image. But too much information of one kind, such as multiple visual images at once, will easily overwhelm the system.

The relationship between attention and immediate memory. Not everyone believes in the working memory concept as laid out by Baddeley and colleagues, but amid the myriad ideas floating around there is a clear trend toward linking memory and attentional processes, as we touched on in Chapter 4.[7] In fact, according to some contemporary theorists, what we think of as working memory can't be separated from the ability to direct attention.

Besides once again driving home the need to capture and direct attention in our learning activities, this attention-memory link steers us away from conceiving of memory as one passive holding tank for information, or even a small set of such tanks. Rather, we're better off thinking of memory as fundamentally linked to how we actively pursue our goals at any given moment. In other words, memory isn't so much "a system" or even "a set of systems," but capacities that serve our needs across different domains. Visual memory capacities are there to help us accomplish visual tasks, verbal memory capacities are there to help us accomplish verbal tasks, and so on. Attention is what helps us allocate resources to goals, so it makes sense that attention would be heavily involved in all aspects of immediate memory, coordinating across different components and constantly redirecting resources where they are most needed from one moment to the next.

Limitations on working memory. You may have read somewhere that we can only hold about seven items at a time in working memory. That's a reassuring enough figure, and might imply that students will do best when we present only seven points at a time—say, seven topics on a web page, or seven bullet points on a PowerPoint slide. But this long-repeated number is now under question as researchers devise ways to measure capacity that factor out rehearsal strategies, imagery, and other mnemonic tricks. Using these updated methods, researchers have found that working memory span is closer to just four items.[8] And even within this set of four things, there may be just one or two that are active enough for us to actually use.[9]

Pinning down the precise number is an important goal for memory theorists, but isn't really germane to real-world teaching and learning—because when we are processing connected ideas, we probably don't hold them in working memory anyway. If we can meaningfully interpret information as it comes in—as we do when we follow a coherent stream of speech—we don't have to hang on to it for any significant length of time before turning it straight into a long-term memory representation.[10] When we are juggling discrete bits of disconnected information, working memory limits can restrict us to handling just a few items in a series, but when we're taking in material with a coherent structure, the limits are much more fluid. The bottom line for teachers and designers is this: Don't worry about counting points on a page, especially when your material is coherently structured. Rather, ask how many distinct and disconnected pieces of information your students have to hold at once while they are completing a learning activity, because those are the things that overtax working memory.

THEORIES OF LONG-TERM MEMORY

There's wide consensus among researchers that long-term memory is essentially unlimited; as theorist James Nairne puts it, asking how many things you can store in long-term memory is like asking how many different tunes a piano can play.[11] Underneath this piano analogy, there's another very nuanced point about how long-term memory works: long-term memory isn't so much a thing that holds pieces of information, but is instead more like a mechanism for *reproducing* information. We reproduce information based on *cues*—fragments of information available to us in the here and now that we can use to reactivate other fragments of information. Then we piece those fragments together into what we experience as a memory.

Storage isn't an issue with long-term memory, but retrieval is. Cues—the information that we use as starting points during retrieval—are critical to retrieving what you need, when you need it, and thus cues underlie many long-term memory phenomena. Consider the experience of having a word "caught on the tip of your tongue." When you're stuck in a tip-of-the-tongue state, have you forgotten the word? Not really—with the right cues, such as a rhyming or similar-sounding word, the word you want will pop right into mind.

Another influence of cues can be seen in the interplay of different kinds of sensory information that we incorporate into a memory. A memory may comprise several distinct sensory aspects, such as what we saw or heard, along with a more abstract representation of meaning. For example, you might remember your spouse asking you to pick up milk at the store. That memory could include, among other things, the abstract idea of milk, the visual image of the empty milk carton sitting on the counter, the tone of your spouse's voice, perhaps even your internal sense of the time of day when you were having the conversation about the milk.

Far from confusing us, these multiple interrelated sensory cues often help us when we go to retrieve the memory. Thus, information with rich sensory associations tends to be better remembered. Visual imagery is particularly powerful; we're more likely to recall a word if it's accompanied with a picture, or if we just see the picture and no text at all.[12] Memory champions—like those in Joshua Foer's best-selling book *Moonwalking with Einstein*—liberally exploit the power of visual imagery, creating outlandish mental images that allow them to accurately encode and recall things like the exact order of an entire shuffled deck of cards.[13]

Another factor that drives recall from long-term memory is what we were doing with the information when we first processed it. In particular, *deep processing*—thinking of information in terms of its meaning—sets us up for much better chances of recall.[14] Let's take as an example a student who is completing an online course in child development. If, as she works her way through the material, she concentrates on how it relates to her goal of becoming a pediatric nurse, whether she agrees or disagrees with the information, or what it says about public policy, she's processing the information deeply. If she just focuses on picking out key words—or worse, truly ephemeral things like the color and layout of the course web site—she's doing shallow processing.

There's an important caveat to this depth-of-processing principle that instructional designers should know. Besides being sensitive to the depth of processing, memory is also affected by the match between the type of processing going on during encoding and the type of processing going on during retrieval. This principle, termed *transfer-appropriate processing*, means that deep, meaningful thought about the course material may not produce superior performance if students are engaged in a very different type of activity when they are tested. Put a different way, memory is best when students are doing highly similar things during their learning activities and during their assessments.

To illustrate, consider the line of research that my colleagues K. Laurie Dickson, Michael Devoley, and I conducted on how different kinds of learning activities affect exam grades.[15] We randomly assigned different sections of our Introduction to Psychology course—all taught with the same book and instructor—to do either multiple-choice practice quizzes or reflective journal writing as part of the required coursework. We found that the quizzes, but not the journal writing, significantly raised exam scores. Journaling is a great example of a deep, meaningful processing activity, so why didn't it raise scores compared to the less-meaningful activity of quizzing? One possibility is that the quizzes produced more transfer-appropriate processing. Journaling emphasizes meaning and personal relevance, but isn't much like the process of taking a multiple-choice test— which is what students were doing on the in-class exams.

One last factor emphasized in the research on long-term memory is *emotion*. Generally speaking, emotions heighten memory.[16] However, the type of emotion matters, and unfortunately for teachers, the less pleasant emotions tend to win out when it comes to memory. In contrast to the classical Freudian view that we repress painful memories, contemporary researchers have discovered that negative emotions—fear, anger, and so forth—actually accentuate memory.[17]

The effect of negative emotions may have to do with the nature of the interconnection between regions of the brain involved in encoding memories and areas involved in emotion. One structure in particular—the amygdala, located deep within the brain—is highly attuned to strong emotions, particularly negative ones. It becomes more active in the presence of emotionally charged stimuli—for example, an angry-looking face.[18] In this highly activated state, the amygdala ramps up the creation of memories via its connections to the hippocampus, a structure that's heavily involved in creating memories, and via its connections to other memory regions in the cerebral cortex. But although the emotion effect is strongest for negative emotions, there is still some benefit for positive emotional tone,[19] so that any kind of emotional charge can help trigger improved memory.

These concepts—cues, sensory influences, depth of processing, and emotion—are the most important points that instructors should know from the established research base on long-term memory. But there is also a new theory on the horizon that can change how we think about teaching, learning, and memory: the *adaptive memory* framework.[20] Formulated by James Nairne and collaborators, the idea rests on the assumption that, like our physical bodies, our cognitive processes reflect the evolutionary adaptations made in response to environmental challenges during our history as a species. Through the process of natural selection, our cognitive machinery was reshaped in ways that gave us a better chance of survival in our ancestral environment, the grasslands where we functioned as hunter-gatherers.

The survival challenges we face in the modern, industrialized environment are very different from the ones our ancestors survived, but vestiges of these ancestral struggles remain, most notably in our memory systems. Researchers have flushed out these vestiges in a number of intriguing experiments, including several that show marked memory superiority for items that people process in terms of "survival relevance." This "survival processing" paradigm asks participants to think of whether a given item—a hammer, say, or a chair—would help them survive living out on a grassland as a hunter-gatherer. Asked later to recall which words they saw in the experiment, participants performed better for objects they thought of in the survival context, compared to a control condition where they had thought of whether the items would be useful moving from one apartment to another, or other more modern survival-relevant activities. Researchers are still hashing out whether these findings can truly be traced to ancestral survival challenges, but for now, evidence suggests that they aren't merely an artifact of some confounding factors such as how emotionally arousing or attention-grabbing the different scenarios are.[21]

Short of turning every course into a savannah role-playing exercise, how do we tap into adaptive memory in our teaching? Nairne places his survival processing research in the context of what he calls the "functionalist agenda," in which he advocates for thinking about memory in terms of what it is supposed to accomplish, rather than as a set of parts to be measured and cataloged without respect to *why* they work the way they do.[22] And this function-first philosophy may be the most important take-home message from the research, because it gives us better general intuitions about what students will remember and what they will forget. Besides retaining obviously survival-relevant information, it's most "functional" for us to remember information we understand and care about—why waste limited resources on disjointed, irrelevant information? To take advantage of adaptive memory in our instructional designs, we need to ask ourselves: Why *should* students remember the information I'm giving them? Does it relate to their goals? Is it tied to motivation? If not, they are likely to forget it—a case of the brain just doing its job the way evolution shaped it to do.

Applied Memory Research

Applied research in memory also offers us important guidance in designing online learning environments. This research directly takes on the questions of what circumstances—individual strengths, pro-

cessing strategies, setup of learning environments—lead to better retention, and how we can replicate those in our learning activities.

INDIVIDUAL DIFFERENCES

Over the course of my career, I've had the opportunity to infor-
mally talk to hundreds of people about memory, and I've found that
most people don't think much of their own memory abilities. But
what constitutes a "good" memory in the first place? People like to
think about memory in terms of inborn ability, but although there
are some disparities in how well different people perform on various
memory tasks, this focus on individual ability is counterproductive.
In particular, it distracts us from a major factor uncovered by applied memory research: expertise. Experts sometimes take advantage of specialized tricks—like the visual imagery mnemonics used
by memory champions—that help with remembering certain kinds
of information. But expertise confers other, more important advantages, most of which have to do with being able to structure knowledge in an organized way.

The idea of "knowledge structures" crops up a great deal in discussions of expertise and learning, but what does it mean exactly?
To illustrate, take the example of a person with expertise in the realm
of professional basketball—a longtime fan who has spent years acquiring knowledge of the sport and its players. This person has vast
stores of information in long-term memory, but crucially, it isn't
just stored piece by piece, like a huge index card file. Rather, it's organized around meaningful linkages, network-style. Players link to
important properties, such as the years in which they were most
famous and team affiliations, and players who are associated in some
meaningful way are linked to one another. It's these complex linkages that lend organization to the body of knowledge stored in the
expert's long-term memory.

Figure 5.1 illustrates what one small part of an expert's body of
knowledge would look like if we plotted it along these meaningful
linkages and relationships. To generate this illustration, I inter-
viewed a lifelong basketball fan, using as a starting point a randomized list of twenty of the most famous players of all time.[23] I asked
my expert to study the list of twenty players, then I asked him to do

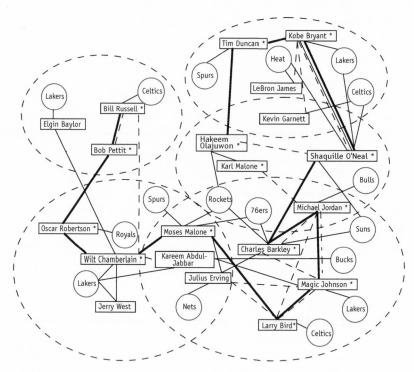

Figure 5.1. Diagram illustrating the organization of an expert's knowledge of twenty famous basketball players. Players (in rectangles) group along chronological lines; eras are encircled within dashed lines. Players who were active during the same era tend to be listed one after the other in free recall, indicated by heavy solid lines. Dashed straight lines indicate rivalries, and light solid lines indicate teammate relationships. Players are also linked to some of their most well-known team affiliations (in circles). Those players spontaneously remembered during free recall are marked with asterisks.

"free recall" of the list, noting the order in which he recalled them. With only a few minutes of study, he was able to list fourteen of the twenty, and recognized the remaining six with minimal prompting— excellent recall for such a long list. Then I asked him to elaborate on factual knowledge he had about each player.

My expert organized the list around the eras in which each player was most active, recalling the players in a roughly chronological order. In the diagram, dashed lines show the grouping by era. Players that were listed one after another in free recall—an indicator that they are strongly associated—are linked with heavy solid lines. Team associations and teammate relationships are marked with light solid lines. Famous rivalries are marked with dashed lines.[24]

What really stands out about this kind of diagram is the complexity of the interrelated knowledge, with multiple different properties that tie groups together. What's also evident is that the groupings are messy and complicated—indeed, diagrams like this are usually pretty hard to make sense of at first, given the multiple, overlapping relationships and representations. And they also show that not all items within a network are created equal—some are much better connected, while some are barely linked in at all. For example, look at the region of the network showing Charles Barkley, Magic Johnson, and Michael Jordan. It's a dense web of associations, overlapping affiliations, and rivalries. Compare that to the region showing Elgin Baylor, Bill Russell, and Bob Pettit—the web of associations around these players is relatively sparse.

So how does a knowledge structure like this impact memory? Imagine someone who isn't an expert—such as myself—attempting to memorize that list of twenty players. Lacking any way to organize the information, I'd probably approach the task with a weak strategy such as just rehearsing the names over and over. But an expert can "divide and conquer" by grouping list items along the lines already laid down by prior knowledge—just as my expert did when he rearranged the randomly ordered players chronologically. These groupings then become effective cues for the information, allowing the expert to get to each name from multiple sources ("was a rival of Michael Jordan's" "played for the Lakers"), thus increasing the chance of retrieval.[25] Indeed, in general, my expert was most likely to spontaneously recall players for which he had a richer set of associations.

Also consider what happens when an expert adds new information to a richly detailed, well-organized network of prior knowledge—such as our basketball expert learning about a brand-new player. Instead of sitting in isolation, this new memory representation can be fused to multiple preexisting structures within the network (team affiliations, where the player went to school, position, other players with a similar style). This too increases the chances that the new knowledge will be remembered.

Knowledge organization is the main reason why experts seem to effortlessly vacuum up new information in their domain of expertise—not a stronger overall memory or higher IQ. In fact, when you throw someone like our basketball expert into an unfamiliar area—hockey, say, or roller derby—that seemingly superior memory ability falls apart. Elaborating on this idea, the authors of the classic work *How People Learn: Brain, Mind, Experience, and School*, explain: "A pronounced difference between experts and novices is that experts' command of concepts shapes their understanding of new information: it allows them to see patterns, relationships, or discrepancies that are not apparent to novices. They do not necessarily have better overall memories than other people. But their conceptual understanding allows them to extract a level of meaning from information that is not apparent to novices, and this helps them select and remember relevant information" (pp. 16–17).[26]

Clearly, prior knowledge scaffolds new memories—and this fact drives home the point that good memory is made, not born. It's also good news for teachers, students, and others who hope to make the most out of the memory ability they have to work with. Above all, the research on individual differences in expertise tells us to foreground conceptual relationships in teaching and learning. To a certain extent, novices can mimic expert performance by imposing conceptual organization on information they are learning. Linking new information to what students already know is another way to build expert-like memory for unfamiliar material.[27]

THE TESTING EFFECT

The testing effect refers to the finding, replicated in numerous studies under a wide variety of testing conditions, that the very act of answering test questions improves the likelihood of remembering that same material later.[28] Especially compared to more passive strategies like rereading, testing produces more benefit for time invested than virtually any other study strategy.

These learning gains aren't just superficial or fleeting. Studies have directly demonstrated that the effect applies to conceptually sophisticated material and lasts at least several months—i.e., as long as the typical college semester. The effect is also robust, holding up across different kinds of test styles, including multiple choice, true-false, and essay. It even holds up when students don't get feedback about right and wrong answers.

The testing effect is counterintuitive for many people, perhaps because we are used to thinking of tests as ways to gauge what's been gained at the end of the learning process, not as part of learning itself. Students, especially, seem to miss out on the power of testing, instead favoring much less effective ways of using study time. In one survey, undergraduates cited rereading as the number-one study method they used; rewriting notes, memorizing, and highlighting notes or book also made the top ten. Follow-up questioning revealed that students were largely unaware that practice testing produced any kind of special benefits.[29]

Indeed, even when the evidence is right in front of them, students tend to doubt the power of tests. In another study, researchers assigned students to do practice tests before some exams, and non-test activities—such as study groups—before other exams. Even though students did better in the practice-testing condition, in hindsight they rated the other conditions higher in terms of preference and perceived effectiveness.[30] When it comes to the real payoff of testing, students' intuitions deceive them, so it's especially important for course designers to step in and make sure that testing is part of studying.

THE SPACING EFFECT

This phenomenon is a bit more intuitive than the testing effect, but still goes against many of the traditional ways we approach teaching and learning. The spacing effect—sometimes also called *distributed practice*—refers to the increased payoff we get from spreading review sessions over time, rather than "massing" them in long, concentrated sessions.[31] Like the testing effect, spacing is robust and holds up under a lot of different variations. There really is no magic number of study sessions or ideal length, as long as spacing is maximized. If you have, say, six hours to spend going over previously learned material, two three-hour sessions beats one big marathon, but three, four, or more shorter sessions are even better.

Memory researchers have cited a number of mechanisms that feed into this effect, including the ability to link up information to a wider variety of cues. More recently, they have discovered that spaced study may override mechanisms in the brain that suppress repeated information, thus allowing the brain to get more out of repeated exposure to information when it's widely spaced.[32]

We've all heard—and likely passed on to students—the injunction against cramming, but we may still end up designing learning experiences that unintentionally steer students in just that direction. High-stakes assignments with infrequent deadlines, a hallmark of traditional course design, encourage bursts of activity instead of steady, frequent engagement with material. This tendency to ignore spacing runs deep; continuing education seminars, language crash courses, and accelerated college programs all inherently push massed practice.[33] Cramming is seductive because it seems to offer fast progress, but these progress gains are quickly lost.[34] So it's especially important to be sure that spacing practice isn't just given to students as study advice, but rather that it is designed into the structure of the course from the outset.

THE INTERLEAVING EFFECT

Like spacing, interleaving has to do with how we organize our study sessions over time. We interleave material whenever we alternate between different topics, categories, skills, and the like, rather than just working with one at a time. To illustrate, participants in one line of research were assigned to learn to identify visual examples, such as different kinds of birds or paintings by different artists. Researchers found that mixing up the exposure to different examples across sessions—different artists, different classes of birds—improved learning.[35] So from a memory standpoint it's best to alternate topics, circling back to previously exposed material rather than working straight through each topic one at a time.

Another series of studies on interleaving focused on mathematics learning, contrasting performance for students who practiced one type of problem at a time in "blocked" fashion with those who alternated different types of problems.[36] Like the students learning about artistic styles, these students did better with interleaving, but for specific reasons that have to do with math. Successfully solving mathematics problems actually involves doing two separate things: first, identifying the kind of solution that's appropriate, then, correctly applying the solution. Interleaving supports both sides of the process, because it requires students to practice identifying the right kind of solution for each problem. Blocking, on the other hand, gives students a free pass on that part of the work, because they simply keep applying the same strategy from one problem to the next. This advantage is an additional reason to mix up topics and problem types when structuring learning experiences.

DESIRABLE DIFFICULTY

As is true for the testing effect, interleaving can be a tough sell to students, who tend to prefer the predictable rhythm of blocked presentation to the more difficult, but more productive interleaved style. Like massed practice, predictability is seductive, producing an illusory sense of increased mastery even as it undermines learning.[37] This false promise of ease brings us to a common thread running through a number of the applied memory findings we've discussed: *desirable difficulty*.

Desirable difficulties are challenging junctures during learning that pay off in better retention[38]—in other words, they engage us in the kinds of productive mental effort that leads to learning. Typical desirable difficulties include taking information presented in one form and turning it into a very different format—for example, synthesizing information from an online tutorial and turning it into a class wiki entry. Or consider the mental effort needed to complete a practice quiz, compared to the more leisurely activity of highlighting a textbook chapter. Desirable difficulty also encompasses the momentary brain-racking that takes place when you are alternating between different kinds of topics, or getting back into material after a hiatus.

For teachers accustomed to prioritizing student comfort and smoothly functioning classes, desirable difficulty can be an unsettling concept. And it is important to keep the emphasis on *desirable*. Otherwise, it can just be a way to excuse busywork, technical frustrations, and other time wasters that don't promote learning at all—or fall into the category of "extraneous load" discussed in Chapter 4. But it is a good idea for teachers, course designers, and—especially—students to get comfortable with the idea that the more demanding learning activities are the ones that pay. Just as athletes need to train on difficult terrain, and musicians need to practice challenging pieces, students need to put themselves in situations where retrieval is possible, but hard. It's one of the best ways to get memory to stick.

What Memory Principles Mean for Online Teaching and Learning

We know a great deal about how to improve memory for course material, and it's clear that these principles can vastly improve instructional design. We constantly relate new information to what we already know, and if we can't relate it to anything, we're unlikely to remember it. Determining what students already know and shaping material to tie into these existing structures is a key component of effective instructional design. Practice quizzing, organizing study into shorter bursts of effort, and alternating among different aspects of the material are all research-tested strategies that create more payoff for time spent.

To produce the payoff, instructors need to assertively guide students, because as we've seen, students have limited insight into which study activities actually work, and are also prone to confusing ease with effectiveness. This is where online learning activities outshine traditional, face-to-face methods. When we break out of traditional class schedules and put work online, we have near-unlimited freedom to change the timing and organization of studying. Online test banks and quizzing systems let us make small-stakes tests an ongoing part of learning. We can also use them to diagnose what students already know, and even make on-the-fly changes tailored to those prior knowledge bases. Getting away from in-class lecture lets us redirect student time into the active, focused effort that makes material stick—and multimedia capabilities let us pull in all the sensory cues that can be part of lasting memory.

Online teaching promotes memory in ways that traditional teaching can't. With this in mind, let's turn to the strategies we can use in designing online learning experiences.

STRATEGY 1: INCLUDE FREQUENT TESTS AND TEST-LIKE ACTIVITIES

Never before have instructors had so many options for harnessing the testing effect, thanks to online quizzing tools. More and more instructors are assigning low-stakes online tests either as an enhancement to face-to-face courses, or as a central part of fully online courses. At my university, there has been a major move toward incorporating features like weekly pre-lecture quizzes, particularly in lower-division "gateway" courses. Our introductory courses in astronomy, criminal justice, electrical engineering, biology, psychology, and more now all include some form of frequent online testing. And as mentioned in Chapter 1, pre-class online quizzes were a key part of the redesign projects in Introductory Psychology carried out at the University of New Mexico and the University of Southern Maine. With the addition of the online quiz feature in these redesigned courses, students earned higher grades, were less likely to fail the course, and learned more material.

The simplest way to go about setting up this kind of online quiz is to import the multiple-choice test bank associated with your textbook into your learning management system (e.g., Blackboard or Moodle). Ideally, this should have enough questions for each chapter—50 to 200, roughly—so that you could pull them at random from the test bank without too much repetition. Then you set up one quiz for each chapter, module, or topic—whatever best fits the structure of the course, but with the guiding principle that it's better to have shorter, more frequent quizzes than the other way around. For each quiz, allow multiple attempts. Unlimited attempts are ideal, but if you're concerned about repeating questions too often, you could limit it to a few attempts and count only the highest grade. This encourages multiple tries with the same material—something that we don't usually think about in association with tests, but that's highly beneficial from a memory standpoint.

Variations on this technique include writing your own test items, something that will allow you to more precisely target your own learning objectives but that can eat up preparation time. Most learning management systems will also let you organize questions (yours or publisher-supplied) in a fairly fine-grained-way, so that you can guarantee that students all get the same proportion of questions on different topics.

For alternative sources of quiz questions, you can mine the MERLOT database for material as well. This free, searchable repository of learning materials is licensed under Creative Commons (creativecommons.org), enabling reuse free of charge, under certain conditions (such as only noncommercial use; see Creative Commons or the MERLOT terms of service for details). Here you can find premade quizzes for a variety of disciplines.

Increasingly, publishers are also beginning to offer stand-alone products that support frequent testing. Pearson's MyLab and McGraw-Hill's Connect products both emphasize quizzes, incorporating different twists such as the ability to customize material or the ability to change upcoming questions based on prior performance. And as we covered in Chapter 4, you can even incorporate intermittent test questions while you're presenting material online, such as by using a Moodle branching lesson with test questions at the bottom of each page. This takes frequent quizzing to a new level, as students get a quick test after every few paragraphs of new material.

Clearly, there are myriad choices for how to bring the testing effect into your online teaching; the problem, if there is one, is how to choose among the options. Some helpful principles for making these design choices include the fact that although feedback isn't crucial for the effect, it does amplify it. Instructors may have concerns about "handing out the right answers," but it may be worth trying to balance this concern in some way—such as by using a larger test bank—in order to maximize feedback. Short-answer questions do produce a moderate advantage over multiple choice, but this shouldn't prevent you from using multiple choice if that's necessary in order to manage grading—plenty of studies have found substantial benefits even for multiple-choice format tests.

In general, the best quiz is one that students will actually *do*—so don't let the perfect be the enemy of the good as you work to create more frequent testing opportunities. Also, it may be worth reflecting on your own beliefs about the meaning and purpose of testing. It is a major shift to think of testing as a learning activity rather than a learning measure, and you'll have to be clear on this mindset in order to pass it along to your students. In our Introduction to Psychology course, we spend a good chunk of class time just explaining this new testing-as-studying view, which students are typically quite dubious about at the outset.

STRATEGY 2: STRUCTURE FOR SPACED STUDY

As with the testing effect, online tools give us unprecedented ability to direct the timing of student engagement with material. No longer limited to swapping hard copies of assignments at preset class meetings, we can arrange day-to-day schedules that balance quizzes, homework, online discussion, and more. Even when we're forced to work within a less-than-ideal accelerated course schedule—a three-week winter session course, say, or a self-paced course with pressure to finish fast—we can set up a schedule of staggered online deadlines that ensure spaced rather than massed class work.

One technique is to set up a recurring weekly schedule where each kind of work (discussion, quizzing, homework, any higher-stakes assignments such as major exams or papers) is due on a different day. You can set things up so that students are welcome to work ahead, but can't fall behind; some will manage to mass their work anyway by turning everything in extremely early, but those students are exceedingly rare.

Using online tools to push spaced study also works well as an enhancement to face-to-face courses. One example comes from my NAU colleague Richard Holloway, who teaches foundational courses in biology. He uses McGraw-Hill Connect for required weekly quizzes over the material that is going to be covered in upcoming class meetings. Every four to five weeks, there is a high-stakes in-class exam as well. He also assigns Connect tutorials that offer more in-depth experience with key concepts, but those are all due right before in-class exams. This structure pushes students to study material weekly before class and actively work with it during each class meeting; attendance is required, and class time incorporates lots of non-lecture, interactive activities. Students then revisit course topics in interleaved, alternating fashion every few weeks as part of the tutorials. It takes extra effort for students to get back into the swing of each topic when they revisit it—but that would qualify as a desirable difficulty.

Bear in mind that when you prioritize spacing and interleaving in your course design, you create a much more complex set of deadlines for students. Compared to the traditional design with just a few high-stakes assignments and exams, a class like Holloway's puts more stress on students' organizational skills. Here too, technology offers us many options for helping students meet spaced deadlines. During accelerated fully online summer courses, I've had success with issuing a daily announcement within the learning management system that lays out what students ought to be doing that day and reminds them of upcoming deadlines. Using a consistent weekly structure (discussions due Thursday, wiki entry due Friday, quizzes due Sunday night, etc.) is another commonsense way to offset confusion and missed deadlines. Text alerts, course calendars within the learning management system, and automated reminder e-mails are other useful tools for helping students stay on top of multiple spaced deadlines.

STRATEGY 3: INVOLVE EMOTIONS (CAREFULLY)

Emotionally arousing material is more memorable than nonemotional material. This seems like a simple enough principle, but the problem is that negative emotions have the most powerful effect on memory. Any teacher would agree that purposely inducing floods of negative emotions in students is problematic to say the least, so can we still use emotion as a useful enhancement to online teaching and learning?

On the one hand, online learning experiences don't have the built-in emotional impact produced by exchanging emotional cues in a traditional face-to-face classroom. On the other hand, resources like YouTube, NBCLearn, and publishers' media repositories give us new ways to show students—not just tell them—the emotionally powerful impacts of what they are learning. Recall that human beings are generally visually oriented—this holds in the emotional realm as well, so visual aids are the way to go for producing an emotional kick.

Using video clips to illustrate material, or to form the basis for assignments, is a great example of how computer-based media can tie in emotions in a way that advances memory for the material. In our online Introduction to Psychology course, for example, we incorporate video of a woman being treated for paralyzing fear of snakes in a brief, intensive therapy method that involves exposure to a live (tame and nonpoisonous) snake.[39] Viewing the video, you feel vicarious anxiety while you watch the woman cringe as the therapist shows her the snake from across the room. Then you feel surprise and relief as you see her go through the desensitization experience, her tension easing with each small step toward the dreaded creature. Within the course, we make the video a focus of one of the class assignments—students watch it at their own pace, then complete a short essay in which they describe the therapy technique and the client's progress, give their opinion of this type of therapy, and explain whether the same approach would be appropriate for treating other kinds of psychological problems.

TED talks are another perpetual favorite. One featuring Indian educator Kiran Bir Sethi conveys her exhilaration at bringing powerful educational experiences to disadvantaged children—an emotional experience that sweeps students right into issues of poverty, education, and social change.[40] Another classic talk features neuroscientist Jill Bolte Taylor recounting the story of her near-fatal stroke and recovery, and its psychological consequences, bringing emotional impact to questions about how the mind arises from the brain.[41] Some caution is warranted in using TED and similar types of video: be sure to vet the content for accuracy (or have a content expert do so), and keep in mind that a static, "talking head" video won't do much in and of itself to heighten emotion. And, as we did with the snake example above, it works best when video is the basis for some required assignment, rather than an optional frill that students can watch if they wish (or not watch, as the case often is with "optional" activities).

Another way to enhance learning with emotion is via public and semipublic sharing of work. Too often, traditional assignments are written for an audience of one—the instructor—losing out on the emotional charge associated with putting the work out there for a wider group to see. Online, you can ask students to share work with classmates, or the general public, if you wish—e.g., by asking them to post work to YouTube.[42] Similarly, rather than just having students turn in work to you, you can have them submit work as wiki pages, then assign the class to comment on one another's work. Many learning management systems now have wiki tools built in, or you can have students sign up for a free wiki site, such as wikispaces.com.[43]

Regardless of the specific tool or technique you use, the key to this strategy is to ask yourself: What is the emotional heart of the material I'm teaching? And how can I foreground this emotional center to my students—especially by using multiple sensory modalities and our natural social connection to other people? At the same time, you have to ensure that the emotional connection is germane to the topic you're teaching—just showing a scary, funny, or uplifting video won't enhance material if the emotions don't connect to content. Lastly, on the practical side, it's important to preface anything that's highly emotional with an explanation of what's to come, and, where appropriate, offer alternatives to students who might have particularly strong reactions. Even something like a video of a live snake—as in our psychology example—can be overwhelming for certain students, so you need to let them know what they are getting into.

STRATEGY 4: STEER STUDENTS INTO DEEP PROCESSING

We've established that mere exposure doesn't do much for memory. Similarly, superficial processing—such as just skimming over the layout and design of a web page—sets students up for forgetting. While designing learning activities, it's therefore important to think through what mental processes students will be engaging in as they complete the assignment.

Left to their own devices, students may stray toward shallow processing, but you can successfully redirect them with the right kinds of guidance. One good example of this comes from a research project on discussion assignments in an online course.[44] In this study, students were assigned to take on specific roles during different online discussions, including "starter" and "wrapper." Starters were assigned to develop discussion prompts that integrated major issues found in the week's readings. It was their job to get the discussion going, and to do this, they had to read materials in advance of the discussion, pull out important issues, and formulate thought-provoking questions that tied into the material. On the flip side, wrappers were assigned to go back over all the posts at the conclusion of the discussion, then tie together the major themes in one coherent summary. Students rotated the roles throughout the semester, so that everyone had the opportunity to participate in these heightened discussion roles. The researchers found that putting the onus of integration and summary onto students—rather than allowing them to always fall into a more superficial, passive role—ensured that all students engaged in very deep processing of material at several points over the semester, and encouraged more meaningful discussions overall.

Psychologists generally agree that the deepest processing of all is *self-reference*—in other words, thinking about information in terms of how it relates to the self. This can be another method for boosting memory—asking students to consider material not just in abstract terms, but in terms of personal examples and personal impact. With the caveat that you don't want to force students to over-share personal information, you can frame assignments, discussions, and similar learning activities by asking students to imagine how the material might play out in their own lives, or by inviting them to provide examples from their own personal histories, personal interests, relationships, and so forth.

STRATEGY 5: BASE NEW KNOWLEDGE ON OLD KNOWLEDGE

Take a moment to read over the following set of instructions:

The first thing you want to do is decide how many items you want to incorporate. Take them out of the container—it doesn't matter which ones, as long as there aren't any obvious signs of damage. Place them somewhere secure, as they tend to move without warning and this can be disastrous. Take the first one you want to deal with, and grasp it lightly along the short axis, then make contact between this and a firm but not sharp object. Be sure you also have an adequate container for the material inside. You can repeat this process up to two times, but after three, you should probably start over. With practice, you will end up with a clean separation, but even experts find that it's difficult to keep the various components totally under control. Remember, this is a skill that gets better with practice, and physical strength is less important than dexterity and finesse.[45]

If you read this paragraph in an online course, do you think you could accurately remember many of the key points? Or would it simply go past you in a swirl of confusing, disjointed details?

But what if I told you that this "mystery process" was a description of cracking an egg? Look back at the paragraph—it probably seems far more memorable with that key piece of context. Framing is important; human memory doesn't seem to fully engage in the absence of meaning and relevance. Thinking back to the "functionalist agenda," this makes a lot of sense—why should we invest scarce cognitive resources on information that doesn't complement what we already know about the world?

In this example, the needed contextual knowledge is already there—it just needs to be cued by the phrase "cracking an egg." In other cases, students don't have the needed contextual knowledge, and thus further material is less likely to stick, even with additional cues and hints. For example, students who start out a biology class without knowing core evolutionary concepts—such as the heritability of variation and the differential reproduction of individuals with different traits—gain less biology knowledge over the course of the semester, even though they're exposed to all the same class materials and activities.[46]

In designing online learning activities, we can cue existing knowledge by prefacing any presentation of material—web pages with written information, say, or an audio podcast—with an overview linking the information to earlier course topics, everyday life, or other familiar experience students can grab on to. Think back to the example of our expert basketball player—students should feel as much as possible like experts assimilating knowledge into existing structures, and rarely like novices struggling to hang on to facts in isolation. The ability to interlink related pieces of information and visualize relationships within online environments is another example of how we can use the qualities of online media to boost memory.

It may also be possible to dig into the data on which parts of the material students are more or less likely to do well on—so-called "learning analytics"—and use that information to shape future iterations of the course. If my Introduction to Psychology students keep missing the same questions about Pavlovian conditioning, for example, that tells me to trim back on some other area where students are doing fine in favor of increased concentration on the Pavlov section.

Taking the idea further, we can assess individual students' preexisting knowledge and use that to personalize subsequent instruction. In the evolutionary biology example above, the instructor could begin the course with an online assessment targeting key concepts such as heritability and differential reproduction. Low-scoring students could be automatically routed into modules designed to target those concepts, rejoining the flow of the subsequent material once they successfully demonstrate mastery. Similarly, some online practice quiz systems allow for re-presentation of questions about concepts that students have missed previously, while skipping material that students have already tested well on. Winnowing questions in this way helps ensure that students have the needed framework to put new information into memory.

Carnegie Mellon's Open Learning Initiative (OLI; oli.cmu.edu) provides an outstanding example of these principles in action. The OLI includes of a suite of freely available, fully online courses, emphasizing mathematics, sciences, and social sciences. Superficially, OLI courses resemble garden-variety massive open online courses (MOOCs), but they are actually highly sophisticated teaching systems built on a coherent design strategy that flows from cognitive principles. In particular, OLI courses emphasize scaffolding of knowledge, i.e., systematically adding new material to what students already know.

OLI courses integrate frequent assessment as the student works through learning activities, and these assessments are personalized according to what aspects of the material the student is having the most difficulty with. During a typical OLI-style quiz, students indicate not just their answers but also their confidence in those answers. Depending on how they are doing, they can access hints that effectively calibrate difficulty level to individual student proficiency while uncovering and remediating missing pieces of knowledge. Another signature OLI move is to continually fine-tune the course itself based on learning analytics—predicting which concepts will be the hardest for students to master, and building more targeted instruction in those areas with each iteration of the course.

Working on our own, few of us could manage the precise calibration, personalized scaffolding, and iterative improvement that you see with OLI. However, OLI's cutting-edge work offers ideas that the rest of us can adapt on smaller scales. It's also worth noting that many of OLI's materials are designed to be incorporated into other courses, or run alongside face-to-face classes in blended or hybrid fashion. Using the courseware for blended course designs has proven particularly effective; one study showed that statistics students who completed OLI in conjunction with a traditional face-to-face class learned a full semester's worth of material in *half* the time of a traditionally taught class.[47] It's strong evidence indeed for what online tools can do when you deploy them in sync with the operating principles of memory.

Chapter 6

Thinking

IMAGINE THAT you're a nurse with a freshly minted degree. You're treating your very first patient, a man who has recently undergone hip replacement surgery. He's breathing quickly, is agitated, and reports chest pain and shortness of breath. What's your course of action?

Back in nursing school, you studied mathematical formulas for calculating IV fluids, memorized anatomy and physiology terms, and learned how to take vital signs. But would you be able to use that knowledge base to accomplish a goal—in this case, developing and executing a plan to address your patient's needs? If so, you're successfully engaged in higher-order thought processes—or what the rest of us call thinking. Thinking, in this context, includes using logic to reason based on the available information, analyzing a problem and developing solutions that are both feasible and effective, and applying creativity in order to come up with new and nonobvious approaches. Effective thinking is one of the main things that sets experts apart from novices. Compared to a seasoned professional nurse, the fresh-out-of-school novice may have a similar amount of knowledge about things like IV fluid calculations, but the veteran will be better able to marshal his or her knowledge to actually help the patient.

Fostering higher-order thinking skills is a top priority for educators, because we want our students to take what we teach them into new domains. Certainly, preprofessional students should apply school-acquired knowledge in career settings, but it doesn't stop there; we want our students to use what we teach them in their personal lives, at the ballot box, and in all other facets of life. Fortunately, we know a great deal about how thinking works and how to strengthen thinking abilities. The research literature tells us that reasoning and problem solving aren't products of unusual inborn ability, nor are they random "strokes of genius." Rather, they are processes that we can build with practice and the right kinds of learning activities. You *can* learn to think better.

As we saw with memory, this is also an area where instructional technology presents major opportunities to take advantage of how our cognitive systems work. Take our novice nurse's chest pain patient. Fortunately for all concerned, he is an early example of instructional technology used to develop higher thought processes. He's a program that runs on SimMan, a computer-controlled mannequin built to provide realistic medical simulations. Since the 1960s, educators have realized the potential of programmable simulated patients for providing exactly the kind of safe, controlled clinical practice most needed by students in health professions. It wasn't until the 1990s, though, that it was feasible to produce such systems on a large scale.[1] SimMan, with its animatronic mannequin, specialized programming, and sound effects is perhaps an extreme example of technology that teaches thinking. But even the typical learning management system allows us to create activities in the same spirit of challenging practice, realistic scenarios, open-ended problem solving, and peer-to-peer collaboration.

That said, there are definite pitfalls in the path from knowledge to application. As experienced teachers know, it can be surprisingly difficult to get students to extend what they've learned to new situations. This, in turn, exposes the difficulty of getting students to understand the deeper principles at work across all the different examples and practice problems we give them. It isn't just the weaker or unmotivated students who have difficulty with some aspects of higher thought—cognitive research has exposed a number of arenas where nearly everyone makes reasoning mistakes.

Transforming thought is one of the hardest things we do as instructors, so it's an area where research and application are especially helpful. As with our other major areas of cognition, attention and memory, we'll start by considering the major findings from research to date, using those to build strategies for online teaching and learning.

Classic Research in Thinking

Cognitive psychologists have traditionally broken down higher thought processes into several discrete areas: formal reasoning, judgment / decision making, and problem solving. These areas also include creativity, subsumed under the general topic of problem solving, and expertise.

REASONING, JUDGMENT, AND DECISION MAKING

Test your reasoning powers with the following scenario: On a long, dull layover somewhere in the United States, you're passing time chatting with your new acquaintance, Joe Bob. Joe Bob proposes a bet: Can you guess where I'm from? Joe Bob says he'll make it even easier by filling you in on some key details about his personal life. He likes to listen to country music while cruising down the open highway in his Ford pickup truck. He makes a living mostly by working outdoors and enjoys spending his free time on target practice, deer hunting, and fishing. Joe Bob's attire fits his rustic lifestyle to a T: cowboy boots, pressed jeans, and a well-worn black wool Stetson.

You're starting to formulate best guesses of Joe Bob's hometown, and then he sweetens the deal even more: all you have to do is guess between two options—Los Angeles, California, or Abilene, Texas. So out of these two options, where do you think Joe Bob is from?

In this scenario, your best bet is to ignore intuition, gut feelings, all common sense . . . and choose Los Angeles. The reason for this has to do with *base rates*, meaning the overall likelihood of a given option, other factors being equal. In the example, base rates correspond to the population of Los Angeles versus the population of Abilene. You know that Los Angeles is much larger than Abilene, so the raw probability of any random person being from Los Angeles dwarfs the probability of that same random person's being from Abilene.

This is not to say that there is *zero* association between Joe Bob's colorful personal details and where he lives. These associations are real, and in your mental calculation you should weigh those associations and the base rates together in making your estimate. But in all kinds of reasoning situations people effectively ignore base rates, focusing solely on descriptive details. When the description matches our representation of a category—such as our representation of a stereotypical Texan—we judge that there's a match, even when it's statistically unlikely.

This mental shortcut—called the *representativeness heuristic*—is one of several well-known quirks of the human reasoning system, together termed *heuristics, fallacies,* and *biases.* First documented by the researchers Amos Tversky and Daniel Kahneman in the 1970s and debated by legions of psychologists since, these phenomena expose gaping holes in our ability to apply quantitative reasoning strategies in judgment and decision making.[2]

Another shortcut that undermines our reasoning ability is the *availability heuristic,* another one of Kahneman and Tversky's discoveries. We use it to judge probability, for example, in situations where we have to weigh the risks of different courses of action. The heuristic works like this: We search memory for examples and then create probability estimates based on how easily we can come up with those examples. If examples easily come to mind—i.e., are highly "available" in memory—we increase our estimate of likelihood.

As shortcuts go, availability isn't that bad. If, say, we can easily recall four different burglaries that happened in our neighborhood, it makes sense to conclude that burglary is likely (and accordingly, lock all our doors and look into installing that security system). The disadvantage, though, is that anything that biases memory will bias our probability estimates accordingly. Vivid, emotional memories are particularly easy to recall, as are things that happened recently—and this disproportionate ease of recollection then exaggerates our probability estimates.

The cognitive psychology research literature is full of different variations on reasoning shortcuts that get us into trouble. What most of them have in common is our deep-seated predisposition to avoid quantitative reasoning strategies in favor of almost *any* other method. Cognitively speaking, mathematical reasoning is a bit like walking on your hands—it's something you can do with deliberate effort, but it's definitely not the natural first choice. Some people can get pretty good at it with practice, but as a species, we're just not that adept.

Formal logic also tends to challenge most people's cognitive abilities. People commonly make glaring errors in applying formal reasoning to do things like test whether a rule is being followed in a set of abstract symbols.[3] Importantly, though, this poor pattern of performance is reversed when people are reasoning within a familiar arena. What seems to be important here is not whether people have actual real-world experience with the reasoning scenario, but rather whether they understand the underlying principles. For example, people usually have a well-established "permission schema," which is general knowledge of situations where you have to meet some criteria in order to do something—being over twenty-one to drink alcohol, having to have a visa in order to enter certain countries, and so on. People can use this kind of general knowledge to reason about specific rules that they haven't encountered before.[4]

Our reasoning systems can perform well when we have some kind of familiar schema to grab onto, but overall, the research on reasoning presents a humbling picture of our limitations. The take-home message for online as well as traditional college teaching is this: Nearly everyone—A-student or not, math whiz or not—experiences occasional failures of reasoning, oftentimes stemming from an aversion to quantitative reasoning but also because fully abstract logic eludes most of us. And people are particularly prone to being sidetracked by memorable details, substituting those for more systematic, mathematical thinking.

It follows that it's unproductive to try to sort students into "good reasoners" and "poor reasoners," given that the general level of ability is typically so low. Furthermore, situational and contextual factors can completely transform performance, as in the case of reasoning about abstractions versus rules we conceptually understand in real life. Especially for those of us who are teaching quantitative subject matter, we should anticipate that mastering formal reasoning will require substantial effort and practice, even for very academically capable students.

PROBLEM SOLVING

In stark contrast to the case of formal reasoning, people as a species are highly adept at working out solutions to problems. As any fan of the movie *Apollo 13* will agree, human beings have extraordinary capacity to use available resources to extract themselves from even the most dire situations. Research on problem solving has focused on pinning down exactly how the problem-solving process unfolds, as well as on the typical ways in which we approach different kinds of problems. Some theorists use a travel metaphor for problem solving, describing it as moving from a starting point, or "initial state," to the desired result, or "goal state." There may be just one pathway or several from the initial state to goal state, and part of what you have to do as a problem solver is select from all the different possibilities, sometimes termed the *problem space.*[5] As you move through the space, there are obstacles to overcome—things that block you, such as rules you have to follow or resources you lack.

Problems can also be viewed in terms of *structural* elements. The deep structure of a problem consists of core elements such as the obstacles involved, goals, and resources available. Surface structure, by contrast, consists of less-relevant superficial details. To illustrate, imagine that you're slated to give a PowerPoint presentation to the campus space allocation committee, a boring obligation but one that could possibly net your unit some coveted new workspaces. The presentation starts in thirty minutes, and you're three miles from campus when your old forest green Toyota 4x4 belches black smoke, sputters, and dies. You have eight dollars in your pocket and a cell phone with about ten minutes of battery life left. What do you do?

In this problem, the structural elements include the time until your presentation starts, the distance from your destination, and resources you have (money, phone, physical mobility, knowledge of engine repair). These are the factors that will guide your choice of solution: trying to make it on foot, calling for a ride, attempting a quick repair, or asking to reschedule. Irrelevant details include the boringness of the committee, the color of your car, the content of the presentation, and so on. If you boil this problem down to its deep structure, it's quite similar to any number of other problems involving time, distance, and delay: hitting traffic on the way to a court date, trying to make a too-tight connection between flights, or racing to your child's school play.

Besides breaking down into deep structural elements, problems break fairly neatly into several distinct types. One dimension on which they vary is *well-defined* versus *ill-defined* problems. Well-defined problems are those in which the constraints (obstacles, rules, resources, and so on) are all clearly evident, and it's possible to say for sure what the goal state is and when it has been reached. Well-defined problems are not necessarily easy—they include things like calculus and physics exercises—but have a feel different from ill-defined problems, in which it's not clear exactly what all the constraints are or even when you've successfully solved the problem. An extreme example would be attempting to answer the question, "What is the best way to have a happy life?" It's not insoluble—just slippery.

Another dimension that differentiates problems is whether they are best characterized as *insight* or *non-insight* problems.[6] Non-insight problems are those in which you can work steadily toward the goal, with intermediate steps along the way to completion. Algebra and chemistry problems are good examples of non-insight problems, as are many real-world situations such as completing a home renovation project or planning a party.

Insight problems, by contrast, are those that are solved in a stroke of sudden inspiration, with little sense of how one arrived at the solution. To try a classic insight problem for yourself, take a piece of scratch paper and draw three equally spaced rows of three equally spaced dots (these should form a roughly square configuration). Can you draw four lines that go through all nine dots, *without lifting your pen from the paper?* If and when the solution comes to you, it will probably come without warning and suddenly. (For an illustration of the problem and several acceptable solutions, see http://www .archimedes-lab.org/How_to_Solve/9_dots.html).

Insight problem solving is closely related to *creativity*—another phenomenon that seems mysterious but is actually governed by a number of fairly well-understood factors. Creativity is generally defined as reaching a solution to a goal that is both novel and useful, i.e., that fits the constraints given in the problem.[7] Consider this story about a particularly astute sanitation manager: In the manager's town, trash collectors did their job by walking to each house, dragging the trash can to the truck, emptying it, dragging the can back to the house, walking back to the truck, and riding to the next house. The manager realized that you could cut about half the time from this process by walking with an empty can to the first house, swapping it for the full trash can, dragging the full trash can to the truck, emptying it, and riding *with* the newly emptied can to the next house. That empty can would then be swapped for the full can, which was then emptied and carried to the next house, and so on.

This creative solution hinges on realizing that a constraint you thought was there initially—that each household get its own assigned can back—was not really a constraint after all. If you successfully solved the nine-dot problem a few paragraphs back, you likely did so in the same way, realizing that (spoiler alert!) you didn't have to stay within the boundaries of the square formed by the three rows of dots.

Figuring out which constraints are illusory is one key to insight and creativity, but there are other factors at work—including some that, as teachers, we have some degree of control over. It is tempting to assume that some students are simply creative by nature, but situational factors make as much of an impact as inborn characteristics, if not more. Creativity is heightened in environments where we are less focused on other people's judgments of our work.[8] It's also enhanced by being in a good mood, and by being motivated more by intrinsic interest than by external rewards.[9] The directions given for problem-solving tasks also matter; students who are given explicit step-by-step instructions tend to produce less-creative work products compared with those who are given less-structured directions emphasizing exploration and the acceptability of different solutions.[10]

It follows that for instructors teaching in disciplines where creativity is a top priority, it is worth putting extra effort into the class atmosphere, directing attention away from grades wherever possible, and setting a positive tone. Emphasizing intrinsic motivation— something we'll return to in Chapter 8—is also particularly important. It may also make sense to structure assignments in less-detailed, more open-ended ways. Fortunately for those teaching in creative fields, it turns out that creativity can be increased through deliberate training and practice, especially when realistic exercises are used.[11]

ANALOGICAL REASONING

Researchers have studied a number of specific techniques that people use to solve problems, but analogy warrants special mention because of its potentially powerful applications to college instruction. Analogical reasoning can be defined as the process that allows us to solve one problem on the basis of another, already solved problem. Applying strategies that work in one situation to a new situation is thought to be one of the key cognitive capacities of the human mind.[12] Examples run the gamut from the mundane (a child's using a Band-Aid to fix a "hurt" doll) to the sublime (a journalism teacher who designs a class to run like a real-world newsroom; a business leader who uses military strategy to dominate a market).

Analogical reasoning is surprisingly complex, involving several discrete cognitive processes that all have to take place for a successful analogy to occur. First, you have to complete an *access* stage, in which you make the connection between the "target" problem you're dealing with in the present and a "source" problem stored in memory. Then you engage in *mapping*, in which you connect the deep structural elements of the source to corresponding elements in the target. Lastly, there is an *inference* stage, where you devise a workable solution to the target based on what worked in the source. Optionally, there may be a *learning* stage, in which the person gains deeper understanding of the principles that tie together both problems.

It's easy to see why educators get excited about analogical reasoning. First, there is the promise of fast, efficient problem solving as students use what they have already learned to tackle new material, instead of starting from scratch. This is particularly attractive for instructors in natural and physical sciences, given the focus on common principles and processes that apply across diverse domains.[13] For example, physics students who have already solved problems in one domain—speeding bullets, say—would ideally be able to apply those same concepts to new domains—rockets, spaceships, and so on—without having to relearn basic concepts every time.

I can attest to the power of the right analogy to instantly illuminate a murky concept, because I frequently rely on this technique to explain "formative assessment" and "summative assessment" to faculty colleagues. This is something I often have to do in my redesign work, and I find that the terms and formal definitions on their own usually provoke confusion. In the analogy, assessment (the unfamiliar domain) is likened to food tasting in a restaurant (a familiar domain).[14] It goes like this: "*Formative* assessment is when the chef tastes the soup; *summative* assessment is when the customer tastes the soup." This simple image gets across the difference between assessment as an intermediate step on the path to improving learning, and assessment as a judgment of the "end result" of learning.

The *learning* stage also holds obvious appeal, as it promises to expand conceptual understanding at the same time that it promotes successful problem solving. In the case of my faculty colleagues, for example, catching on to the tasting analogy can trigger productive reflection on why assessment is important and the different functions that testing can serve within a single course. Furthermore, the choice of analogy can transform a person's perspective on different aspects of the problem. In a study conducted during the early stages of the first Gulf War, researchers asked participants to draw an analogy between that conflict and World War II. Some participants were encouraged to map the Gulf War–era United States to World War II–era Britain, while others were pushed to map it to World War II–era United States. This mapping affected how participants saw the leaders of the different countries involved; mapping the United States to Britain predisposed participants to see George H. W. Bush as analogous to Winston Churchill, while mapping the United States to itself predisposed them to see Bush as analogous to Franklin D. Roosevelt.[15] It follows that by suggesting a specific analogy, we can get our students to break out of one viewpoint and adopt a different one—a persuasive power that we really need for teaching some kinds of material.

Analogies can be powerful teaching tools, but they are no magic bullet. One major caveat is that learners, particularly novices in a field, are fairly unlikely to spontaneously generate target-source mappings.[16] Even when presented with two clearly analogous problems in a short space of time, people commonly fail to make the connection.[17] In one classic study of analogical reasoning, volunteers were provided with a problem and solution in the form of a story about a general who broke up his force into small groups and had them converge on a military target. The purpose of this "convergence" strategy was to defeat a system of land mines that would be tripped by the force of large groups, but not smaller groups. Volunteers were then asked to generate solutions for a new problem: how to attack a tumor with radiation without damaging surrounding tissue. When volunteers were given an explicit hint that the problems were connected, over three-quarters of them were able to use the analogy to generate a convergence solution for the radiation problem: send small beams of X-rays from different angles so that they converge on the tumor. But without the hint, fewer than a third hit on the analogy.[18]

Explicitly pointing out analogies helps, but it isn't a guarantee that analogical reasoning will take place. And when less-advanced students attempt to draw analogies, they are prone to mapping across problems based on surface features rather than on deep structure. One study of analogical reasoning in mathematics instruction presented students with short probability lessons framed in the context of two different real-world situations—runners in a race and students trying to get tickets to a lecture. Although students did benefit from having the instructor explicitly point out the mappings between different problems, they were still sometimes thrown off by the context, inappropriately applying the strategies learned in the racing example to other problems involving races, and strategies learned in the lecture example to anything else involving lectures.[19] The power of analogy to guide thought can also backfire rather spectacularly when people choose inappropriate mappings[20]—as with psychology students who think about the brain as exactly analogous to a muscle, or economics students who think about the nation's budget as exactly analogous to a household budget.

There are several strategies that can help instructors avoid these pitfalls. Actively engaging students in the source problems, rather than just showing the problems to them, increases the chances of successful mapping later down the line. Novices also need more than just one or two source problems. Instead, they require extensive practice in order to reliably perform access, mapping, and inference.

The mathematics-learning study with the "racing" and "lecture" examples further revealed that having the instructor physically point out the structural correspondences in different problems— i.e., which parts of one problem map onto which parts of other problems—was the best strategy for maximizing analogical reasoning capability and making sure that students didn't fall prey to inappropriate surface analogies.[21] Other studies suggest that only a few structural similarities should be presented at a time, because multiple structural relationships quickly overwhelm working memory.[22] One potentially productive variation on teaching with analogy is to push students to generate their own analogies, which tend to promote deeper understanding of problems than teacher-presented analogies (with the caveat that the teacher needs to monitor such analogies closely in order to correct any inappropriate ones).[23]

Applied Research on Thinking

EXPERTISE AND PROBLEM SOLVING

Experts solve problems better, but not because they are smarter or just because they have more stored knowledge. Experts do have a repertoire of problem-solving strategies memorized from experience, but this is not the sole foundation for their better performance. Rather, as people become experts, there are qualitative shifts in how in they think about problems in the domain of expertise.[24] One major shift has to do with how knowledge is organized.[25] Think back to our basketball expert in Chapter 5, who classified players in a highly conceptually sophisticated way compared to how a novice would. The expert's knowledge structures captured meaningful factors like chronology—how different players fit into the history of the game—cause and effect, and interrelationships between different players, transforming the information from twenty different names into a rich, interconnected narrative.

These conceptual relationships not only support memory— making it easier to encode and recall the names of the top twenty players—but also help experts apply the right knowledge in the right way during problem solving. In particular, experts are better at sorting out irrelevant details (surface structure) from relevant (deep structure) information, which helps them make the most of limited cognitive resources during problem solving.[26]

Experts also use stored knowledge to determine the best approach to problems, as well as to identify source problems (i.e., previous experiences) that could be applied to the present situation. Compared to novices, they also tend to spend more time gathering information in order to make an informed "diagnosis," and less time engaged in trial and error. For example, imagine that you had the choice of bringing back any basketball player from any era to play for your favorite team. Who would you pick? Nonexperts might just pick the one they like the best, but an expert would ask questions first—who else is playing on the team, the weakest and strongest aspects of the current lineup, and so on. And so, even when working with essentially the same set of options, the expert will produce a better solution.

For teachers hoping to build expertise, there is no way around the need to create extensive opportunities for deliberate practice, as we've discussed earlier in this book. Students with less natural aptitude (visual-spatial ability, say, or working memory) should be particularly encouraged to persist past the novice stage, as inborn cognitive abilities begin to matter less as a person progresses toward expertise.[27] Emphasizing the organization and classification of knowledge, as well as conceptual interrelationships between different pieces of information, may accelerate the development of expert-like knowledge structures. Ways of doing this include asking students to explain how one event led to another or what two things have in common. Students may also benefit from emulating expert-like problem solving. You can ask them to do this by asking them to identify and apply appropriate analogies, think about underlying concepts like cause and effect, and encouraging them to spend time diagnosing and strategizing before offering any solutions.

TRANSFER

Closely related to theoretical research on analogical reasoning, research on transfer focuses on how we get students to take what they've learned and apply that knowledge to new domains, problems, and situations. Transfer is one of the most central problems in the entire realm of education, one that researchers have now grappled with for over a hundred years.[28] Transfer is what allows that nursing student to use a case study she did with her classmates to help a patient in her real-world career, it's what lets a computer expert quickly pick up the latest programming language, and it is how a teacher applies techniques learned at a workshop to novel challenges in a classroom. Without transfer, learning is just a collection of facts frozen in time.

Like analogical reasoning, transfer doesn't just flow naturally from the mere existence of knowledge in memory, as we see in the case of people who can do "everyday" math (making change, calculating sale prices) quite capably, but who fall apart on formal mathematical problem solving.[29] Transfer is remarkably hard to achieve, a particularly unsettling fact given that it is also such a high-stakes issue; after all, an education that doesn't transfer isn't worth much.

Given the stakes and the challenges, researchers have put a lot of effort into identifying transfer-promoting teaching techniques. What this research reveals is that in general, the main influence on transfer is how thoroughly students learn material in the original domain.[30] This makes a lot of sense, given that only deep, extensive learning creates the conceptual knowledge that students can effectively extend into new arenas. And this "original" knowledge has to be well organized, again to support the conceptual reasoning that is the basis for successful transfer.

To illustrate, think back to the basketball expert described in Chapter 5. What would happen if he tackled an unfamiliar subject that has some connection to his domain of expertise, such as the history of baseball? In theory, this student could whiz through the task by using some of the features of his basketball knowledge—the chronology of the game, interrelationships between players, contrasting styles of play, and so on—to organize knowledge in the new arena. Transferring from one realm to the other would not only create great deal of memory efficiency, but would also allow for more insightful reasoning. However, this would work only for someone who had learned about basketball to the point where this conceptual organization was fully developed. In other words, knowing a lot about basketball might help you learn about baseball, but knowing just a little bit about basketball wouldn't help much at all.

The research suggests several other major points of advice on how to build transfer:

TEACHING METACOGNITIVE STRATEGIES

Metacognition refers to one's own insight about learning and ability to self-manage the learning process[31]—namely, the awareness of how your own learning works and the skill of deliberately maximizing your own learning. Metacognition can be strengthened by teaching students effective study strategies as well as by having them self-reflect on learning. This works best when metacognitive strategies are integrated alongside the material being taught, rather than pieced out as a separate thing to learn. Teaching metacognition does not have to be highly technical or theoretical in nature. I encourage the faculty I work with to simply introspect about how they approach material, as disciplinary experts, as a way to uncover what they should teach their students about thinking in a discipline. You can also incorporate learning principles, such as the testing effect, into the material you teach your students as a way to build metacognition. Essentially, infusing metacognition into teaching means focusing on the "process as well as the product" of thinking through a problem in the discipline.[32] When students have strong metacognitive ability, they are better able to see relations between old and new problems, and maximize transfer between the two.

Emphasize how knowledge is organized.[33] Point out classifications, hierarchies, interrelationships, and the like. Doing this when you teach the original material helps students transfer that information later on, because it makes conceptual linkages easier to spot.

Go for depth rather than breadth.[34] If you teach a select few foundational areas very thoroughly, students will be able to transfer from those foundational ones to subsequent ones much more easily. This is better than having to start from zero (i.e., no transfer) as you skate superficially across a larger number of topics.

Emphasize underlying principles and conceptual structure.[35] Continually draw students' attention to abstract, general aspects of the material. You want students to focus on abstract, potentially transferrable principles, rather than surface features that are tied to specific contexts. One way to do this is by assigning exercises or asking questions that emphasize structure—for example: draw a diagram that organizes the information; explain why you picked a particular multiple-choice answer; identify the second-best multiple-choice answer, and explain why; explain what additional information would be useful in answering the question.

Frequent quizzing.[36] Besides promoting memory, testing increases the likelihood of transfer.

Tell students why wrong answers are wrong.[37] Explanatory feedback is more effective for building transfer compared to feedback that just says whether an answer is right or wrong.

CRITICAL THINKING

Besides hoping that what they teach will transfer, educators also fervently desire that their students will adopt generalizable critical-thinking skills. Critical thinking involves a number of cognitive processes such as evaluating evidence, analyzing arguments, and appreciating the context associated with information.[38] Some researchers believe that critical thinking is also fundamentally *dispositional* as well as cognitive—meaning that you have to be willing to do it, as well as able.[39]

Critical thinking is serious business. In the United States alone, *billions* of consumer dollars are spent on the basis of unscientific marketing claims for products ranging from athletic shoes that supposedly build muscle to worthless homeopathic remedies—claims that collapse under the most minimal critical scrutiny.[40] Unsupported, illogical arguments are also a hallmark of political movements that promote hostility and violence toward other groups.[41] Critical thinking may also have important consequences for individual well-being; one study found that people who score lower on critical-thinking tests are more likely to report consequences stemming from poor life choices ranging from sunburn to bankruptcy to unintended pregnancy.[42] On the positive side, critical-thinking skills are commonly reported among the top qualifications sought by employers, suggesting that students who acquire these skills will have a competitive edge in their future careers.

Cognitively, critical thinking has a lot in common with transfer and analogy, as it requires you to first recognize the underlying structures and principles in new problems, then solve those new problems by applying strategies you learned previously. And as with analogy, this retrieval and mapping process can easily fail. Diane Halpern, an expert on critical thinking, offers this example: "Students may be able to explain why correlation is not causation when presented with this question on an exam but still not recognize that this same principle is operating when they read that children who attend religious schools score higher on standardized tests than those who attend public schools" (p. 72).[43] This happens, according to Halpern, when students lack adequate practice at identifying the structural characteristics of an argument—e.g., how to know when someone is making causal claims on correlational evidence. These structural characteristics are the cue for applying critical thinking, so without the cue, critical-thinking processes don't come into play. The problem isn't just that students are unskilled at critical thinking—they often don't know when to do it in the first place.

Other barriers to critical thinking include the fact that we sometimes have strong psychological motivations to uncritically accept certain kinds of ideas. As psychologist Scott Lilienfeld explains, "Many paranormal claims, such as those concerning extrasensory perception, out-of-body experiences, and astrology, appeal to believers' deep-seated needs for hope and wonder, as well as their needs for a sense of control over the often uncontrollable realities of life and death" (p. 4).[44] For example, believing in the ability to foresee catastrophes—plane crashes, illnesses, horrible accidents—might help some people manage anxiety by giving them the false assurance that if anything really bad were about to happen to them, they would be able to sense and avoid the danger. So sometimes, critical thinking isn't just about picking apart logic, but rather about examining belief systems, deep-seated emotions, and worldviews.

The kind of cognitive biases outlined earlier in the chapter—availability, representativeness, and so on—can also powerfully distort our thoughts in illogical ways.[45] And critical thinking is plain *hard*—requiring far more taxing mental effort than other, uncritical modes of thought.[46]

Teaching critical thinking is a tall order, and researchers are still working on devising and testing effective strategies. However, we can pull out several concrete points of advice from the existing research literature. The first is to give students explicit practice in recognizing the kinds of critical-thinking problems that are typical for your discipline. For example, what are the cues that let you know something is a correlation-versus-causation problem, an ad hominem argument, or pseudoscience? Lilienfeld advises explicitly listing for students the specific features that characterize pseudoscience—red flags such as focusing on confirmatory rather than disconfirmatory evidence, relying on anecdotes and testimonials, and avoiding peer review.[47] So as a psychology instructor, I might explain and give examples of what each of these critical-thinking triggers looks like, then ask students to work through some practice scenarios. In this way, they can learn to identify the right times when critical thinking should come into play.

Another strategy is to draw students' attention to the *structural elements* of arguments that should trigger critical thinking—in other words, pushing students to look beyond superficial differences to find what these problems have in common. Halpern illustrates this with the example of "sunk costs" arguments. Sunk cost reasoning, i.e., arguing that resources already spent must justify investing additional resources, can play out in a very diverse array of real-world situations, from pouring money into a broken-down car because you've already spent so much on repairs, to marrying a less-than-ideal partner because you've been dating for years, to spending money on an ineffective military project that's already cost billions.[48] Students need to be able to identify all these as examples of sunk cost reasoning, despite the fact that on the surface, the scenarios are completely different. Instructors can build the ability to do this with techniques that explicitly ask students to identify what the situations have in common, explain cues that suggest sunk cost reasoning is at work, or otherwise pull out underlying, abstract aspects of the argument.

In many situations, instructors should also tread cautiously around the motivational side of irrational beliefs—i.e., the personal and emotional reasons why students believe illogical things in the first place. Lilienfeld suggests handling emotionally charged beliefs—ESP, astrology, visitation by ghosts—with "compassion and sympathy," being mindful that any perceived condescension or ridicule will just provoke backlash. It might also help to acknowledge that we *all* experience cognitive biases to one degree or another, so falling into the occasional cognitive trap doesn't make you dumb, just human.

Finally, we instructors need to manage our own expectations about critical thinking, especially given the tendency to underestimate just how hard it is to effectively teach this type of thinking skill. Don't expect that it will naturally fall out of teaching the course content; it takes a lot of concerted effort—both yours and the students'—to achieve real gains in critical thinking that have any chance of transferring beyond the course. Accordingly, it's best to present multiple examples of arguments that should trigger critical thinking, spaced throughout the term, instead of segregating critical thinking off in its own one-shot module.[49]

What Research on Thinking Means for Online Teaching and Learning

Online teaching and learning methods provide powerful avenues for carrying out strategies for highlighting deep structure, using analogy, fostering transfer, and other important aims discussed thus far. It's more feasible to offer multiple practice opportunities—case studies, argument analyses, and many more variations—in the virtual environment, compared to doing them face to face in the classroom setting. Increased practice opportunities also help online teachers make better use of analogies. Analogies work best when multiple source problems are presented, which is easier to do systematically online, compared to the hasty single analogies we're prone to throw out in a traditional face-to-face class setting.

The asynchronous online environment also affords more opportunity for deliberate reflection, whereas in-class discussions tend to reward immediate, off-the-cuff responses. Online, students can take as much time as they need to thoughtfully formulate responses, and it's this kind of effortful analysis that best supports coveted intellectual habits like critical thinking. Similarly, putting thoughts into writing in the virtual environment can push students toward clarity and attention to argumentation.

Educators and researchers have come up with some remarkably creative and effective online tools that target thinking skills. Many, as we'll see, directly tie in to cognitive principles of higher thought.

STRATEGY 1: ASSIGN STUDENTS TO PRACTICE THE THINKING SKILLS YOU WANT

To strengthen thinking abilities, practice needs to be frequent, challenging, and specifically targeted to the desired cognitive processes, whether those be critical thinking, formal reasoning, identifying deep structure, solving problems, analyzing arguments, or some combination of these. If critical thinking is a priority in your course, consider including interactive reasoning activities in which students explicitly break down the components of an argument and supporting evidence. One example is the Rationale software system for argument mapping (http://rationale.austhink.com). Rationale provides a graphic workspace where students can use drag-and-drop graphic tools and text boxes to lay out the structure of arguments, arranging them hierarchically to denote, e.g., the supporting evidence feeding into an overarching claim.[50]

Besides providing an intuitive way for students to visualize all the parts of a well-structured argument, Rationale encourages students to develop better argumentation skills by forcing them to fully specify all the parts of an argument, indicating not just what the evidence is but how it fits into the overall argument structure. Researchers in one study found that undergraduate introductory psychology students assigned to complete argument-mapping exercises within Rationale showed increased improvement on a standardized test of critical thinking before and after the exercises, compared to a control group.[51]

Similarly, there are computer-based graphic tools designed specifically to map cause-and-effect relationships, something that is highly relevant to critical thinking and other analytical reasoning skills. The jMap system uses the Autoshape tools within Excel to allow learners to easily create graphic representation of how multiple factors feed into an outcome.[52] It also features a group collaboration function, combining information from multiple students' maps into a single graphic representation. Carnegie Mellon's Causality Lab (http://www.phil.cmu.edu/projects/causality-lab/) is another system specifically designed to teach causal reasoning through interactivity and graphic representations of cause-and-effect relationships. Causality Lab allows students to engage in simulated experimentation and data analysis to determine whether two factors (for example, tar-stained fingers and lung cancer) are actually causally related.

Among the instructors I consult with, one of the commonest complaints is that students lack the ability to engage in critical reading, something that's essential for evidence-based reasoning and argumentation in virtually any field. Students tend to have difficulty pulling out the key points from the text, as well as discerning how different parts of the text fit together to support the authors' message. This is another area to target with practice exercises, made much easier with online collaboration tools. One example is HyLighter, a program that allows individual users to highlight, tag, and annotate a text, then aggregates all the marks across group members (http://www.hylighter.com/hybar/site/index.html). There is some evidence that using HyLighter and similar instructional methods to have students highlight, comment on, and reflect on one another's work is associated with gains in critical thinking.[53] Instructors who don't want to use a specialized commercial product like HyLighter could replicate some of the same functionality with word-processing programs such as Pages or Microsoft Word, which also have mechanisms for annotating text documents.

What these online exercises have in common is explicit focus on building critical-thinking processes, drawing on the capability of online tools to support graphic visualization, easy rearranging of different elements, and collaboration. They also have in common a

strong *scaffolding* component, i.e., providing some preexisting elements for students to work with as they do the exercise.[54] It's possible
for novice learners to complete these kinds of exercises just using
basic software or pencil and paper, but they will get much farther in
an environment that gives them preset options and a framework to
work within.

STRATEGY 2: SET UP VARIED, REALISTIC SCENARIOS FOR REASONING

Besides assigning structured practice with the formal components of
reasoning, another effective approach is to use scenarios drawn from
the real world. The real world aspect requires students to transfer
knowledge into the kinds of situations they might encounter in their
later lives. It's also a good way to vary the surface structure of problems, another technique that promotes effective transfer.

One well-established method for doing this is *problem-based learning*, a technique for having students work through realistic questions
that tie in to course material. Problem-based learning (together with
other kinds of "experiential learning" approaches such as *project-
based learning*) is a hot area in education; there is even a scholarly
journal entirely devoted to this one method (the *Interdisciplinary
Journal of Problem-Based Learning*, http://docs.lib.purdue.edu/ijpbl/).
Problem-based learning is especially effective for promoting transfer,
such as transfer between strategies learned in school and problems
encountered much later in work environments.[55]

Generally speaking, problem-based learning (PBL) involves assigning students an open-ended, ill-defined problem situated in a
realistic context, such as how to reduce the number of bike-car colli-
sions in the surrounding community or how to increase mathematics achievement in a local elementary school. Students collaborate
in small groups to work out a solution via discussion and information gathering.[56] The instructor functions as a discussion facilitator,
monitoring the groups' progress and pushing discussion forward
where needed.

Crucially, the problem-solving process in PBL isn't totally free-
form. Rather, the instructor delineates how the groups are to go
about analyzing the problem and recording their progress. One way
to do this is via the "whiteboard" technique, in which a group rec-

ords important aspects of the problem and solution in a writing space divided into pre-labeled columns. The columns consist of Facts (essentially, the deep structure of the problem), Ideas (possible solutions or parts of solutions), Learning Issues (questions raised about the problem), and Action Plan (things the group needs to do or information the group needs to gather). As the activity unfolds, groups write down main points in these columns—a great way to make discussion more productive, direct attention to deep structure, and avert the novice move of zipping straight to solutions before the problem is fully understood.

Problem-based learning is designed to accomplish an ambitious list of educational goals. It is intended to be highly motivating, given the ties to real-world concerns and the satisfaction of creating an original, potentially useful solution. Other goals relate specifically to thinking. Engaging with a complex problem spurs students to integrate knowledge—that is, build meaningful connections, as opposed to just learning collections of disjointed facts. This integrated knowledge, in turn, supports transfer. Lastly, PBL requires students to directly practice problem-solving skills.[57]

There are still a number of unanswered research questions about PBL, but the growing body of literature suggests that it does indeed produce gains in thinking skills, particularly critical-thinking skills. As far as being an effective way to teach course content, the jury is still out. A number of studies conclude that PBL increases content knowledge, while a minority indicate no difference, compared to traditional methods.[58] At the very least, research suggests that PBL doesn't seem to *detract* from content, despite the fact that it redirects substantial class time away from presenting content, e.g, through lecturing.

Also encouraging is the finding that PBL translates well into online learning. In fact, given how online methods force students to record their work in writing, they may even be superior for implementing PBL, compared with traditional face-to-face classes.[59] In one study, students in a fully online course about educational technology used chat and discussion-board tools to identify the best kinds of software to buy for various educational purposes. Compared with students who engaged in more traditional, instructor-centered learning activities, the PBL students showed equal gains in content knowledge and superior gains in critical thinking.[60]

If you're thinking of setting up an online PBL activity, consider taking advantage of online databases of problems—resources such as the Problem-Based Learning Clearinghouse maintained by the University of Delaware, https://primus.nss.udel.edu/Pbl/. Besides posting an online description of the problem and setting up group-discussion threads, you'll also want to incorporate some ways for students to first discuss what you expect as far as their behavior and contributions, and give students opportunities to interact with one another online before jumping into the exercises. You might also assign groups to work out their own guidelines and agreed-upon norms (e.g., what's the minimum level of participation, how should disagreements be handled) before beginning. Also, remember to include reference materials (or links to reference materials) that you want students to use. Lastly, in the online environment it's especially helpful to give a detailed structure of how you want students to use their time, such as intermediate deadlines for each stage of the process.[61]

Case studies have a long history of effective use in both online and traditional formats. Less formal than problem-based learning, case study assignments present students with a compelling, realistic narrative, coupled with prompts asking for conclusions, interpretations, or possible solutions.

The narrative aspect of case studies is important; as the Vanderbilt University Center for Teaching explains, "Good cases generally have the following features: they tell a good story, are recent, include dialogue, create empathy with the main characters, are relevant to the reader, serve a teaching function, require a dilemma to be solved, and have generality."[62] With all these considerations in mind, setting up good case studies can be a daunting task. Fortunately, this is another area where there are a number of good-quality online databases to use for inspiration; the National Center for Case Study Teaching in Science, http://sciencecases.lib.buffalo.edu/cs/, and MERLOT's searchable materials collections (www.merlot.org) are two good places to start.

Case studies are particularly well suited to applied and preprofessional fields, given how they make students practice exactly the kind of problem solving they will do later on. They also work well on-line, although they do take work to set up. Because case study teaching is based on storytelling, it's necessary to write (or find) a well-elaborated story with lots of descriptive details. Online, you also have the option of using multimedia to enhance the story; recall that humans are particularly moved by visual stimuli, so you might try putting the story in video or slide-show form to maximize the narrative impact.

You'll also need to think through exactly what you want students to do with the assignment, and lay out those requirements in detail for students. One instructor who frequently uses the technique offers a set of example case studies of varying complexity and format that she uses in her fully online courses, ranging from a city council that's debating whether a new Walmart will hurt local jobs, to an adult woman who wants to prosecute her own father for sexually abusing her during childhood. She lays out three different ways to structure the assignment: *discussion* (e.g., how would you classify a hypothetical patient's disorder using standard diagnostic criteria?), *debate* (e.g., should parents have their infants sleep with them or not?), and *trial* (e.g., play assigned roles in the sexual abuse trial, such as attorney, father, mother, witnesses). The trial method, in particular, can engage students in deep analysis of the issues as hand, because students tend to treat trial scenarios with an especially high degree of realism.[63]

The case study method does present some challenges. Foremost is the need for a compelling, relevant case to kick off the activity. Also, as with problem-based learning, it's best to avoid unstructured discussion. Rather, the instructor needs to give a fair amount of direction by assigning roles, asking specific prompts, and so on.

Case studies can also really bring out the communication and collaboration glitches that are possible in any kind of online teaching and learning. One reason for this is that compelling cases, such as the sexual abuse vignette above, can provoke strong emotional reactions. This is not necessarily a bad thing, but means that students will need coaching on appropriate tone in online communication before jumping into the assignment.[64] There are also all the problems inherent to group work—slackers, disappearing team members, hyper-controlling leaders, and so on. One creative way to head these off is to use a warm-up case study as a way for students to strategize about group dynamics. Here is one example:

"Learning Team A is made up of Frank, Omar, Lisa, Jackie, and Shawn. Frank volunteers to be the team leader and takes control rather easily. He notices Lisa is the last person to make comments and suggestions. Also, she shows up in the main folder but not the group folder. The deadline for the first project is in two days and Lisa has not contributed much. If you were in Learning Team A, how would you first define the problem?" (p. 144)[65]

STRATEGY 3: USE ANALOGIES (THE RIGHT WAY)

Recall that analogies are powerful teaching tools, but that they are easy for students to misinterpret or miss out on altogether. They work best when students actively work through multiple examples rather than just hearing one or two, and when the instructor explicitly points out the correspondence between problems.

There has not been a great deal of empirical research on the use of analogies in online learning. However, the combination of replay capability, interactivity, and illustrative multimedia suggests that online environments are promising for effective teaching with this powerful reasoning strategy.

The MERLOT database (www.merlot.org) has a number of example activities that show this promise in action. Standouts include Elizabeth Miles's tutorial called "Inside the Body: Fluid Pressures and Processes."[66] Designed for nursing students, the activity uses the analogy of a garden soaker hose to teach how different factors affect the buildup and release of fluids within tissues. In it, students see video and hear explanations of how the soaker hose maps onto systems in the body. Then, they click on different analogous processes—turning up the water pressure, kinking the hose—to see how those affect fluids. In this way, the analogy doesn't just wash over students in a passive fashion—they have to get involved. The video and graphics are also a great example of how to use multimedia to illustrate a fairly complex analogy, helping ensure that students make the correct conceptual mappings.

George Burruss's "Analogy for Testing Statistical Significance" uses the analogy of a horse clearing jumps of different heights to explain how statistically significant results are determined using the chi-square statistic.[67] In it, students are asked to enter different values of chi-square, then an animated horse and rider demonstrate whether that value would make it over the hurdle—i.e., achieve significance— or not. More-complex study designs are represented by more jumps and higher jumps, showing how the ability to find significant results goes down as complexity of the study design goes up.

The activity requires the student to be actively involved. It also encourages multiple attempts, because something different can happen each time, depending on the parameters the student puts in. The accompanying animation is also particularly compelling; the horse and rider gallop toward the jump, and if unsuccessful, the horse slides to a dramatic stop, hurling the rider to the ground. An additional thoughtful design feature is a prominent explanation of one potentially problematic conceptual mapping. Prior to the anima-tion, it's stated that a nonsignificant statistical test does *not* repre-sent a failed research project, in the same sense of a horse and rider making a failed attempt on a jump. With that issue out of the way, the rest of the analogy holds up well.

Although they are not, strictly speaking, online learning activi-ties, a series of mathematics modules developed by the researchers Lindsey Richland and Ian McDonough serve as very informative examples of how to construct and present instructional analogies.[68] Because they consist of video lecture and demonstration, this kind of module would translate smoothly into an online format. The re-searchers created the video lectures to experimentally test the best ways to apply theories of analogical reasoning to mathematics in-struction. Each module focused on one mathematical concept, such as permutation. In the critical experimental condition (termed "high cuing"), the instructor, using a whiteboard and verbal expla-nation, illustrated the concept using explicit cuing of how the source problem mapped onto the target problem—meaning that he or she pointed out exactly how one problem corresponded to the other. The explicit mapping was further heightened by lining up the prob-lems so that each step in one problem visually corresponded to the other problem.

Compared to other modes of presenting the same information, the high-cuing condition produced some consistent advantages.

Students solved subsequent problems more accurately, and further-more were less thrown off by problems that seemed similar but actu-ally weren't analogous to the previously solved problems. Not only does this suggest that explicitly cued analogies are effective; it also implies that students developed more flexible, less context-dependent knowledge representations. The moral of the story is that if you want to use an analogy, it's important to make mappings as obvious as pos-sible, not just via verbal explanations, but also by visually aligning corresponding elements wherever possible.

STRATEGY 4: USE DISCUSSION TO BUILD THINKING SKILLS

Peer-to-peer student discussions are a core part of online teaching. This component can even be the heart and soul of the whole class, carrying the majority of interaction and reflection. I feature discus-sion prominently in my own online classes, not so much to "cover the content" but to give students an opportunity to share personal stories—within their comfort zones, of course—that tie into course topics. I find that having active discussion threads going on adds an important dynamic element to the class experience; something is always new and different each time students log in, encouraging frequent engagement. Students echo this sentiment, with many commenting that discussion boards are the first place they go when they log into the class. In a study of participation patterns conducted with my colleague Linda Neff of the NAU E-Learning Center, we found that the single best predictor of final course grade was the number of discussion posts made over the course of the semester—even though these posts made up only a small proportion of the course points.[69]

Other researchers attest to the effectiveness of online discussion. Online discussions offer advantages over traditional face-to-face class discussions, which suffer from time limitations, too many peo-ple in a class at once, and domination by a few highly verbal students at the expense of quieter, more reflective types.[70] In one comparison of educational psychology classes taught with and without required online discussions, the discussion component produced significantly higher gains in critical thinking over the course of the semester. Student posts also displayed pronounced changes in the direction of

higher-order thinking skills, with students characteristically showing more sophisticated thinking with each subsequent round of
posts.[71]

Online discussions are ideal vehicles for the kind of thought processes we've considered throughout this chapter. Depending on how
they are set up, discussions can require students to construct persuasive, well-supported arguments, analyze the underlying aspects of a
question or problem, reflect on their own learning (thus promoting
metacognition), and apply knowledge to new scenarios. And as we've
also seen, a number of the strategies I've suggested incorporate some
kind of discussion as a key component of the assignment. Problem-
based and case study assignments, in particular, revolve around substantive communications with peers.

That said, discussions can easily spin off into unproductive
chitchat—or worse, hostility and hurt feelings. Therefore, keep in
mind some of the "best practices" to use in designing discussion to
foster thinking skills. Before you get into any of the specifics of the
activity, identify exactly which thinking skills you want the discussions to reinforce: Formal argument analysis? Critical thinking?
Problem solving? Metacognition? This will guide your assignment
design in a purposeful way. For example, remember that critical
thinking has a lot to do with identifying the underlying structure of
a problem, then identifying the supporting evidence needed and any
typical fallacies (e.g., sunk costs, causation vs. correlation) associated
with that kind of problem. It follows that the assignment should require students to talk about problem structure and explain the reasoning, being sure to identify any missing evidence or faulty logic.

Best-practices guides also recommend detailed explanation of
what you expect from each post, tied into a grading rubric for the
quality of contributions. For example, is it OK to make brief superficial comments ("I totally agree"), and do those count for credit?
What are the acceptable ways to respectfully express disagreement or handle conflict? How many original posts should students
make, and how many responses should they make to other students' posts? Is there an "end product" (solution, summary, study
guide) that should come out of the process, or is the discussion itself sufficient?

The NAU E-Learning Center's comprehensive online database (http://www2.nau.edu/d-elearn/support/tutorials/) is one good source of advice on designing, conducting, and grading discussion assignments. These include Linda Neff's Designing Effective Online Discussions slide show, which focuses on specific best practices.[72] One of the key strategies Neff suggests is to create a "welcome forum" of some kind, where students get to know one another in a low-stakes, casual environment before jumping into the more challenging assignments. She also explains that, in general, good discussion-prompts meaningfully relate to student experiences, preferences, and life activities, link to course content, and are "short and purposefully vague." In contrast, the kinds of review and summary questions you find at the end of textbook chapters don't tend to stimulate good discussion.

Other best practices address how to facilitate and moderate discussions once they are under way. Effective moderation is certainly challenging, particularly with respect to how frequently you post in the discussion.[73] There aren't hard-and-fast rules about when you should post, but most experts agree that you shouldn't respond to every single student post. In fact, there is some evidence that the more frequently an instructor posts, the *less* students participate.[74]

Even if you aren't constantly posting, you still need to make your presence known. In particular, be sure to check on active discussions frequently (once a day, minimum), and intervene in any discussion that's gotten off track or where posts have gotten even a little bit hostile. Hints can also be a good way to recharge a stalled discussion.

Because online communication tends to be more negatively interpreted than face-to-face communication, it is important to address any conflicts quickly. Modeling a positive tone is also important. Neff advises, in particular, that you scrupulously avoid sounding sarcastic, threatening, or bitter. She also warns against taking a "devil's advocate" stance, because it tends to move the discussion away from a spirit of inquiry and toward defensiveness—something that would be even harder to sense and moderate in an online environment devoid of the usual nonverbal and interpersonal cues.

Although you do want to use a light touch as a discussion moderator, there's also evidence that the right kind of guidance can move discussion in some desirable directions. In one recent study, researchers compared online discussion-based group work in groups with and without supportive moderators who were trained in different moderation strategies. Students in the supportive-moderator group were significantly more likely to engage in productive, collaborative interaction, as opposed to less-productive patterns such as following one self-appointed leader or stating positions without any follow-up discussion.[75] Supportive moderation can include posts that direct students as they construct knowledge, such as the following:

> To solve this problem we need to . . .
> What else can we do for our following tasks?
> Would you please tell us more about your idea?
> Why is this message important? (p. 1710)[76]

Supportive prompts can also just serve to motivate students to keep persisting, as in "Great job, this idea sounds reasonable!" or "What might we need to know more about next?"[77]

In sum, if you want to build thinking skills with discussion assignments, the key is to take aim at those skills, designing and executing assignments in ways that tie directly to the desired skills. And in this way, they echo the themes of all our other strategies. Thinking skills are perhaps the most challenging thing we ever tackle as teachers. The frameworks provided by cognitive psychology—and the tools of online learning—can help.

Chapter 7

Incorporating Multimedia Effectively

A STUDENT DROPS in on the Chinese department of a large university, engaging a helpful department staffer in conversation about the department and its facilities. "Is that the library?" he asks. "No, it's the reading room," the staffer answers, assuring him that students from any department are welcome to use the large, inviting space. The visitor inquires about the number of professors and whether there are any foreign students in the department. The staffer describes these for him—two professors, several foreign students—and invites him to come by any time. The pair exchange pleasantries, thank one another, and the visit comes to an end.

Students in the Centre for Teaching Chinese as a Foreign Language at the University of Oxford also take part in the scene—not by traveling to China, but via the Chinese Multimedia online course, created by Kylie Hsu. The course features brief video vignettes like the visit to the Chinese department,[1] which serve as springboards for detailed instructional modules. In these multipart modules, students review the dialogue written out in both Chinese and English and can replay audio of each individual line of dialogue. Then students tackle learning how to write characters associated with the vignette. In the tutorial, each character is explained as well as visually illustrated, with animated diagrams showing, in dynamic, step-by-step fashion, exactly how the character is created.

These online Chinese lessons demonstrate the power of multimedia. Short of having a personal one-on-one tutor or completing a full-fledged immersion program, it's hard to imagine a learning activity better suited to the challenging task of mastering the Chinese language and writing system as a second-language learner. Even a dedicated in-person tutor would soon tire of repeating dialogue and explanations as many times as needed, but dynamic multimedia such as video demonstrations, animations, and simulations offer infinite, learner-controlled iterations of the lesson.

The tutorials also show the full range of the types of computer-based multimedia typically used in higher education. *Text* is used to present instructions and transcriptions of the dialogue. *Audio* is used for the line-by-line replayable dialogue, and *video* to show the dialogue taking place in a realistic setting, with props and nonverbal cues enhancing one's understanding of what's going on. *Animations* and *diagrams* help teach the character writing component.

The contemporary era of educational technology offers a wealth of multimedia bells-and-whistles we can add to our learning activities. Most of us have an intuitive sense that these media engage students beyond what we can do with plain text. And conceptually, some topics are nearly impossible to explain without some kind of illustration. Can you imagine trying to explain in words to an English-speaking student the correct way to write the Chinese character for *library*, or describing to a beginning biology student how cell division works, using just plain text?

Intuitions, however, are not always right, and so we need to look at multimedia with a critical eye, asking what it will add to any given learning activity. We also need to be sure we get educational mileage out of multimedia because these can be some of the most costly and time-consuming educational materials we ever create (just think about the time, equipment, expertise, and resources that went into Oxford's Chinese learning modules). Multimedia components also add a layer of technical and user-support complexity. Within a course, they are another thing that can crash, stall, or otherwise go wrong, so we need to be sure that they are worth the potential headaches.

And just adding multimedia to a course doesn't guarantee improved learning. A U.S. Department of Education report concluded that, according to the majority of research studies available at the time, adding multimedia such as video modules rarely produces improvement.[2] There's also some indication that multimedia used in the wrong way can detract from learning.[3] As it turns out, effectively adding multimedia is much trickier than simply taking a standard lesson and tacking on lots of colorful graphics, sound effects, and engrossing videos. Each modality of media—audio, visuals, video—affects learning in its own particular way.

There are also individual differences among students that we need to consider when thinking through the role of multimedia, especially those students with sensory limitations. We will return to the accessibility issue later in the chapter, but first, let's consider: Is it true that individual students learn differently depending on the modality of presentation? Does it matter whether students are visual, auditory, or kinesthetic learners?

Sensory Modalities and Learning Style

According to the "perceptual learning styles" or VAK (visual-auditory-kinesthetic) idea, visual learners learn best from materials such as diagrams, artwork, and pictures. Auditory learners learn best from lectures, music, and spoken explanation, while kinesthetic learners do best when they can physically manipulate materials or act out a lesson. One twist on the theory includes a fourth group, "reading" learners, who learn best from written text. Other theorists use a binary classification, with "visualizers" on one end of the spectrum and "verbalizers" on the other.

Perceptual learning style is an incredibly pervasive concept, one that's become widely accepted as common knowledge.[4] Primary and secondary schools now routinely test students' VAK learning styles; the idea has also made significant inroads elsewhere in the culture, e.g., in the form or employment screening for different VAK styles.[5] But despite its popularity, VAK may go down as one of the greatest psychological myths of all time—something that "everybody knows," but simply isn't true. Like the notion that we use only 10 percent of our brains or that people can be classified as right-brained or left-brained, perceptual learning style is a seductive but demonstrably incorrect idea.[6]

If the VAK idea were true, it would have a strong implication: that presentation mode fundamentally drives learning. Specifically, it predicts that matching presentation mode to style—diagrams and pictures for visual learners, audio clips for auditory learners, manipulatives for kinesthetic learners—would boost learning. From a cognitive psychology perspective, this notion seems fishy, because people constantly translate, or "recode" information from one modality into another during cognitive processing. We do this all the time when we read, converting a visual experience (looking at marks on a page) to an auditory one (representations of word sounds). Likewise, we're perfectly capable of describing a diagram to ourselves in words (i.e., recoding visual to verbal) or creating a visual mental image based on a verbal description (recoding verbal to visual).

Within the brain and mind, different sensory modalities don't "dominate" one another in the sense that individuals have a dominant right or left hand. Rather, sensory information typically combines across different senses, and when there is some kind of mismatch, vision usually wins (provided that the person has typical sight abilities). We know a lot about how people perceive the world based on their senses—in fact, sensation and perception is the oldest subfield of scientific psychology. Time and again, this research has demonstrated broad similarities across individuals with respect to the basic machinery of sensory processing, barring major deviations in typical sensory ability (blindness, colorblindness, deafness). With these patterns of processing in mind, it doesn't seem right to sort students into rigid categories of sensory dominance.

One study of learning style used functional magnetic resonance imaging (fMRI) to determine if there were qualitative differences in brain activation patterns associated with visual versus verbal learners. When presented with verbal information, visualizers showed more activation in areas of the brain that support visual processing.[7] On the surface, this finding might appear to support perceptual learning styles, but in fact, it points back to the recoding concept. It suggests that there may be qualitative differences in style, but rather than *limit* what people pick up from their senses, style leads us to recode information from a less-preferred modality to a preferred one—such as "visualizers" turning verbal information into imagery.

Other researchers point out that written materials aren't even properly classified as "visual"—they may "enter" the brain through the eyes, but are processed and stored using verbal, not visual working memory systems.[8] If we're constantly recoding information across different modalities, it makes little sense to assume that we're locked into whatever presentation modalities the teacher happens to choose.

And this is exactly what the best empirical studies of VAK learning style have concluded. One project focused on the key implication of the theory for instruction, that matching modality of instruction to perceptual learning style would result in better learning. In this formulation, "visual learners" should retain the most from visually presented materials and "auditory learners" should retain the most from aurally presented materials. But in fact, matching style didn't produce this pattern at all.[9]

Another piece of bad news for VAK theory is the mismatch between people's self-professed learning preferences and their results on commonly used learning-style inventories. In one study, participants were queried about their perceived learning styles and why they believed their learning style fell in that particular category. People tended to answer based on whatever personal experiences happened to come to mind (there's the availability heuristic at work!) rather than on any systematic analysis of their learning patterns. This haphazard self-assessment led to big disconnects between the learning styles people thought they had and the learning styles indicated by the formal inventory.[10] In sum, people don't even know what their "true" learning styles are, and tend to have poor intuition about how to self-assess style. Small wonder, then, that matching those supposed styles does nothing to improve learning.

Even if we accept that the VAK idea is unscientific, what's the harm? Couldn't it still be useful as a way to create variety in learning activities or draw in students with the appearance—if not the reality—of truly personalized instruction? Unfortunately, there are real downsides to incorporating VAK into our teaching. Students are prone to feeling locked into one mode of presentation once they've received a learning-style label. Rather than encouraging students to see themselves in charge of their own academic success, learning style encourages them to make excuses—or disengage when confronted with activities that contradict their learning-style label. Furthermore, the effort needed to assess style and personalize instruction around those styles is considerable, thus detracting from other, empirically supported methods such as adding in more testing opportunities or assessing prior knowledge.[11]

VAK is a bad theory, one that doesn't just fail to support good teaching with multimedia, but may actively hinder us in trying to do so. So what *does* matter with respect to different ways of presenting information? The best resource for answering this question is the extensive body of research on how to effectively bring together auditory and visual information in teaching, known as *multimedia theory.*

Multimedia Theory and Applications

Most associated with researcher Richard E. Mayer, this school of thought draws on both a theoretical side, focused on understanding the cognitive processes that allow us to integrate across different modalities during learning, and an applied side, concerned with empirically testing the effectiveness of different design approaches in multimedia learning materials. Central to the framework is the *multimedia principle,* which holds that adding pictures—or diagrams, or other similar representations—to text produces enhanced learning compared to text alone.

This may seem like a simple enough idea—add pictures and, voilà, learning happens. But in his comprehensive book *Multimedia Learning,*[12] Mayer explains how a host of variables interact to create enhanced learning through multimedia. One of the major directives that comes out of Mayer's research is that narrated animations work better than animations paired with text, most likely because the latter arrangement requires the learner to shift visual attention back and forth between these two visually presented sources of information. Auditory input can be processed somewhat independently from visual input, a claim that makes sense given what we know about separate brain mechanisms used for visual and auditory processing. It follows that the two can complement one another when presented in paired fashion.

Not all kinds of narration are helpful, though. Verbatim narration of written text—i.e., just reading aloud exactly what's on the screen—tends to hinder learning, something called the *redundancy effect*. In a study of narrated slides, one research team discovered something of a "Goldilocks" principle with respect to the discrepancy between the narration and visually presented slide. They found the usual redundancy effect for verbatim narration, but also noted worse performance when the narration was highly discrepant from the visuals. In contrast, a moderate level of difference between the two was "just right."[13]

Furthermore, narration works best when it uses conversational, everyday language, compared to when it's formal and academic in tone.[14] Pictorial materials, too, are maximally effective only within a fairly constrained set of parameters. Generally speaking, pictures seem to work best when they carry the conceptual information that's going to be tested later—they don't enhance learning by their mere presence, even though many people assume they do.[15]

Mayer and colleague Eunmo Sung lay out a useful taxonomy of different kinds of lesson illustrations: seductive, decorative, and instructive.[16] *Seductive* illustrations are those that are interesting, but unrelated to the material in any meaningful way. Sung and Mayer offer the example of a picture of a current celebrity added to a lesson on early mail delivery systems. Seductive illustrations aren't just harmless diversions—they actually do damage by siphoning off limited cognitive and attentional resources from the substantive material being presented. Accordingly, students retain less from lessons featuring seductive graphics, compared to lessons without any graphics at all.

Decorative illustrations are those that, like seductive illustrations, have no conceptual link to the material, but aren't inherently interesting. An example would be a picture of a waterfall added to the lesson on early mail delivery systems. Decorative illustrations don't detract from learning, but they don't add to it either. *Instructive* illustrations, by contrast, directly relate to the concepts being taught—such as a photo of a pony express rider added to the lesson on mail delivery. And these graphic enhancements do, in fact, promote retention.

The moral of the story? Don't bring in graphics *except* those with a substantive connection to what you are trying to teach. Pictures for picture's sake make your lesson prettier, but less effective.

Multimedia Learning offers a number of other best-practice principles, all backed by extensive empirical research. Here is a summary:

Signaling principle. Visually highlight the most important points that you want students to retain, so that they stand out from less-critical aspects of the material.

Spatial contiguity principle. If using captions or other text to accompany graphics, place them as close to the graphics as is practical, to offset the cost of shifting between the two. If you're using diagrams or animations, try placing captions right next to the relevant parts of the graphic components, instead of putting them in one big block of text at the bottom.

Temporal contiguity principle. Present spoken narration and graphics as close in time as is practical—presenting both at once is better than presenting them one after another.

Segmenting principle. Especially when presenting a long sequence of material or when students are inexperienced with the subject, break up the presentation into shorter segments and let students control how quickly they advance from one part to the next.

Pretraining principle. If students won't know the major concepts and terminology used in your multimedia presentation, set up a module just to teach those concepts and terms, and make sure they complete that module beforehand.

Modality principle. Students learn better from pictures plus audio narration than from pictures plus text, *unless* there are technical words or symbols, or the students are non-native speakers.

ANIMATIONS

Animations are a special case of multimedia theory at work. This form of multimedia is useful for explaining how a complex process unfolds, illustrating magnitude and direction of changes over time, or how multiple factors interact during a process. They are also ideal for illustrating important processes that aren't visible in the real world, such as air flow or the movement of electrons.[17]

Take for example the computer animation of obesity trends produced by the U.S. Center for Disease Control and Prevention.[18] This relatively simple dynamic display, which was used to great effect in the movie *Supersize Me*, drives home the dramatic changes in obesity that took place between 1985 and 2008 while simultaneously highlighting marked regional disparities. You *could* lay out the same facts and figures in text or a static graph, but the impact would be radically lessened.

Or consider the narrated, illustrated animation of the Latin American debt crisis of the 1980s created by Laura Tedesco and Tara Wernsing of the IE Business School.[19] The module uses simplified icons to represent how different players in the crisis—banks, oil producers, totalitarian governments—interacted to produce the crisis. A voice explains the actions taking place on screen, taking advantage of the dual auditory and visual channels to enhance understanding of the complex dynamics at work.

One caveat to using animations is that they introduce more working-memory demands on the viewer, compared to static displays.[20] Rather than staying on screen for easy reference, concepts and terms disappear as the animation unfolds, forcing the viewer to depend on memory. This is something to consider as you design animations. If there is any information that your students need to keep in mind in order to understand the unfolding narrative, then you may want to keep it somewhere in view, even if it's off to the side or bottom of the display. Pacing is another design issue with animations, which can easily run too rapidly for novice learners. Adding easy ways to stop, start, speed up, and slow down can help address this limitation.[21]

Narrated diagrams are a bit simpler than animations, but they are another option for bringing audio and visual information together to create a powerful learning experience. When it's not crucial to get across how dynamic processes unfold over time, narrated diagrams—with their reduced complexity—may be an ideal way to get information across without causing cognitive overload.

An example of effective educational diagrams comes out of current trends in doctor-patient communication. In lieu of the traditional hasty hand-drawn sketches, physicians can now use specialized iPad technology to create personalized illustrations, superimposing their own drawings on quality medical illustrations and recording themselves talking the patient through medical processes and procedures.[22] Just as they would in other teaching and learning contexts, the "students"—patients, in this case—benefit from being able to take the narration home with them and replay it as many times as they need to. This practice is also a good example of the multimedia principle in action—the doctor can explain a process verbally while simultaneously highlighting (via arrows, circles, underlining, and so on) the relevant graphics in the visual channel. Taken together, these synchronized inputs have more impact than either could alone.

In summary, we know that visual, auditory, and text presentations have great power to heighten learning, but that they have to be paired in a fairly precise way to work. Concurrent auditory and visual presentation is particularly effective, as long as the two don't exactly replicate one another. Restricting audio and graphics to just those that directly tie in to course material is also important—that means no purely ornamental soundtracks, sound effects, pictures, or animations. Narrated diagrams and animations are two powerful twists on this idea; each has its own advantages, disadvantages, and guidelines for best practice.

SIMULATIONS

Simulations are a class of multimedia that warrants special attention. They can be loosely defined as computer-based media that replicate aspects of a process, object, or scenario from the real world. Simulations typically go beyond illustrations, giving the user the ability to interact with the media in some way. They offer the repeatability and user control that's a big advantage of other well-designed multimedia, and—depending on how they are designed—can take advantage of the multimedia effect. On a practical level, they can also be a way to offer some of the advantages of a hands-on physical lab experience, in a way that's less dangerous, less expensive, or not as time-consuming compared to their real-world counterparts.

Interactive simulations can definitely be engaging, as evidenced by wildly popular open-ended computer games such as The Sims. In this way, they offer some of the same advantages for motivating students as learning games do, a topic we'll take up in Chapter 8. Besides the fun factor, simulations have been shown to make several distinct contributions to learning. Well-designed simulations make major concepts more obvious to learners, e.g., by animating or enlarging key parts. They also give immediate, easy-to-interpret feedback. Instructors can use them to connect "textbook" concepts to more familiar real-world situations—illustrating physics in the setting of a skate park, for example.[23] Simulations don't have to be used as solitary, one-off activities—they can be woven throughout a course as supports for other pedagogies, such as being used as springboards to stimulate discussion or as the basis for group inquiry projects.[24]

Simulations are currently being applied to teaching in a wide variety of disciplines. Simulations used to teach anatomy are one example that particularly highlights the potential of this tool. Special hand-held interface devices allow the user to manually rotate virtual anatomical structures—such as human bones—onscreen, allowing users to explore and learn about the structure. These computer-presented materials may even have advantages over traditional materials, in that the display can include "orientation references" (lines that show the major axes of the object), to show how objects are usually oriented in space and highlight the spatial arrangements of all their parts.[25]

The University of Colorado's Physics Education Technology (PhET) project is one of the most well-elaborated efforts to create and disseminate effective simulations for teaching. The PhET web site (http://phet.colorado.edu) features dozens of freely available interactive simulations of science and mathematics concepts, with options suitable for kindergarten through graduate students. The materials are developed according to a research-driven design process that assesses accuracy (from the perspective of disciplinary experts) as well as engagement and user-friendliness (from the perspective of student users).[26]

This painstaking design process has produced some impressive empirical results. A team of researchers compared learning in introductory physics courses across students whose laboratory component was run entirely through PhET simulations and a "control" group who did traditional hands-on laboratory assignments. The simulated-lab students didn't just match the performance of the traditional-laboratory students—they significantly exceeded it, as evidenced by performance on end-of-semester exam questions tapping conceptual understanding. Surprisingly, the simulated-lab group also showed better ability to build, describe, and explain actual physical circuits.[27]

Acknowledging that it may be hard for traditionalists to believe that simulations could outperform "real" labs, the researchers offer several possible explanations for the advantage. Paradoxically, students may benefit from the reduced complexity of computer simulations versus physical models—so, for example, they aren't as distracted by extraneous factors such as the color of different wires, which are all the same in the simulation but vary in the physical lab materials. Here, too, the "invisibility" factor was a plus: Simulations can explicitly show components (e.g., electrons) that aren't normally visible, thus providing important scaffolds for novice students. Simulations, in this study, seemed to support the same kind of free-form experimentation instructors like to encourage in physical laboratories; according to instructor observation, the simulated-lab students regularly engaged in productive "messing about" with their simulations. Truly nonproductive experimentation (such as making bracelets out of wire intended for the lab activity) was also less likely in the simulated lab group.

Online, you can find a wealth of other simulations to use or just explore for inspiration's sake—consult the MERLOT database or teaching journals in your discipline for options. Here are some illustrative examples:

Packet Tracer. This is a simulation program created by Cisco Systems to teach students how to troubleshoot problems and accomplish other tasks relating to computer networks.[28]

eLucy. This site lets you explore "Lucy," the famous *Australopithecus afarensis* fossil, and compare different elements of it to modern-day humans and chimpanzees. Other skeletal anatomy learning activities can be found on the parent site, eSkeletons.org, maintained by the University of Texas at Austin.

Sniffy the Virtual Rat.[29] Sniffy is an animated white rat in a "Skinner box," a specially designed cage where animals can be trained ("conditioned") to perform behaviors, using a food dispenser for rewards. Prior to training, Sniffy patters around his cage randomly, much like the real thing. Then, students choose to reward some of these random behaviors ("shaping") to produce the desired responses. My NAU colleagues, like many psychology instructors, find Sniffy an indispensable tool for teaching students how learning principles affect behavior in nonhuman animals—without the headaches of maintaining a rodent lab.

ACCOMMODATING DIVERSE LEARNERS WITH MULTIMEDIA

Most of what I've presented in this chapter about teaching through multiple modalities has presumed that the students have a typical range of sensory function, with full visual and auditory capability. There are other sides to the accessibility issue as well, as in the case of students with dyslexia, processing-speed deficits, or other characteristics that have traditionally been termed "learning disabilities."

In truth, the question of access for diverse learners touches on every part of this book, but teaching with multimedia—where we're intentionally drawing on multiple modalities—throws into high relief the need to make sure that our materials accommodate diverse students. Class-linked multimedia resources are also subject to legal requirements governing accessibility, such as the need to provide alternatives to graphics for low-vision students and captioning for hearing-impaired students. So how do we design multimedia for maximum inclusivity?

Creating fully accessible, legally compliant materials is an educational subspecialty in its own right, so to get a grounding in all the relevant considerations and techniques, you'll want to consult a comprehensive overview. One good example is Norman Coomb's *Making Online Teaching Accessible: Inclusive Course Design for Students with Disabilities*,[30] a guidebook geared to faculty without technical or legal expertise in the field.

One of the nice things Coombs does in this book is try to reframe the anxiety-provoking, legalistic impression many faculty have about accessibility regulations. Although laws such as the Americans with Disabilities Act carry an enormous amount of legal weight, it's extremely rare for them to be used against educational institutions in punitive fashion over accessibility of course materials. Rather, these issues are usually treated with a problem-solving approach, where the institution is given plenty of latitude to come up with mutually acceptable solutions. The relevant laws also set limits on how far institutions must go to create full access for all individuals to all coursework; "undue" modifications or fundamental transformations of course material aren't required. With these reassurances in mind, it makes sense for faculty to approach accessibility in a nondefensive fashion—concentrating more on meeting students' needs and less on the threat of legal action.

Coombs reflects that "multimedia has both benefits and deficits for people with disabilities. On the one hand, due to multimedia's use of multiple senses, some elements will be totally inaccessible to people with a specific disability. On the other hand, the use of redundant multimedia modes makes it possible to reach all disability groups—provided the multimedia was designed to do that" (p. 1753). One facet of Coombs's design philosophy nicely echoes Mayer's: multimedia should be limited to graphics and other media that tie directly to course concepts. Besides being distracting, things like busy slide backgrounds and nonessential animations create accessibility problems—giving instructional designers yet another reason to eschew purely decorative multimedia frills.

Beyond this overarching principle—keep multimedia content-relevant—Coombs offers a number of other helpful guidelines, including:

Formatting text documents with headings and other organizational "landmarks." These are particularly useful for visually impaired students using screen readers. It's best to create this kind of formatting using automated methods, such as Styles and Headings in Microsoft Word, because these can be more easily picked up by screen-reading software.

Avoid using color to convey meaning in text or graphics. Keep in mind that some students are colorblind; therefore you should use alternate ways to convey meaning, or back up color-coding with some other explanation.

Hide or delete any learning-management elements that you don't need. For example, if you won't be using the chat tool, take it off of the course menu. Keeping screens free of unnecessary "stuff" is helpful to those using screen-reading technology, as well as to students with processing speed or attention deficits.

Allow self-pacing whenever possible. Set up narrated slide sequences so that students control when to advance to the next slide.

When making a video, include as much narration of the on-screen action as possible, in which you describe what's going on while it's happening. This will reduce the need to fit in additional audio description when the video is made accessible to low-vision students.

Making technical science and mathematics content—equations, graphs, and the like—accessible to low-vision students presents special challenges. Don't despair, though—there are ingenious systems for transcribing many of these kinds of materials. Consult an accessibility expert at your institution, or see Coombs's book for more details. One last point of advice is to *rely on expert guidance* when navigating accessibility issues. Specialized disability resource centers, where expert staff work with special tools for transforming multimedia materials, are standard issue in institutions of higher education today. If you haven't yet introduced yourself to the disability resource staff that support your disciplinary area, make it a point to do so—and go to them first when you need to convert materials, accommodate specific student needs, or gather suggestions about how to design new online materials for maximum accessibility. You'll save time and be more likely to deliver the best-quality student experience.

In sum, multimedia introduces some very real concerns about accessibility, but you shouldn't let that put you off of trying it. Thinking ahead about accessibility during the design process—especially with respect to the commonest types of sensory limitations, such as low vision and hearing impairment—may inspire you to make a few design decisions that ease access later on. There are also some truly amazing tools out there that can convert nearly any type of media to something that's usable in a different modality. Given the range and the pace of technological innovation, it makes sense to work with accessibility experts during the design process and any time you have an accessibility concern.

Takeaway Points on Using Multimedia

Contemporary multimedia technology makes it easier than ever to bring in graphics, video, animations, and audio that enhance online learning experiences. The idea that individuals have "dominant" perceptual learning styles is an appealing one. However, this popular notion has been fairly thoroughly debunked. Matching presentation modality to perceptual learning style does not aid learning, and focusing on supposed learning styles may discourage students from persisting.

Multimedia theory provides a powerful, empirically supported framework for getting the most out of varied media, particularly text, narration, and graphics. In general, pictures enhance learning when added to text or to audio narration, but the devil is in the details: graphics can't just be decorative, and have to be combined cautiously with text, because having to switch between two visual inputs at a time disrupts attention and overloads memory. A particularly effective alternative to text plus graphics is audio narration plus graphics.

Simulations are one exciting option for using multimedia, allowing students to experience some aspects of real-world application in a safe, inexpensive, and infinitely repeatable format. There's some empirical evidence—primarily from physics education—that simulated labs can not only meet, but exceed the benefits associated with traditional in-class physical labs. The best simulations tie closely into course material, visually highlight the most important conceptual elements of the activity, and encourage active engagement.

Because it explicitly ties into specific sensory modalities, multimedia highlights the need to offer access to diverse students, including those with sensory or cognitive processing limitations. For faculty designing multimedia materials, an inclusive mindset and willingness to work with disability support specialists are the main things they need to address this important aspect of online teaching. And fortunately, many of the same best practices that benefit typically abled students—such as sticking to germane graphics, providing clear organization, and offering materials in multiple modalities—also ease accessibility.

Chapter 8

Motivating Students

I PROBABLY SHOULDN'T, but in my online Introduction to Psychology course, I open the topic of motivation by asking a series of provocative questions about why the students chose to log into the course that day, instead of choosing to do something easier. I ask them: Why did you even get out of bed this morning? What drove you to abandon that warm, comfortable environment in favor of less pleasant, more energy-demanding pursuits? Fortunately, as far as I know, no student has ever reflected on these questions and decided, on second thought, to hop back into bed. My intent is to open their minds to some of the big questions about the motivational side of human psychology: What is it about our psychological makeup that allows us (sometimes, anyway) to choose the harder path over an easier one—like logging in to our online course when we could spend the time relaxing instead?

The word "motivation" derives from the same Latin root as the word "to move," and this reflects the way in which psychologists have traditionally conceptualized the topic. It is the study of the mechanisms that put you in motion, pushing you toward certain things and pushing you away from others. It's closely tied to the study of emotion, which makes sense given that our emotions revolve around attracting us to things that are beneficial to our survival and the survival of our genes—food, sex, attachment to loved ones—while repelling us from things that threaten survival, such as physical danger and social exclusion. However, people are not just motivated by basic survival; our motivational systems also incorporate "higher" aims such as the drive to create, to master challenges, and to engage in intellectual inquiry.

Motivation and emotion have traditionally been treated as a subfield distinct from cognitive psychology, so I've studied the process of motivating students as a bit of an academic outsider. For many years, cognition and emotion were considered to be separate, even antagonistic processes: like oil and water, they coexisted but didn't mix. However, psychologists have recently begun reconsidering how emotions shape our thinking, and conversely, how thinking shapes our emotions.

The *social cognitive approach* to motivation, which underlies much of our current understanding of academic motivation, is one outgrowth of this newer, more inclusive view. In this framework, our behavioral choices—what we are motivated to do, or not do—stem from a complex interplay between what we feel and what we believe. In particular, we're motivated by what we believe about our own capabilities, how those capabilities compare to other people's capabilities, and how our capabilities allow us to exert influence over the environment. Social cognitive theories tell us a lot about motivation in college students. As we will see later in this chapter, motivational problems that look purely emotional in nature—avoiding academic effort, reacting poorly to feedback, procrastination—are in fact heavily rooted in beliefs. The good news is that, as with any beliefs, it's possible to modify these dysfunctional thoughts with the right persuasive techniques.

Theories of motivation and cognition are enormously useful for informing our teaching, but like many of you, I've also learned a lot about motivation as a practical part of my teaching career. As most of us learn early on in our teaching lives, college instructors are *all* professional motivators to some extent. Being professional motivators, we intuitively know that it isn't enough just to put learning opportunities out there for students—we have to entice them into the material. Nor is it enough to set up "carrot and stick" point systems to get students to really maximize effort and engagement. Beyond just rewards and punishments, motivating students has an elusive, inspirational quality to it—something that skilled teachers seem to be able to do just by their mere presence.

Online, motivational issues are complicated, as it's easy for students with motivational barriers to simply avoid engaging with the course. This "out of sight, out of mind" problem undermines success for many otherwise-capable students. It is one of the most challenging—and occasionally disheartening—things about orchestrating online learning experiences. And how are we supposed to translate that inspiration factor into a virtual environment—where we can't rely on all the normal social signals to convey enthusiasm, approval, and encouragement? It's daunting, especially if we believe that ineffable personal qualities are what allow us to motivate students. But there are many aspects of motivation that aren't mysterious at all, but rather systematic principles that we can deliberately design into our courses. Doing so requires us all to think like psychologists, getting into students' mental processes to figure out how to spark the forces that move them.

After opening with that risky thought experiment about why we don't all just stay in bed, I pose another big question to students in the motivation module of my Introduction to Psychology course. In the discussion forum, I place an open invitation for students to explain to their classmates what motivates them to stay in school. This one question taps into a deep reserve of all the things that drive students to persist, while connecting motivation to students' life circumstances. Many of the students at my institution, especially those in online courses, juggle schoolwork while simultaneously managing paid employment, caring for children, and obligations to extended family. Many are also from historically disadvantaged backgrounds, including rural communities where just accessing a reliable Internet connection can be a struggle.

Students jump into this assignment wholeheartedly, posting stories that belie the stereotype of the hard-partying college student who just wants to graduate with a credential and a lucrative job offer. A handful of students say that they're motivated by the prospect of moving up financially, but the more striking trend is how many cite the goal of inspiring the important people in their lives. Setting an example for one's children, younger siblings, even parents is a powerful incentive for many students—as for one young woman who wrote that her academic progress inspired her mother to go back to complete a long-unfinished bachelor's degree. Now *that* is moving.

As teachers, we all benefit from building our insight about motivation. Classic research in motivation delineates several important influences on motivation and identifies the kinds of environments and situations that promote motivation. These concepts have also been extended to apply specifically to college students in research that focuses on motivation in academic environments. There is relatively little work to date specifically on motivation and online learning, but there are some emerging findings that do suggest the best ways to maximize motivation in this uniquely challenging environment.

Classic Research on Motivation

If one thing emerges from decades of psychology research on motivation, it's that there is no single, universal motivating force. Rather, theorists concur that any given behavior on any given occasion reflects a combination of multiple contributing factors. There are many theories of how these multiple motivating forces work, but these theories are not all mutually exclusive or even in competition with one another. Instead, they often describe processes that go on at different levels of specificity, or that happen simultaneously.

One of the most influential frameworks for understanding motivation is *self-determination theory*, or SDT.[1] SDT grew out of the work of psychologist Edward Deci, who made a number of important discoveries in the 1970s contrasting the effects of *intrinsic* motivation, i.e., inherent interest in and valuing of an activity, and *extrinsic* motivation, i.e., external consequences such as rewards and punishments. Deci discovered that, in contrast to the prevailing psychological wisdom of the time, external consequences could actually detract from people's motivation. In one particularly counterintuitive set of findings, he showed that giving people a desirable reward to engage in activities like puzzle solving reduced their interest in doing the task; conversely, just asking them to do the activity without a concrete reward of any type increased the likelihood that they would spend more time on it, and they actually enjoyed the activity more.[2]

Later research suggested that the extrinsic/intrinsic distinction also applies to types of goals.[3] For example, we might strive to do well in a research placement because we want to get a good letter of reference from the supervisor (*extrinsic* goal), or because we want to contribute to knowledge, advance our intellectual growth, or be good colleagues to our lab mates (all *intrinsic* goals). Deci and colleagues also came to believe that not all extrinsic motivators are counterproductive. When people fully internalize the value of something they are externally pressured to do, they can begin to engage in that activity in a self-determined fashion—as in the case of a student who doesn't particularly like a required class but immerses herself in it because it connects to a long-term career plan.[4]

This focus on self-controlled behavior laid the groundwork for the overarching SDT concept, which posits that people are motivated by the need for three basic things: competence, relatedness, and autonomy.[5] We strive to be good at things, to develop bonds with other people, and to make our own choices. People are the most intrinsically motivated and experience the most growth in environments that support these three basic needs. When we're cut off from any of them, motivation suffers. In an alternative interpretation of how the self shapes motivation, other theorists state that we are powerfully motivated to do things that protect our self-worth.[6] Wanting to avoid failure, for example, is a powerful motivator because failure threatens our self-concept as a worthy, capable person.

Other researchers have focused on how personality shapes motivation. Early in the scientific study of personality, researchers realized that one major personality difference among individuals is their level of *achievement motivation*.[7] Achievement-oriented people seek out—and are very motivated by—the opportunity to set and accomplish goals, as well as the opportunity to be evaluated on their own individual work. You'd know which of your students were highest in achievement motivation if you were to tell your class "How about instead of giving out individual grades, I just pick one grade and give that to everybody? Are you OK with that?"

Students with low achievement motivation might find the prospect of one flat grade rather appealing, but students high in achievement motivation would absolutely hate it. It follows that high-achievement-motivation students are more motivated in settings that emphasize evaluation of individual progress toward goals. Individuals also have distinct personality profiles with respect to *need for cognition.*[8] People with high need for cognition are drawn to activities that allow them to do mentally effortful things, like analyzing information and solving puzzles. In contrast, people low in this personality trait are less motivated by opportunities for mental effort.

Traits like achievement motivation may be fairly stable across time and situations,[9] but other personality factors play out differently in different situations. Self-efficacy has to do with the belief that you have the ability to create a desired effect through your own actions.[10] Like the Little Engine That Could, people with high self-efficacy "think they can." Self-efficacy isn't necessarily one global trait that applies in all domains; people can have self-efficacy associated with different realms of life, such as academic self-efficacy or computer self-efficacy. Not surprisingly, self-efficacy figures into motivation as well—believing that effort will pay off is highly motivating, while believing that one's efforts are fruitless is powerfully demotivating.

Turning now to another view of motivation, researchers have recently stepped up their interest in what is commonly called "willpower," namely, the ability to intentionally pursue one's goals in the face of short-term discomfort. Studies of situations where people have to exert self-control have exposed some surprising facts about willpower. Our ability to exert willpower is oddly analogous to our ability to exert muscle power.[11] Self-control is a limited resource—we can keep it up for only so much time before it fails, a psychological process known as *ego depletion*. Much in the same way that different exercises can all tap the same muscle power, self-control over different domains taps one central reserve of willpower.

Ego depletion created by exercising self-control in one arena reduces our self-control in completely different arenas, leading to some surprising crossover effects. A dieter who is depleted from resisting a tantalizing buffet spread at work is more likely to give in to the temptation of online shopping later that night; a parent who has been working all day to keep his temper with the kids might lack the will to turn off the TV after dinner and go finish his term paper. Stress, too, seems to drain our central stores of willpower, so that it's harder to exert self-control even when the stressful situation is over.[12]

The muscle metaphor is bad news for self-control, in that it means willpower is essentially finite; much as we would like to, we can't just conjure up new reserves for every different challenge we face. The good news is that, like a muscle, willpower may be something we can build up with repeated practice.[13] So, as a student keeps returning to that challenging online course at the end of each tiring day, it's possible that he or she will begin to build up greater reserves of personal willpower.

Another encouraging finding from ego depletion research is that *habits* are a powerful weapon in the battle for self-control. Habits compensate for low levels of self control; we fall back on them when self-control is low, as they don't drain our central self-control reserves in the same way as more consciously motivated behavior.[14] Positive habits, then, are a kind of behavioral "safety net" that can keep us from falling too far when we're depleted. So, a student who has established a positive habit of always logging on to an online course after dinner is in a far better position than one who hasn't established such a habit, as the student with an established habit will probably manage to check in even after an unusually depleting day.

In sum, the classic research emphasizes that there isn't any one "root cause" of motivated behavior, but that motivation is the sum total of different driving factors, both those that originate within the person and those that come from the surrounding environment. Motivation has a strong cognitive component; our beliefs about ourselves and our ability to make an impact guide the actions we'll take. Extrinsic factors like rewards and punishments also guide us, but don't have the same long-lasting, powerful effect as intrinsic motivations. Many theorists believe that the most important motivating factor of all is the intrinsic drive toward growth and the pursuit of individual interests and values. Additionally, under self-determination theory, people are thought to all share three basic needs—mastery, relatedness, and autonomy—and are most motivated in situations that offer pathways toward those three things.

SDT emphasizes what people have in common, while other theoretical perspectives focus on the factors that make individuals different. Some people are inherently more disposed to enjoy—and be motivated by—the prospect of goal setting, and these are the same people who thrive when they are judged on individual achievement. There are also major individual differences in how people respond to situations that demand mental effort. You can expect that a class—like any group of people—is going to contain a mix of these different motivational styles.

Regardless of personality or situation, we all struggle with getting our behavior to line up with our good intentions. This is especially tough because we can't expect to be perfectly self-controlled in all situations at all times; self-control applied to one willpower challenge simply depletes the amount available for the next challenge. Habits can help, but only if they are positive ones that are well established before we are in a situation that tests our willpower.

Motivating College Students

Much of the applied work in motivation has focused on motivation in academic settings, including higher education. Academic self-efficacy, in particular, has attracted a great deal of attention. In general, students who think that they can do well are the most motivated; multiple studies have all concluded that academic self-efficacy is a powerful predictor of academic success.[15] This suggests that raising students' academic self-efficacy could be the fast track to motivation.

In theory, there are several main ways that self-efficacy beliefs can be shaped. These include "mastery experience," i.e., experiencing success oneself, but also watching someone who is similar to you succeeding (vicarious experience), as well as verbal persuasion.[16] Researchers have explored intervention strategies that put these theories into practice in teaching situations. One team harnessed the vicarious-experience effect to address the low self-efficacy that characteristically plagues psychology students taking required statistics courses. At the beginning of the semester, researchers arranged for a student who had successfully taken the statistics course to make a class presentation about what taking the class was like for her and what strategies she had found helpful. Mindful of the fact that people are most affected by role models they see as having aptitude similar to their own, the researchers picked a presenter who appeared and described herself as a typical psychology student, rather than a "star student." This intervention succeeded in raising students' self-efficacy beliefs about being able to succeed at statistics.[17]

The question of intrinsic versus extrinsic motivation is tricky when applied to teaching and learning in college classrooms; as the educational psychologist Paul Pintrich observed, grades and point systems are not going away anytime soon, so it isn't practical to try to implement motivational systems for students solely based on intrinsic rewards.[18] Even so, there are better and worse ways to manage intrinsic motivation within the constraints of the traditional grading system. One strategy is presenting grades in a way that is "informational" rather than "controlling"—advice that makes sense in light of the motivational power of autonomy and perceived choice.[19] Also, using grades for motivation doesn't necessarily detract from intrinsic interest, as long as the classroom environment minimizes student-versus-student competition for grades, and grades are linked to assignments in meaningful ways. Examples include framing grades as feedback that is useful for improving future performance.[20]

Pushing students to internalize extrinsic motivations is another way to offset the motivation-undermining effects of grades. This can mean refocusing students away from purely external incentives like getting a marketable degree, and toward big-picture life goals, such as the wish to improve the lives of others through one's career. Even subtle reframing can have an impact on getting students to take goals to heart. For example, student motivation improves when course materials are worded in a way that emphasizes how the course ties into students' long-term intrinsic goals. This effect is strongest when the language also foregrounds student autonomy, such as by saying "you might" or "we suggest" instead of "you must"—just as predicted by self-determination theory.[21] In sum, the combination of an atmosphere of self-determination and a connection to students' personal goals and values is a potent formula for motivating college students.

But when achievement and effort begin to touch on students' self-regard, things get more complicated, because achieving success in challenging academic contexts can engender conflict between one's drive to succeed and one's fear of failing. Thus, protecting self-image can make students view different kinds of academic efforts—jumping into a class discussion, signing up for a "killer" course—in light of potential risks and rewards. Aiming high for an academic goal may seem like a straightforward enough path to improved self-regard, but as one group of researchers puts it, academic challenges always involve some level of risk to one's self-concept: "Success without trying can indicate one has talent, but failure following effort is often viewed as compelling evidence that one lacks ability" (p. 1).[22]

Especially in students who simultaneously value success and fear failure, this risk to self-concept can set students up for dysfunctional coping patterns. Avoidance is a prime one, as it allows students to escape (at least temporarily) what they experience as an overwhelming and painful dilemma. Another dysfunctional pattern is defensive pessimism, in which students downgrade their own potential for succeeding—"I'm sure I didn't get better than a C on that test," "I never do well on papers," and so forth. This pessimistic stance takes some of the sting out of failure when it does happen, but erodes motivation over time. There's also self-handicapping, an even more worrisome dynamic in which students put up barriers to their own success—everything from procrastination to psychosomatic illness to drug use—as a way to shield themselves from the pain of trying hard and failing anyway.[23]

The question of how to manage psychological consequences of academic failure is central to one of the most influential lines of research on motivation in college students, Carol Dweck's work on implicit theories of intelligence. Sometimes termed "mindset," these implicit theories are beliefs we have about the nature of human intellectual abilities.[24] People with a "fixed mindset" carry around a belief that people have a set amount of intelligence that is essentially unchangeable, and that this fixed aptitude determines whether you succeed or fail. Those with a "growth mindset" believe that intelligence (1) isn't set in stone and (2) isn't the main determinant of success or failure. In the growth mindset, it's effort, not inherent ability, that is the main explanation for why some people succeed and some don't.

Closely linked to people's concept of intelligence is how they think about the purpose of doing academic work in the first place. Some people interpret academic tasks in terms of "performance goals," where the ultimate purpose of assignments is to document and demonstrate one's ability. Others see them in terms of "mastery goals," where the point is to help you get better at the discipline.[25]

Dweck's work has uncovered an astonishing array of implications. Most important among these, for college teachers, is the way in which a fixed mindset undermines motivation, particularly the way in which fixed-mindset students interpret the meaning of assessments and the feedback they get on them. In the fixed-mindset view, tests and other graded assignments reflect on one's inborn, unchangeable intelligence, and thus become anxiety-provoking ordeals. Trying to raise your scores through extra effort presents a psychic catch-22: You need to study to get the good grade that proves you're smart, but needing to study must mean that you aren't actually all that smart to begin with.

Feedback—in the form of any grade that's less than perfect—then becomes something to fear instead of an opportunity to improve. Students caught up in this cycle of psychological threat may begin gravitating toward "easy" subjects and assignments, thus avoiding intellectual challenges that risk exposing their less-than-adequate intelligence; or, they might disengage from entire arenas of academic work that make them feel threatened.[26] With this dysfunctional dynamic at work, you can see why some students thrive in college, while others—equally smart, dedicated, and capable—flounder, become unmotivated, and fail.

It's not totally clear why some people develop fixed mindsets and others don't, but we do know that the environment plays a major role. Teachers and parents foster mindset simply by how they talk to students about their performance. Insidiously, *positive* comments can be the worst offenders for pushing students into a fixed mindset. Dweck is an outspoken critic of what she terms "praise for intelligence," pointing out that statements like "You did great on that test—you are really smart!" or "Wow, you're a real whiz at math!" carry with them a huge payload of implicit assumptions, such as that test results reflect how smart you are or that intelligence is the most important thing that determines grades. Offhand comments like these have been shown to have powerful negative consequences, shifting students into a fixed mindset and deterring them from taking on more-challenging work.[27] Even comforting struggling students in the wrong way—e.g., by telling them, "It's okay, not everyone is a 'math person'"—can demotivate them by engaging a fixed mindset.[28]

It's unnerving to think that our well-intentioned words have such power to throw students into a maladaptive pattern of belief and behavior, but the flip side is that the right kind of commentary is also powerful. In lieu of harmful "intelligence" praise, Dweck advocates a different kind of encouragement: "process" praise, or feedback that highlights factors like working hard, choosing good strategies, taking on a challenging assignment, or improving one's performance.[29]

Fortunately, mindset is quite malleable with the right kind of communication and support. In one intervention carried out with college undergraduates, researchers used a time-tested persuasion technique—writing a supportive letter to a younger "pen pal"—in an effort to get students to adopt a growth mindset. Students who explained to their "pen pals" why effort, not fixed intelligence, was the main determinant of success not only changed mindset in a positive direction, they also achieved significant gains in GPA.[30]

More direct approaches to changing mindset can work as well. Educating students about the realities of how the mind and brain work, emphasizing the plasticity of the brain and the importance of effortful practice, can help. Dweck and colleagues created a set of multimedia educational modules called "Brainology" (http://www .mindsetworks.com) to teach this kind of applied cognitive science to middle schoolers, but even a basic overview would be a step in the right direction for a college-age audience. Every teacher—online and offline—should be aware of mindset, as its presents a real and powerful threat to our students' motivation. But mindset's message is also fundamentally optimistic: sometimes transforming motivation is just a matter of repairing faulty beliefs, which can happen remarkably quickly under the right circumstances.

Applying Motivation Research to Online Learning Challenges

Motivational challenges are one of the main differences between online and face-to-face teaching. Especially if the class is fully online, learners have to be highly self-reliant to get the work done.[31] Even the most sophisticated forms of online communication can't replicate the motivating force of being in a classroom surrounded by other students engaged in the work, their enthusiasm sustained by the personal presence of a dedicated, inspiring instructor. It's possible for students to "check out" of face-to-face courses, just as they sometimes do in online ones, but the rhythm of scheduled class meetings requires a more concerted intention to avoid. Putting online work out of mind is easy by comparison; you can do it just by not turning on the computer. Or, if you happen to be online already, there are plenty of tempting sites waiting to spirit you away. Online instructors also have a harder time knowing when students are losing motivation, because they can't rely on telltale signs like facial expressions, fidgeting, or high absenteeism.[32] The motivation issue is concerning, so much so that the increased need for student self-discipline is one of the major factors cited by university leaders as a barrier to online learning.[33]

Knowing what we do about the dynamics of student motivation, let's consider how they might play out in an online course. A student signs up for a course that holds little intrinsic interest—something he's taking just to earn a couple of credits. He looks over the syllabus the day before the semester; it reads like a long to-do list of student responsibilities and does little to draw him into the topic. The first assignment looks intimidating, requiring skills our student doesn't feel confident about, but fortunately—or so he thinks—it's not due for quite some time. There's not much else going on anywhere else in the course, so there's no need to get into the habit of checking in each day.

Our student really does want to earn a good grade on the big assignment, but given the disconnect between his self-perceived skills and what the assignment seems to require, it's not looking likely. As day after day ticks by, he starts to get a familiar knot in his stomach while he thinks of all the points he'll lose when it finally comes due. Just logging in to class makes this sinking feeling worse, all the more so given the instructor's ominous-sounding announcements about how the assignment is mandatory and worth a substantial portion of the grade. Overwhelmed with anxiety and not sure what to do next, he busies himself with other things until the day the assignment is due. "I didn't really have the time to do my best work on this," he tells himself. "Who cares, I knew I wasn't going to get a good grade in this class anyway."

Our hypothetical student should have made some different choices in this scenario, but the setup of the class didn't help. Like many of our students, he came to the class without the intrinsic interest that would have bolstered motivation. The first impression of the class is a onetime opportunity to shape the intrinsic appeal of the course, but in this case the opportunity was lost. The introduction to the course could have also done a better job at foregrounding student autonomy, one of the "big three" motivators according to self-determination theory. We generally don't want to give our students total free rein in setting up a course, but it's possible to create an atmosphere of autonomy by giving students some choices and using wording that frames them as free agents. The lack of opportunity for social relatedness—even something like a getting-to-know-you discussion thread or personal welcome message—is another missed motivational opportunity. At least in the student's mind, he didn't have the opportunity for mastery either, given his doubts about being capable of successfully completing the work. Low self-efficacy and anxiety combined to deter him from even attempting to succeed, creating a cycle of procrastination and, ultimately, failure.

What could the instructor have done differently to prevent this disaster? Intrinsic interest is tough to convey to students; enthusiasm, no matter how sincere, doesn't just automatically leap from one person to the next. But it is possible, in those all-important first moments of contact between students and course material, to steer the focus toward the "why" of a course—*why* anyone would study this topic, *why* this area of study could change the world for the better, *why* you will be a more capable person after you complete it—and away from the "what"—*what* is required, *what* you have to do and in *what* order, *what* the grading policies are. Both can and should be covered early on, but foregrounding the "why" topics provides a motivational advantage.

Besides doing your best to sell students on the subject matter, you can also target self-efficacy. Offering small-stakes assignments at the outset can be one way to demonstrate to students that success is within reach. (If you make one of these small-stakes assignments a syllabus quiz, this also does double duty in getting students to master the "what" information, freeing you to focus on the "why.") Pushing students, early on, to routinely check in also serves as motivational insurance policy; later on, when students are facing challenges—fatigue, competing demands, frustration, or lack of interest—having an established logging-in habit may ensure that they don't stall out. These frequent check-ins, in turn, can help keep them out of the cycle of anxiety, avoidance, and procrastination that spells doom in online coursework.

Motivating students online is a high-stakes endeavor. A lot can go wrong, and you can't fall back on your engaging classroom persona to pull students back in once they go astray. It follows that your instructional design process for online courses should include developing at least an informal game plan for motivation. This plan can be informed by the general research literature on motivation, as well as work that focuses specifically on motivation in online learning. Below are some points to consider as you build your plan.

PROCRASTINATION

Online classes present more opportunities for procrastination, compared to face-to-face classes.[34] This means increased potential for serious damage to learning (and grades). The lectures that predominate in face-to-face courses are relatively ineffective ways to teach, but they probably contribute to spacing material over time, because they unfold in a set schedule over time. In contrast, depending on how the courses are set up, online students can sometimes avoid exposure to material altogether until an assignment is nigh.[35]

Although there is wide agreement that online classes are breeding grounds for procrastination, there is less consensus about specific design strategies for preventing it. One research team uncovered a somewhat surprising role of discussion forums in mediating the relationship between procrastination and success in an online course. They found that procrastinators are particularly unlikely to participate in online discussion forums, and this reduced participation, in turn, is correlated with worse grades. A possible explanation for this correlation is that procrastinators are especially hesitant to join in once the discussion is under way, perhaps because they worry about being perceived as newcomers in an established conversation. This aversion to jumping in late causes them to miss out on the important learning and motivation benefits of peer-to-peer interaction.[36]

Ways to get students to participate "early and often" in online discussion include "getting to know you" assignments worth just a few points at the beginning of the term. Setting up lots of briefer conversations as well (e.g., weekly topic discussions) that open and close on specific dates is another anti-procrastination strategy. In these time-limited settings, students will be less shy about getting into the conversation, as opposed to one that's been going on for weeks and weeks.

Because habits support us when willpower fails, we should also intentionally design for positive habit building. This means making a conscious decision about how often we want students to check in—daily is good for a fully online course, or, for hybrid or blended courses, two or three times per week will work—with the idea that we are designing a schedule that students can realistically keep to on a consistent basis throughout the term. Then, we would convey this expectation explicitly to students, and let them know about the incentives for following the schedule as set (e.g., quizzes due at certain consistent times per week, windows of opportunity for participating in discussions for credit). Lastly, ensuring that there is a steady flow of new information, so that something is new and different every time a student checks in, creates a psychological pull toward the course. Discussions are wonderful for this purpose, but even things like daily reminders and announcements can help. Consider Facebook: it may not be a great teaching tool, but it's a useful model for how to get people compulsively clicking by doling out a steady stream of status updates, commentary, news, and other tidbits.

Other commonly suggested anti-procrastination techniques include getting away from the traditional infrequent schedule of high-stakes assignments and exams, and instead setting more "proximal" goals: small chunks of work that build toward larger goals or projects. This works for a variety of reasons. For one, students are less inclined to work themselves into a frenzy of anxiety and avoidance when they are working with smaller, more manageable tasks. They also get more opportunities for feedback, which helps refocus them if they're off track, and, if they are on the right track, gives doses of efficacy-boosting encouragement. In general, structure is the enemy of procrastination—so setting up these small-stakes assignments with clear timetables, instructions, and rubrics can also be part of designing for maximum motivation.

DIVERSE MOTIVATIONAL STYLES
Recall that there are substantial individual differences in what kinds of situations and incentives motivate people. If you are a typical hard-charging academic, you are probably driven both by achievement motivation (the opportunity to pursue goals and be individually recognized for meeting them) as well as by need for cognition (the opportunity to engage in mentally challenging activities). Your students, by contrast, will likely fall along a more diverse spectrum of styles. This means that you can't rely solely on your own intuitions for what incentives your students will find most appealing. Some will relish the opportunity to compete with classmates, while others are put off by a competitive atmosphere; some will inherently gravitate toward work framed as puzzles, while others would find this kind of thing exasperating.

Given this diversity, it makes sense to introduce variety into the motivational side of your online learning activities. On some assignments, you can emphasize the opportunity to earn points (appealing to achievement-oriented students as well as those who aren't inherently motivated by need for cognition). Other activities can allow—but not force—students to showcase their work to classmates (another thing that's appealing to the achievement-oriented). Having some component of group work can draw in the less achievement-oriented students.

ACADEMIC SELF-MANAGEMENT SKILLS

Another side of individual differences in motivation is the fact that some students, particularly ones earlier in their college careers, are unskilled at channeling their motivation into effective learning strategies. These strategies fall under the concept of "self-regulated learning."[37] Self-regulated learning, or SRL, broadly comprises a number of positive practices of effective students, ranging from being able to manage time to valuing learning and believing in one's own academic abilities. SRL is strongly linked to success in college courses, a relationship that holds true for online courses as well as face-to-face ones.[38]

SRL tends to increase over time as students mature and become more experienced, but there are some things online instructors can do to speed the process along. Because students do vary so much along this continuum, it may make sense to do targeted SRL interventions for students who need them the most.[39] There are established survey tools that measure SRL, such as the Motivated Strategies for Learning Questionnaire (MSLQ).[40] You can administer such a survey early in the semester to identify students who will benefit the most from SRL coaching, such as a time management or study skills tutorial.

Other course design factors encourage all students to develop good SRL practices. These include being maximally transparent about grading through techniques such as keeping a user-friendly, up-to-date grade book that students can use any time.[41] Online rubrics, which you can easily set up in most learning management systems, also help you teach students to align their efforts toward the instructor's objectives for the assignment. These tools make it easy to show students exactly what you will be looking for as you evaluate their work, and show them—for future reference—the stronger and weaker parts of what they turn in.

Academic self-efficacy is closely related to SRL, and is another area where some of your students will need extra help. Recall that motivational research tells us that we tend to feel demotivated in situations where we don't feel competent to achieve what we want through our own actions. Here's another arena where small-stakes "proximal" goals are helpful—these small "wins" help ingrain in students the expectation that they *can* successfully do the work.[42] Building self-efficacy by providing relatable role models is a bit tougher in an online environment, since you can't just call in a guest speaker for the day. But there are options: you can post video testimonials from successful former students, and encourage any teaching assistants you have to establish a personal presence, e.g., by posting a photo and a bit of background, instead of just lurking invisibly. Lastly, something that I've employed with some success in my online courses is to include a discussion thread where students are asked to post their own most successful study strategies—the idea being that reading this advice from a peer might just hit home in a way that advice from me might not.

GROWTH MINDSET

One of the many good things about the "mindset" research discussed earlier in the chapter is that it's easy to act on. The research itself suggests a number of concrete, easy to implement teaching practices that can help our students move toward a healthy "growth" perspective on their academic abilities. There has not been extensive work on how mindset plays out in online settings, but we can extrapolate several general design principles from the theory. One principle is to be scrupulously careful with the language we use in communicating with our students (something that is a bit easier to do in an online environment, compared to speaking off the cuff in a traditional classroom). Words like "talent," "ability," being "naturally good" at a discipline—these should all be expunged from our teaching vocabularies, as they telegraph a fixed mindset. Similarly, when we praise and encourage students—which we should be doing frequently—we must watch our language, being sure to cite specific things we liked about their work and/or the effort put forth, rather than making global statements about how good they are at the subject or skill.

Mindset can be shaped by the instructor's actions as well as by his or her words. Certain course designs reinforce the idea of building skill with effort—getting across the idea that it doesn't matter how good you are at the outset, but rather, how much incremental progress you make over the entire term. Once again, the small-stakes, frequent-assignment design proves superior, as it sends a message that we instructors value and reward sustained effort over the long haul. By contrast, the traditional system of infrequent, term-end assignments gives the impression that we expect students to produce A-plus work in a short spurt of effort crammed in during finals week.

Similarly, including some assignments and assessments that can be repeated for credit, such as repeatable online quizzes or multiple essay drafts, communicates that we expect and value revision. This kind of setup reinforces the core idea that successful students aren't just the ones who can do brilliant work in one shot; rather, the real superstars are the students who keep trying. Online tools for quizzing and tracking changes in documents, such as the Track Changes tool in Microsoft Word, make this teaching strategy easier to carry out than ever before.

Motivational Strategies in Action: The First Year Learning Initiative

Getting students moving and keeping them moving throughout the term requires planning and concerted effort. This is especially true for classes with less-mature, less-experienced students. For an example of what a coordinated strategy for motivation looks like, consider the First Year Learning Initiative, a program my colleague Blase Scarnati and I developed for optimizing the design of courses serving primarily first- and second-year college students. Although the First Year Learning Initiative (FYLI) isn't a technology initiative per se, several fully online and blended courses participate in the program, and the design features we promote tend to draw heavily on instructional technology.

When we first accepted the charge to create a large-scale course redesign initiative that would specifically target success in foundational courses, our first move was conduct a number of focus-group-type meetings with faculty who taught early career students day in and day out. We asked them what, in their experience, differentiated successful students from unsuccessful ones. The answers were striking: not one person cited a lack of intellectual ability as a barrier to success. Rather, opinions came down squarely on the side of motivational factors. Of all the factors faculty cited, some related to self-regulated learning (time management, coming to class), some were more in the realm of mindset (understanding that their own effort was the most important determinant of success), and some had to do with intrinsic motivation (students' getting "hooked in" to the discipline by relating it to their own interests).

Through this discussion, Blase and I came to understand that courses for early career college students must be designed not just to convey information, but also to motivate students by "socializing" them to the college environment. However, we knew from experience that the majority of foundational courses simply never addressed this issue, or addressed it only weakly and indirectly. We also identified design features that would specifically support self-efficacy and self-regulated learning, while being general enough to work across multiple disciplines and across different delivery formats (online, face-to-face, blended).

To date, over forty courses are "FYLI-certified," meaning that they have undergone an intentional redesign process during which faculty revamp the course to meet criteria having to do with socializing and motivating early career college students. Hallmarks of FYLI-certified courses include the following:

"EARLY AND OFTEN" ASSESSMENT PHILOSOPHY

First impressions are priceless, and so FYLI courses get off to a brisk start: to be certified, courses must have some small-stakes, graded work due within the first two weeks of a standard fifteen-week term. Some of our courses take this even further, asking for homework to be turned in by the second class meeting. This isn't intended to scare students or discourage them, but rather to let them know, in a very tangible way, that active involvement is expected from the get-go. It also establishes a healthy habit of frequently checking in with the course. This small-bites design philosophy is then carried throughout the rest of the course, with frequent assessments and lots of opportunity to revise and improve.

BRIDGING, SCAFFOLDING, AND HOOKS

With quite a few construction metaphors in play, we ask FYLI faculty to consider how the course intentionally meets students where they are and leads them into the material. This means understanding how students' idea of the discipline differs from that of experts, and "bridging" that with explanation and activities that bring them closer to expert understanding. For example, students who are new to the study of history probably assume that it revolves around dates, timelines, and names. But professional historians see the discipline completely differently, with an emphasis on evaluating historical sources and thinking critically about events and their causes. Addressing this disconnect head-on, early in the semester, can do a lot to prevent students from disengaging when expectations are not met.

Scaffolding, similarly, means addressing the gap between the skills and knowledge students need in order to succeed, and the skills and knowledge they have when they start the course. For example, we might ask students to write a five-page research paper, and assume they can do that as long as they understand the material. However, writing a paper really comprises a number of different subtasks, all of which the student has to have mastered in order to write a good paper. There's finding and evaluating research sources, formulating a thesis, organizing and elaborating the supporting evidence for the thesis, and revising for mechanics, just to name a few. Scaffolding a paper assignment means providing opportunities for students to practice and get feedback on all the component parts before turning in the final paper draft. This scaffolding, like the "early and often" approach, provides more opportunities for students to be successful, gives them the tools to be successful, and fights the cycle of procrastination and disengagement that sets in when students are left to "sink or swim."

"Hooks" tie in to intrinsic motivation by asking faculty to deliberately strategize about what might pull students into material—in other words, what is it about the discipline that might appeal to the life experiences and interests of the typical students? A musicology course, for example, might start by referencing students' own experience of music, what their preferences are, and what it is they like about certain performers. From there, it can lead into the formal analytical skills students need to develop in order to begin appreciating music the way a musicologist does. Another "hook" that is enormously popular in psychology is to use current and classic films as springboards for discussion about phenomena ranging from dreams (*Inception*) to memory (*Memento*) to mental illness (*A Beautiful Mind*).

PUBLIC RUBRICS

Self-efficacy thrives on clear, attainable goals, and so FYLI courses feature rubrics, meaning structured guides to grading that spell out exactly what the instructor is looking for and how these criteria factor into an overall grade. Furthermore, these rubrics are not only accessible to students, but instructors also actively promote them to students as something they should consult as a matter of course when completing an assignment. Students gain a sense of control and mastery when they have this information up front, plus they also establish the important habit of consulting rubrics before doing any assignment. Future classes they take may have rubrics, or they may not, but when they do it's more likely that our FYLI students will make use of them. Rubrics are particularly easy to use in online learning environments, as rubric tools that automatically total up grades and show feedback are now a standard feature of most learning management systems.

PEER TAS

One last distinguishing feature of the FYLI motivation plan is that FYLI courses have a *peer teaching assistant* (PTA), an undergraduate student who works under the instructor's direction to help with tasks like supervising group problem-solving activities, checking in on online discussions, and grading small-stakes quizzes. FYLI faculty know that these assistants aren't just a way to ease workload, but can also serve an important motivational function in the course. Because PTAs are all undergraduates, and generally have completed the course themselves fairly recently, they are the kind of relatable "role model" that builds self-efficacy.

Taken together, these features establish a maximally motivating learning environment, and they are adaptable to a wide range of technologies, styles, and settings. The approach is working, as evidenced by high endorsement of academic values and self-management by students in FYLI courses, and by the fact that FYLI participation is associated with significant improvements in course completion rates.[43]

Motivating with Games and "Gamification"

Recently, I visited the Musée Mecanique in San Francisco, a converted warehouse containing over 200 mechanical and electronic entertainment devices, including some that are over 100 years old. Amazingly, they are all still playable, albeit for the inflation-adjusted price of twenty-five cents per game. And every one—from Pong to Whack-a-Mole to a preelectronic driving game that uses a metal car suspended over a drum painted with road markings—still draws in its share of delighted players. It's tangible proof of the almost primal human drive to take the technology of the day and use it to create new forms of interactive entertainment. There is something incredibly motivating about the ability to play a game with a machine—a force that drove the development of the multi-billion-dollar electronic gaming industry we know today.

To get a sense of this motivational power, consider an astonishing fact relayed by game developer Jane McGonigal in her book *Reality Is Broken: Why Games Make Us Better and How They Can Change the World.* The "massively multiplayer online roleplaying game" World of Warcraft has been played for a total combined amount of time of about *5.9 million years* to date—roughly the same amount of time that human beings and our hominid ancestors have been walking upright.[44]

People all over the world willingly pour vast amounts of time and effort into games, acquiring enormous amounts of game-related skill and knowledge along the way. And so, educators have developed a keen interest in harnessing the power of games to create online learning experiences that students actually want to do—an interest that only continues to increase along with new developments in gaming and learning technologies. *Gamification*—a major buzzword in online education today—means somewhat different things to different people, but in general, designers use it to denote a new approach to online teaching that pulls elements of gaming into online learning activities, with the goal of creating a more motivating and memorable learning experience.

As we touched on earlier in this book, educational researchers have theorized that there is overlap between game play and engaged learning, with both being characterized by multiple attempts, the ability to overcome early failure, intrinsic interest in the "story" (be that course material or game narrative), and pursuit of a clear set of attainable objectives.[45] Other researchers have delved into the details of how to develop games for different learning and training applications, establishing a fairly extensive body of literature documenting best practices and effective examples from different domains.[46]

Would-be "gamifiers" need to decide early on whether they are more interested in constructing a full-fledged learning game or, conversely, infusing some game-like qualities into conventional online instruction. For the former, it's important to realize that game development is more daunting than it may appear. The development team, at a minimum, should involve a content expert, instructional designer, graphic designer, and programmer, all working together on a structured plan with benchmarks and multiple testing phases—hardly the lone person we might picture putting a game together in his or her spare time.[47] It's a worthy activity, given the value of well-designed instructional games, but well beyond the scope of this book.

Game-*inspired* instruction, in contrast to game building, is attainable with a much more modest investment of time and expertise. The literature on gaming suggests a number of principles that are reasonably easy to adapt in the design of online learning activities. One of these is the theory of *flow* proposed by psychologist Mihaly Csikszentmihalyi.[48] This idea actually predates the contemporary era of computer gaming, but has been highly influential in game design circles. Csikszentmihalyi's work seeks to identify and explain the distinct psychological experience of being fully absorbed in a pursuit—a state of optimal engagement termed *flow*. Flow states are characterized by pleasure, exhilaration, and seemingly effortless concentration—clearly a desirable thing whether your goal is recreation or something more serious.

Most of us intuitively understand what flow states feel like; Csikszentmihalyi's master stroke was the discovery that flow states aren't idiosyncratic to the individual or just random happy moods. Rather, certain qualities of the environment can fairly reliably produce flow states. Two of these qualities are particularly relevant to games and learning. First, flow activities have an optimal level of challenge—goals are neither too easy to attain, nor too difficult, for that individual participant. Optimizing challenge means that the participant has to stay fully engaged (not too easy), yet keep attaining enough small successes along the way to feel a sense of mastery (not too hard). Second, flow activities provide abundant, rapid feedback, so that it's immediately clear whether one's actions are having the desired effect. Abundant feedback encourages continued engagement as the participant quickly learns how to adjust his or her responses for better results.

Game designers have seized on these concepts as tools for making game play both pleasurable and "addictive." Computer games feature myriad sources of feedback, from sound effects to heads-up displays of game data like number of kills, lives remaining, levels, and powers. They also feature an optimal and usually high level of challenge, with opportunities to fail balanced against reasonably attainable goals. This design principle is actually somewhat counterintuitive, as it goes against the idea that players just like playing games that give them lots of wins and no losses. As Jane McGonigal observes, "Roughly four times out of five, gamers don't complete the mission, run out of time, don't solve the puzzle, lose the fight. . . . Which makes you wonder, do gamers actually *enjoy* failing? As it turns out, yes" (p. 66).[49]

From flow theory, game designers have learned to set up highly interactive environments with multiple opportunities for failure as well as success. Instructors can also learn from the theory, though the applications are a bit less obvious. We can think of different learning activities not as culminating in one big "ah-hah" moment at the end, but as unfolding in a series of smaller challenges, all of which give feedback to the learner. Flow theory also highlights the importance of optimizing difficulty, so that whenever possible we are calibrating content and questions into the "sweet spot" where the learner will be challenged but still feel that success is in reach.

Flow provides a good overarching framework of the kinds of learning activities that provide a motivating environment. What other principles and practices can we borrow from game design? One answer gamers might agree on is *quick start with multiple tries.* Today's gamers rarely read manuals before playing for the first time, or, really, at any point thereafter. Instead, the preferred method is to jump in and start experimenting with the properties of the game. Contemporary game builders accordingly consider it a hallmark of good design for a game not to need any kind of extensive explanation as a condition of starting play.[50] This only works when initial failure isn't catastrophic, and there is lots of opportunity to try again.

With the repeatable online quizzes we use in Introduction to Psychology, we encourage students *not* to wait until they've fully mastered the textbook material to start their attempts. This is totally contrary to the usual advice students get about tests, but the repeatability factor means that they can use them to reflect on learning, shape questions about the material, and for other nontraditional purposes—all while relaxing a bit about the grade factor. Other instructors apply this principle by having students tackle a group case study activity before reviewing the relevant concepts, with failed analysis of the case study treated as a learning experience just as valuable as success.[51]

SENSE OF MISSION

"To look at the majority of games today, one might think that gamers care only about saving the world," comments game developer Trent Polack in *Reality Is Broken.* This tongue-in-cheek characterization shows how having a central mission powerfully motivates game players. Once they buy into the mission, the sky is the limit, motivationally speaking. We see this in the wildly popular game Halo, in which millions of players rally behind the cause of saving the planet from malevolent alien invaders—a premise that's compelling but simple enough to explain in a short paragraph.[52] Students, as well, get moving when they know not just what's required but why.

It's especially powerful when they can collaborate to accomplish that goal together—a principle we see applied in World of Warcraft, with its organized guilds and collectively fought campaigns.

Within a class, the sense of mission can also be reinforced not just by spelling out the different course objectives, but by continually reminding students of how each part ties back into the "big goals" of the class. Tying learning to the "big goals" of humanity contributes, too. As McGonigal points out, sense of mission is ultimately about the opportunity to be a part of something that is larger than oneself, something that is also true of helping apply academic knowledge to real-world problems. Even in a course without an applied focus, students can be inspired by the opportunity to become a part of the discipline's community of scholars—a group of people collectively motivated by an intellectual quest.

On a more pragmatic note, I find that sense of mission benefits from chopping up material into moderate-size, discrete modules, so that students can treat each one as a challenging but attainable mission unto itself. This is especially easy to do in learning management systems, as you can separate different topics not just chronologically but also visually, by grouping module-related material in folders and using graphic icons to differentiate each one.

STORY/NARRATIVE

Many psychologists have observed that the human mind is particularly attuned to stories, so that information we encounter in story format tends to be particularly compelling (as well as memorable). Game developers have taken this narrative principle to heart, building player interest via familiar elements of story: characters and settings, complications and conflict, transformation, and resolution. By fully elaborating story-based teaching activities like case studies and role-play activities, filling them out with specific characters, settings, and conflicts, we take advantage of this gamification principle.

KNOWING WHERE YOU STAND

Good games make individual standing salient. Standing can include things like relative strengths and weaknesses (e.g., your game character's special powers), as well as your overall prowess compared to other players. Halo takes this transparency to the extreme, compiling massive dossiers of play statistics for every player, every session—documentation that players find highly motivating as they seek ever-higher levels of accomplishment within the game.[53]

Classes can also be designed to make standing salient. However, even with online grade books and similar tools, this can be surprisingly complicated in classes that are designed with numerous small-stakes assignments. Even when students know their grades on individual assignments, it may be unclear how those combine into an overall grade. It can also be hard to pick out important patterns, such as doing well on written work but poorly on factual test questions, or excelling at textbook material but missing points from primary source reading. Some instructors, such as my NAU colleague Beverly Amer of the Franke College of Business, create custom online calculation tools that show students their current overall grade as well as performance in different categories. This can be one way to address the transparency issue and make standing more obvious to students.

Another, potentially more controversial way of adapting gamelike transparency to the classroom is the concept of a *leaderboard*.[54] Computer games frequently feature some kind of public display of one's standings relative to other players. The ability to climb the leaderboard, vying for position with one's peers, is no doubt a highly motivating aspect of game play, and it's possible that the same could be true for maintaining visible leaderboards in classes. Clearly, though, you would need to put some kind of mechanism into place to protect student privacy—code names, for example, or a voluntary opt-out system. Even then, you have to consider what would happen if and when a student fell down the leaderboard, something that would be a fairly public, and disheartening, display for the affected student.

One possible way to offset this issue could be to set up the leaderboard display to obscure all of the names except one's own. Thus, each student could see his or her standing relative to the other students, but not who is displacing each person—and no one could track the decline of any individual student. It might also be a good idea to have the leaderboard show only the upper part of the rankings—such as the top 25 percent—so that no students are visibly stuck in the bottom few places. In sum, introducing the kind of extreme transparency, and therefore the intense competitive atmosphere, associated with gaming would no doubt add to motivation in a class setting—but with other repercussions that have to be carefully weighed first.

Take-Home Points on Gamification

The gaming and gamification movements can add a number of things to our repertoire of motivational techniques. We can think about flow and how that might come about at different points in the learning process, keeping in mind that flow happens when challenge is optimal and the activity is dynamic, providing moment-to-moment information on how we are doing and giving lots of opportunities for incremental improvement. It gives further impetus to move away from the traditional schedule of infrequent, high-stakes assessment in which failure is catastrophic, and instead strive for learning environments in which failures lead toward future success. Purpose, mission, and story can carry the learner along, allowing individuals to transcend their own reality and be a part of the lives of others. Lastly, the opportunity to achieve and have those achievements be publicly known can light a fire under students and gamers alike.

Also important are the features that *don't* appear in this list of readily adaptable principles. Although commercial games do tend to have impressive production features such as quality soundtracks and incredibly realistic graphics, in general, these features don't make substantial contributions to learning.[55] In learning-oriented games, blocky graphics can be just as effective as photo-realistic ones, as long as the major conceptual information still comes across. This is good news for those of us without the technical know-how (or substantial dollars) needed for the artistry of professionally developed game environments. It's even possible for games to be effective without being particularly entertaining. While elaborated storytelling elements do add to the effectiveness of things like case studies, it isn't necessary to have the dramatic abilities of a professional screenwriter in order to promote learning. In other words, don't worry that your learning activities lack the surface appearance of a Halo—it's the deeper aspects of a game, such as feedback, transparency, and multiple attempts, that truly matter for a gamified learning experience.

Chapter 9

Putting It All Together

THROUGHOUT THIS BOOK, we've examined ways in which cognitive and brain sciences inform teaching with technology. Attention, memory, and higher thought processes are all areas of cognition that we can target by bringing cognitive theory together with technology. In many cases, there are aspects of these cognitive processes that we can't get at nearly as well with solely face-to-face teaching methods.

We've covered quite a range of specific technology-aided learning activities that draw their power from underlying principles of human cognition. What would these look like put together into a fully "cognitively optimized" course? This final chapter includes planning guides and examples that will show you how to teach in ways that take advantage of both technology and cognition. It's my goal that seeing all the pieces working together integrates and illustrates the concepts from throughout the book. I also hope that what you've seen here inspires you to use future technologies—tools we can't even envision yet—to serve, inform, and inspire students, all with an eye to the cognitive processes that drive learning.

Designing for "Cognitive Optimization"

Applying cognitive principles to technology-aided learning begins with the course design process. This is an opportunity to plan how you will integrate cognition into the building blocks of the course—learning objectives, learning activities, assessments, student-to-student peer interactions, and grading schemes. The design phase is also an opportunity to apply research findings on the psychology of student motivation, creating the "active management of motivation" that's crucial for effectively deploying online teaching tools.

As you envision (or reenvision) your course, there are key questions to ask yourself about each of the major parts. These are laid out below, along with a brief recap of the cognitive principles behind each question. Then I've listed specific tools and techniques that can help address each question.

1. LEARNING OBJECTIVES: WHAT WE WANT STUDENTS TO KNOW

When we first sit down to plan a course, it makes sense to start with the "big picture" questions, identifying the highest-priority things we want students to get out of the experience. These priorities, in turn, help us choose the right kinds of activities and online tools. As you identify and articulate the skills, knowledge, and abilities students should gain from the course, ask yourself:

Question: How will the course ensure that students gain the right kind of thinking skills?

THE PRINCIPLE: Skills such as critical thinking, reasoning, and argument analysis are relatively unlikely to emerge just as a result of engaging with intellectually challenging material; a more effective approach is to first identify the thinking skills that are needed, then assign students to practice those skills frequently and in a focused manner.

TOOLS AND TECHNIQUES:
- Collaborative highlighting tools such as HyLighter
- Scientific reasoning tools such as Carnegie Mellon's Causality Lab
- Argument mapping software such as Rationale
- Problem-based learning
- Case studies

- Online problem and case study databases, such as the University of Delaware's Problem-Based Learning Clearinghouse

- Simulations, e.g., "Sniffy the Rat"

- Multiple opportunities to work through problems

- Configuring multiple-choice test questions to include an area where students can explain why they chose a particular answer

Question: How will the course ensure that students *transfer* what they have learned?

THE PRINCIPLE: Transferring knowledge—correctly using analogies, extending knowledge to new kinds of problems, or using school-acquired knowledge in real-world situations—is particularly difficult for novices unless they have had the kind of practice that allows them to understand the deep structure of problems within the discipline.

TOOLS AND TECHNIQUES:
- Interactive, replayable media illustrating analogies, such as those available in the MERLOT database

- Visually arranging examples so that common elements line up, making conceptual relationships easier to spot

- Explanatory feedback

- Assignments that feature multiple problems with the same deep structure but different surface features

- Graphic tools, such as Autoshape, used to diagram arguments or problems

- Asking students to explain structural elements of problems

Question: Are there any skills students need to be able to carry out *automatically* if they are to succeed in the discipline?

THE PRINCIPLE: With practice, students can achieve automaticity for some kinds of routine tasks, which frees up cognitive resources for higher-level thought processes.

TOOLS AND TECHNIQUES:

- Timed online assignments graded on speed as well as accuracy

- Assignments that are repeatable for credit

- Using auto-grading to provide rapid feedback

- Mastery learning: Setting the learning management system to open more-advanced assignments only after students have earned passing grades (or better) on lower-level assignments

2. LEARNING ACTIVITIES: HOW WE WANT STUDENTS TO SPEND THEIR STUDY TIME

Once you've figured out the framework of major objectives for the course, the next question is how the learning assignments will feed into those objectives. As you design assignments and other activities, ask yourself:

Question: How will you *keep students focused* as they do the learning activity?

THE PRINCIPLE: We encode very little information in the absence of focused attention, so capturing and holding attention is critical.

TOOLS AND TECHNIQUES:

- Lessons that alternate text with student responses, such as quiz questions or reflection on the reading

- Interactive branching lessons or "choose-your-own-adventure" style lessons that change as a function of student choice

- Synchronous chat

- Dynamic multimedia such as animation or narrated diagrams

- Working with technical staff to maximize speed and stability of instructional technology

- Instructional modules or demonstrations that teach students about the dangers of "multitasking" (e.g., the "The Amazing Color Changing Card Trick" YouTube video)

Question: How will you *minimize extraneous cognitive load* while students are doing the activity?

THE PRINCIPLE: People have very limited capacity to switch focus among different inputs, so the learning environment should be free as much as possible from extraneous information, and all the information needed to do the task should be pulled together in one place.

TOOLS AND TECHNIQUES:
- Designing diagrams and graphics so that text labels are integrated, rather than putting text off to the side or underneath
- Graphics that convey substantive information about the material, rather than merely adding decoration
- Audio explanations of diagrams and animations (not text)
- Instructional modules that teach needed technology skills *before* students tackle content knowledge

Question: How will learning activities *maximize spaced study?*

THE PRINCIPLE: Spreading out study time across shorter, more frequent sessions improves recall.

TOOLS AND TECHNIQUES:
- Assigning online work on alternate days with face-to-face meetings
- Staggering deadlines so that different assignments are due on different days of every week across the term
- Interleaving: Arrange material so that you revisit topics over time
- Frequent quizzes covering just single chapters or even parts of chapters
- Publisher-supplied tutorials and online labs that incorporate material drawn from different units or modules

Question: How will learning activities *use emotions to promote learning?*

THE PRINCIPLE: Emotions boost memory—with the caveat that *negative* emotions are the most powerful.

TOOLS AND TECHNIQUES:
- Video and movie clips (with alternatives for students with sensitivities or special concerns)
- TED talks
- Wikis and web pages where students view one another's class work
- Class-constructed publicly viewable work products, such as web pages
- Visually rich multimedia
- Role playing
- Narrative case studies
- Games and "gamification" techniques

Question: How will learning activities promote *deep processing?*

THE PRINCIPLE: Focusing on meaning, rather than superficial qualities, promotes memory as well as understanding; this is particularly true when people relate information to themselves.

TOOLS AND TECHNIQUES:
- Discussion assignments that require leading and/or summarizing discussion threads
- Online discussions built around experiences from students' own lives
- Quizzes that include application and integration questions as well as factual ones

Question: How will you *build on existing knowledge* as you introduce new concepts?

> THE PRINCIPLE: Memory for new information is powerfully shaped by what we already know; when people can't fit new information into a conceptual framework of some kind, they are unlikely to remember it.

> TOOLS AND TECHNIQUES:
> • Online pre-assessments
> • Instructional modules aimed at just those students with demonstrated deficiencies in an area
> • Adaptive quizzing systems that automatically revisit material missed in earlier attempts
> • Discussion prompts asking students to relate new information to old information

3. ASSESSMENTS: HOW STUDENT LEARNING WILL BE MEASURED

Assessments—i.e., tests—are one of the things students focus on the most as they work through a course. Testing is a fact of student life, but some approaches to testing are better than others when it comes to boosting learning and motivation. As you design the assessments for your course, ask yourself:

Question: How will assessments take advantage of the *testing effect?*

> THE PRINCIPLE: Tests and any activities resembling tests are highly effective at promoting retention of studied material, but students rarely take advantage of this fact when left to devise their own study routines.

> TOOLS AND TECHNIQUES:
> • Repeatable, auto-graded online quizzes
> • MERLOT quiz database
> • Publisher-supplied customizable quizzing tools

- Randomly selected spot-graded tests, for questions that can't be auto-graded—select a set proportion of answers at random for detailed grading, and grade nonselected answers for completion alone
- Framing tests as learning opportunities, not just measures of learning
- Interspersing test-like components into other learning activities, such as questions to answer while reading

Question: How will assessments function to *motivate, not demotivate* students?

THE PRINCIPLE: Students' experiences with tests and test feedback powerfully shape mindset (growth versus fixed) and can also affect academic self-efficacy.

TOOLS AND TECHNIQUES:
- Frequent, small-stakes assessments
- Early and frequent opportunities for success
- Test instructions and feedback that emphasize effort, rather than talent, intelligence, or other inborn factors
- Opportunity to compensate for early failures; multiple attempt options
- Rapid feedback, e.g., via auto-grading
- Adaptive quiz systems that automatically calibrate difficulty according to performance
- Rubric tools within learning-management systems
- Frequently updated online grade books
- Spreadsheet and calculator tools students can use to calculate their own grades

4. PEER-TO-PEER INTERACTION: HOW STUDENTS WILL LEARN
FROM ONE ANOTHER

Collaborative learning in one form or other is part of most contemporary college courses, so mindful planning of these activities is another necessary step. As you consider how you will incorporate discussion forums, group work, and other social components, ask yourself:

Question: How will you maximize the amount and quality of *online discussion?*

> THE PRINCIPLE: Discussions can be surprisingly powerful learning experiences when designed and managed the right way.
>
> TOOLS AND TECHNIQUES:
> • Discussions that start and end at set times
> • Short, tightly focused discussions that unfold over two weeks or less
> • Icebreaker or "getting to know you" discussion threads
> • Explicit civility guidelines
> • Frequent "lurking" and as-needed intervention by the instructor to keep threads on track and civil
> • Grading rubrics for discussion posts
> • Discussions tied to structured activities such as problem-based learning or case studies

Question: How will the online peer interactions *reinforce thinking skills* associated with the course learning objectives?

> THE PRINCIPLE: Through collaborative learning, students can practice many forms of higher thought, such as reflection, debate, problem solving, and critical thinking.
>
> TOOLS AND TECHNIQUES:
> • Warm-up case studies illustrating ways to head off difficulties that arise in group work

- Problem-based learning

- Group case study activities

- Role playing, with roles and supporting materials assigned by the instructor

- Wikis, such as those you can create at wikispaces.org

- Case study databases such as the National Center for Case Study Teaching in Science

- Discussion guidelines that emphasize critical thinking and presentation of evidence

5. GRADES AND OTHER INCENTIVES: HOW TO GET STUDENTS MOVING IN THE RIGHT DIRECTION

The final major course component to plan is the grading scheme, and more generally, how you will use grades and other incentives to draw out students' best efforts. As you consider how to motivate students, ask yourself:

Question: How will you discourage *procrastination?*

THE PRINCIPLE: Online coursework is notoriously subject to procrastination; unfortunately, you can't eradicate procrastination simply by imposing heavy grade penalties.

TOOLS AND TECHNIQUES:
- Small-stakes assignments

- Syllabus quizzes

- Using learning management systems' tracking functions to identify and intervene with students who don't log on early or often enough

- Intermediate work products, such as outlines, bibliographies, or rough drafts

- Getting-to-know-you discussion threads

- Expectations for how early and often students will log on

- Regular updates, active discussion threads, and other "dynamic" components on course web sites

Question: How will you balance grades with other incentives?

THE PRINCIPLE: Grades aren't the best or the only way of motivating students—rather, a complex mix of intrinsic and extrinsic motivations, self-efficacy, and self-regulated learning abilities all influence how hard students are willing to work.

TOOLS AND TECHNIQUES:
- Online pre-assessment of self-regulated learning (SRL)
- Instructional modules or other early interventions targeted at low-SRL students
- Video testimonials from successful former students
- Opportunities to remedy real or perceived deficiencies in needed skills
- Online interactions with relatable role models, such as peer TAs
- Web sites and online resources connected to real-world concerns and interests
- Web sites and online resources connected to career goals, such as professional organizations
- "Leaderboard" that shows relative student rankings in real time
- Discussion threads and other mechanisms for social connectedness among students
- Building choice and options into assignments
- Narrative-based assignments, such as role playing

Connecting Theory and Practice: A "Cognitively Optimized" Sample Course Plan

In this final section, I've laid out a fully articulated syllabus showing how the principles in this book would look when implemented in an actual course. To illustrate the connection between syllabus components and cognitive principles, I've arranged the syllabus and explanations so that the syllabus appears in the main text of the page, with explanations in boxes that link course features to specific sections from earlier in this book.

For the subject matter of this hypothetical course, I chose Introduction to Psychology. The reason for this choice is not just that it's a good match to my own disciplinary expertise; it's also one of the most popular college courses in the world, taken by about one million students annually in the United States alone.[1] I created my first fully online Introduction to Psychology course in 2003, and have worked extensively on fine-tuning it since then. The sample course here reflects not just my own work, but also my collaboration with Michael Rader. Together, we coauthored an article in the *Journal of Online Learning and Teaching* about special features of our online Introduction to Psychology course,[2] which resembles this sample class in many ways. It also draws on the ongoing course redesign project for the face-to-face version of the course, which I've worked on with a number of collaborators, including Melikşah Demir, Derrick Wirtz, Melissa Birkett, Chad Woodruff, and K. Laurie Dickson.

I chose to make this hypothetical course fully online, but it includes components that could easily be incorporated into a web-enhanced, hybrid or blended course, such as repeatable online quizzes and discussion assignments. And while some parts of it are necessarily specific to psychology, I've intended most of the examples to be adaptable to a wide array of other disciplines. For example, the course puts a big emphasis on "practical application" assignments, in which I ask students to apply material to different real-world scenarios using role-play techniques such as writing an e-mail offering advice to a friend or drafting a memo to one's supervisor. This type of technique—asking students to role-play advice-giving based on course material—would fit well in a variety of disciplines with an applied side, such as environmental science, geology, or education.

Another versatile component is the "reading matrix" students complete as part of their reading assignments. Lack of critical-reading skills is a common complaint I hear about students, especially among faculty who teach introductory-level courses. Like other thinking skills, critical reading is best taught through frequent and deliberate practice, with explicit explanation and scaffolding that bridges the gap between expert academic readers and novices. The reading matrix consists of a set of prompts students respond to as a way of summarizing what they read—questions such as *Why was this research conducted? Did the results support the researchers' hypotheses or predictions? What are the practical applications of the study's results?*[3] With minor revision, the same questions could apply to research articles in social sciences, or even the natural sciences; with some more drastic reenvisioning, you could set up a similar matrix for journalistic or fiction writing as well.

I've left out some of the logistical minutiae you'd usually see in a syllabus, such as policy statements about late work, academic honesty, and so on. In a real course syllabus, there would also normally be language or links relating to accessibility, but I have omitted these from the sample syllabus given that such information tends to vary according to local policies and resources.

The structure and scope of my hypothetical "cognitively optimized" course is reasonably realistic, but involves a bit more work for students than an introductory course typically would. This was a conscious decision on my part, intended to allow room for a wider range of activities and assessments. In a real course, the workload might be toned down by having students choose from among the different kinds of assignments, turning some weekly assignments into capstone or term projects, or offering some as extra credit.

■ SYLLABUS

PSY 101: Introduction to Psychology
College of Social and Behavioral Sciences
3 Credit Hours

About the Course

Psychology is a social science focused on understanding why individuals feel, think, and behave the way they do. When most people think of "psychology," they tend to think of psychological disorders, emotional difficulties, and therapy. It's true that these are all areas within psychology, but it's far from a complete picture of the field. Psychology focuses on all

> *Motivation: Bridging, Scaffolding, and "Hooks."* Especially at the introductory level, there are major gaps between students' conception of what psychology is about and what's actually true of the field today. Addressing this gap helps keep students engaged and motivated.

kinds of other questions about people: why the same person might act completely differently in different situations (an elevator, a classroom, a riot); whether kids turn out the way they do because of their environments, their genes, or both; why we remember some things and forget other things; how best to cope with the stresses in your life, and many more.

This course will introduce you to how psychologists use evidence to create theories about behavior and the mind, and will give you a grounding in major discoveries psychologists have made in different areas of the field. In the course, you will also have opportunities to practice applying psychological research to real-world problems, and to build critical-thinking skills as they relate to behavior and the mind.

Student Learning Outcomes for This Course

After you've successfully finished this course, you'll be able to:

- Describe and explain the major theoretical frameworks used in psychology
- Describe and explain the major discoveries and important facts from within different subfields of psychology
- Describe and explain the research methods psychologists use to gather evidence
- Apply critical thinking skills to questions about behavior and the mind
- Apply concepts and findings from psychology to real-world situations and problems

Course Structure/Approach

This is a fully online class. All activities are *asynchronous*, meaning that you don't have to be online at a set time or day. You do, however, have to complete your assignments according to firm deadlines, which you can see in the Course Schedule.

I have organized our material into five modules. Here is the breakdown of the course in terms of content (material you read), assignments (work you do), and assessments (tests):

Content

1. Textbook: D. G. Myers (2011), *Exploring Psychology* (8th ed.).
2. M. Demir, M. Birkett, K. Dickson, & M. Miller, eds. (2012), *Psychological Science in Action: Applying Psychology to Everyday Issues* (San Diego: Cognella). This reading is a compilation of brief research articles from psychology journals. The articles are all brief and relate to real-world topics such as video games, psychology in the legal system, and bullying. It also contains a guide to how to read and interpret research articles, as well as short "practical application" assignments that relate

the research articles to solving problems in the real world, such as how to reduce the incidence of bullying in the schools.

3. Interactive online multimedia lectures. These are web pages with content that helps explain and extend the material covered in the textbook. At the bottom of each page, there is a question that checks for your understanding or asks you to draw connections between different concepts that were presented. Each lecture also contains diagrams with audio narrations.

Assignments

1. Critical-Thinking wiki
2. MiniQuest assignments
3. Research application assignments
4. Discussion posts

Assessments

1. Repeatable multiple-choice quizzes (1 per chapter)
2. Non-repeatable exams (1 per module)
3. The answers you give during interactive online multimedia lectures

There is also an introductory module that orients you to the course, ensures you have the needed computer skills for the course, and introduces you to your classmates.

Grade Calculation

There are 1,000 total points in the course, assigned as follows:

ASSIGNMENTS   600 points total
Critical-thinking wikis 5 @ 20 points = 100
MiniQuest assignments 5 @ 30 points = 150
Research application assignments 5 @ 40 points = 200
Discussion assignments 15 @ 10 points = 150

ASSESSMENTS   350 points total
Repeatable multiple-choice quizzes 15 @ 10 points = 150
Non-repeatable module exams 5 @ 30 points = 150
Interactive online lectures 5 @ 10 points = 50

INTRODUCTORY MODULE   50 points total
Syllabus quiz 10 points
Discussion assignment 10 points
Online lecture: Managing Your Mind for Learning 20 points
Scavenger-hunt assignment 10 points

GRADE CUTOFFS
900–1000 A
800–899 B
700–799 C
600–699 D
599 and below F

Motivation: Procrastination. The grading scheme in the
course is built around frequent, small-stakes assignments,
which tend to be less procrastination-prone than infrequent,
high-stakes assignments. Small-stakes assignments also
provide more opportunities for success, which can enhance
academic self-efficacy. No single assignment in the course is
worth more than 4 percent of the total course grade.

Course Schedule

The course has a modular structure, with one module due every three weeks. Each module works the same way, so once you've done one, you follow the same plan every three weeks throughout the semester. The only exception is the beginning of the course, where we will also be doing a brief introductory module.

Work is due every Wednesday, Friday, and Sunday throughout the semester, always by 11:30 p.m. Repeatable quizzes and online lectures are due on Wednesday, discussion assignments are due on Friday, and all other work is due on Sunday.

> *Motivation: Sense of Mission.* Discrete, moderate-size chunks of work can build a sense of attainability and help sustain student persistence.
>
> *Attention: Assess Cognitive Load.* Especially in courses with many small-stakes assignments, just staying abreast of deadlines requires significant cognitive effort. Using the same routines and timelines for work wherever possible frees up cognitive capacity.

WEEK	MODULE	CHAPTER TOPIC	REQUIRED READING
1	Introductory and Module 1	Overview of the Field	Course Syllabus, Myers Chapter 1
2	Module 1	The Brain and Nervous System	Myers Chapter 2 Demir Chapter 1
3	Module 1	The Nature-Nurture Question; Genetics and Behavior	Myers Chapter 3
4	Module 2	Development Over the Lifespan	Myers Chapter 4
5	Module 2	Perception	Myers Chapter 6 Demir Chapter 5
6	Module 2	Consciousness, Sleep, and Attention	Myers Chapter 7
7	Module 3	Learning	Myers Chapter 8
8	Module 3	Memory	Myers Chapter 9 Demir Chapter 2
9	Module 3	Thinking and Language	Myers Chapter 10 Demir Chapter 4
10	Module 4	Motivation	Myers Chapter 12
11	Module 4	Personality	Myers Chapter 15 Demir Chapter 4
12	Module 4	Social Psychology	Myers Chapter 18
13	Module 5	Stress and Health	Myers Chapter 14
14	Module 5	Psychological Disorders	Myers Chapter 16 Demir Chapter 7
15	Module 5	Therapy	Myers Chapter 17

Week 1 works a little differently because of the introductory module, but there is still work due on Wednesday, Friday, and Sunday that week. After that, the assignments are staggered across weeks, like this: Week 1, critical-thinking wiki; Week 2, Research application assignment; Week 3, MiniQuest assignment. Module exams are always due Week 3 of each module.

> *Memory: Structure for Spaced Study.* This system of staggered deadlines takes advantage of the spacing effect and discourages extended cramming sessions.

How to Pace Your Work in This Class

This is a fast-paced class that requires you to work consistently and in a self-directed way. To succeed, you'll need to **log in to the course at least once** every weekday.

We hit the ground running, so our deadlines begin the first week of class. Work is consistently due on certain

> *Motivation: Procrastination.* Online courses need to establish clear expectations about how often students should be logging in, to discourage procrastination and help establish good habits.

days throughout the week, and we go through the same sequence of assignments and tests with every module. Below, I've made up a suggested schedule of how to pace your work across the three weeks of one module. Remember, you can always turn in work early if this schedule doesn't fit well around your other commitments. You can choose to turn your work in on Sunday, rather than on Friday, but I set up this suggested schedule so that you don't have to work on the weekend unless you prefer to.

> *Motivation: "Early and Often" Assessment Philosophy.* Having small-stakes work due as soon as practical creates a tangible demonstration of your expectations for frequent engagement, and creates opportunities for the small "wins" that support motivation.
>
> *Motivation: Procrastination.* Structure is the enemy of procrastination, so even a suggested study schedule can be helpful in an online course environment where there is a great deal of student-directed work.

WEEK 1

Monday	Read the textbook chapter for the week.
Tuesday	Complete the online lecture and repeatable quiz for the week.
Wednesday	Begin working on the *critical-thinking wiki*.
Thursday	Continue working on the critical-thinking wiki; read and participate in the week's discussions.
Friday	Complete your work on the critical- thinking wiki and turn it in. Finish participating in discussions.

WEEK 2

Monday	Read the textbook chapter for the week.
Tuesday	Complete the online lecture and repeatable quiz for the week.
Wednesday	Begin working on the *research application* assignment.
Thursday	Continue working on the research application assignment; read and participate in the week's discussions.
Friday	Complete your work on the research application assignment and turn it in. Finish participating in discussions.

WEEK 3

Monday	Read the textbook chapter for the week. Choose which *MiniQuest* assignment you'd like to do.
Tuesday	Complete the online lecture and repeatable quiz for the week.
Wednesday	Begin working on the MiniQuest assignment.
Thursday	Continue working on the MiniQuest assignment; read and participate in the week's discussions. Study for the module exam.
Friday	Complete your work on the MiniQuest assignment and turn it in. Finish participating in discussions. Complete the module exam.

Extra Credit Opportunity: Calculate Your Current Grade

You can earn 10 extra-credit points for sending me an e-mail with the following: today's date, total points earned in the class so far, percent points earned out of the possible maximum points to that date. I'll give full credit for a complete and accurate estimate; there is no penalty for inaccurate answers. You can do this up to four times for a maximum of 40 extra-credit points.

> *Motivation: Self-Directed Learning, Knowing Where You Stand.* I got this idea from my colleague James Palmer, a computer science instructor. It is a way to reward and encourage good self-directed learning practices, while getting students to practice applying the course's grading scheme. It also incorporates the "gamification" feature of full transparency / knowing your score at all times.

Details on the Assessments and Assignments

ONLINE LECTURES

The purpose of the online lectures is to extend and deepen the knowledge about psychology that you get from the textbooks. They are my way of giving you a more personalized explanation of the major concepts, adding things that the textbooks leave out, and offering demonstrations that you can do on your own. They also illus-

> *Thinking.* People reason better when they understand the purpose behind the information. Therefore, all the detailed explanations of the assignments lead with what the assignment is supposed to accomplish.

trate some of the more challenging concepts through *narrated diagrams*. Research shows that graphic narrations with audio narrations are an effective way to learn, as an alternative to just reading text.

Here is how the online lectures work: Each one is a sequence of web pages containing a combination of text, narrated diagrams, and demonstrations of different concepts in psychology. There's one lecture to go along with every textbook chapter. You read the pages in order and at your own pace. As you do so, please make a note of any questions or unclear points that you'd like to discuss with me; we can do that by e-mail or online chat.

You'll notice that at the bottom of each page, there is a short-answer question. These may ask you to explain, in your own words, a concept that was presented, offer an example, or otherwise reflect on what you just read. Keep in mind that some of these short-answer questions will show up on the module exam—so it is good practice to do your best work on these questions!

Attention: Ask Students to Respond. Alternating between presentation and student input helps keep students attentive and engaged—necessary conditions for learning.

Memory: Transfer-Appropriate Processing. Note that some of the module exam questions are short answer, not multiple choice. This practice activity helps students practice the material in the same format as the test.

Because of the large number of short-answer questions generated as the class completes the online lectures, I won't provide detailed feedback on every answer you submit. Rather, I'll give you full credit for any good-faith answer for most of the questions. I'll select a subset of answers at random for detailed grading and feedback.

Memory: Include Frequent Tests and Test-Like Activities. Frequent feedback is ideal, but the testing effect produces benefits even when there is no feedback. Thus, you can adjust grading based on your class size and other demands of the course. Choosing only some answers for detailed grading is one way to do this.

CRITICAL-THINKING WIKI

The purpose of this assignment is to build your ability to apply critical thinking to situations involving psychology. The American Psychological Association lists critical thinking as one of the main goals of psychology instruction. Critical thinking includes a number of different skills having to do with how we analyze claims and their supporting evidence. Here are some especially important ones cited by the American Psychological Association:[4]

Thinking: Critical Thinking. Research suggests that building critical-thinking skills doesn't just happen as a side effect of engaging with intellectually challenging material. Rather, it's most likely to emerge when it's intentionally targeted.

- Evaluate the quality of information, including differentiating empirical evidence from speculation and the probable from the improbable
- Identify and evaluate the source, context, and credibility of behavioral claims
- Challenge claims that arise from myth, stereotype, or untested assumptions
- Use scientific principles and evidence to resolve conflicting claims
- Recognize and defend against common fallacies in thinking
- Avoid being swayed by appeals to emotion or authority
- Evaluate popular media reports of psychological research
- Demonstrate an attitude of critical thinking that includes persistence, open-mindedness, tolerance for ambiguity, and intellectual engagement
- Identify components of arguments (e.g., conclusions, premises/ assumptions, gaps, counterarguments)
- Distinguish among assumptions, emotional appeals, speculations, and defensible evidence
- Weigh support for conclusions to determine how well reasons support conclusions

For this assignment, we will be building a "class wiki" about critical thinking—that is, a collection of web pages that you add to, plus discussion about the content of the pages. The wiki assignment works like this: For each module, I will assign a choice of critical-thinking skills from the above list—e.g., "Avoid being swayed by appeals to emotion or authority," "Identify components of arguments," "Weigh support for conclusions to determine how well reasons support conclusions." I will make a page for each skill that you can choose from.

Many learning management systems, including Blackboard Learn, have wiki tools. Alternatively, you can use freestanding wiki tools such as wikispaces.org. Wikis are particularly good for pulling together lots of student-sourced materials. They also make this material viewable to other students or even the general public, depending on what tools you use; this public display can be one way to Use Emotions (Carefully), as described in the Memory chapter.

Then it is your job to find at least one online source that illustrates this skill in the form of some claim, urban legend, or product marketing—Snopes.com has some excellent ones, or you can find your own on YouTube or similar places.

Thinking: Use Varied, Realistic Scenarios for Reasoning. Online media and web sites offer more realistic materials to work with, compared to contrived scenarios. You can put the "work" of finding them on students, making the search a part of the assignment.

On the wiki page for that skill, link in the source you found, then write a short description of it. Explain how you'd analyze or evaluate it using the critical-thinking skill. Lastly, comment on at least two of your classmate's contributions.

Thinking: Use Discussion to Build Thinking Skills. If properly set up and managed, peer-to-peer online discussion can be a particularly effective mechanism for promoting thinking skills, such as critical thinking.

Note that these sources may include topics where there is heated disagreement among individuals, such as the existence of the paranormal, social stereotypes, and so on. For this reason, I expect your comments to display the "attitude of critical thinking" described above. I'll grade your wiki assignments on the basis of how well you applied the assigned critical-thinking skills and how well your comments display the "attitudes of critical thinking" described above.

> *Memory: Involve Emotions (Carefully).* Issues like these do tend to be emotional. This emotional charge can boost memory, but has to be managed so that it doesn't become hurtful or damaging to the class atmosphere.

RESEARCH APPLICATION ASSIGNMENTS

This assignment is intended to do two main things: build your ability to critically read psychology research articles, and help you draw connections between psychology research and important real-world problems. The assignment is based on your Demir et al. textbook, *Psychological Science in Action: Applying Psychology to Everyday Issues.*

For each research application assignment, you'll read one assigned article out of this book. Then you'll do one of the assignments listed after the article. These assignments let you simulate what you'd do about a real-world problem based on ideas from the article, using techniques such as role-playing.

> *Thinking: Assign Students to Practice the Thinking Skills You Want.* These two activities tie directly to the learning goals of the course. Like critical thinking, the ability to do critical reading doesn't necessarily occur as a byproduct of doing other activities in the class, so this assignment provides deliberate practice. Nonexperts also tend to struggle with extending what they have learned to new situations and scenarios, so this assignment offers explicit practice in doing so.

> *Thinking: Set Up Varied, Realistic Scenarios for Reasoning.* Because novices at problem solving in a domain need lots of opportunities for practice, and because they have a hard time noticing commonalities in deep structure, it's helpful to vary the surface structure of examples to promote more focus on deep structural elements.

You'll also complete a reading matrix for each article. The purpose of the reading matrix is to guide you as you learn how to critically read and evaluate empirical research articles in psychology. In this matrix, you'll briefly summarize all the different parts of the article by responding to a set of questions about the purpose and conclusions of the article.

Thinking: Assign Students to Practice the Thinking Skills You Want; Expertise and Problem Solving

Memory: Include Frequent Tests and Test-Like Activities. The reading matrix assignment accomplishes at least three aspects of cognitive optimization. One, it gives focused practice on the skill we want—the ability to read, understand, and evaluate primary-source material within the discipline. Two, it gives an organizational structure to the information contained in a research article—something that experts naturally have, but novices don't. This structure, in turn, makes the information less overwhelming, more memorable, and easier to apply. Third, the question-and-answer format is similar to a short-answer self-quiz, which is an effective way to promote memory for concepts in the reading.

If you find you can't answer any of these questions, go back and reread the article until you can!

Reading Matrix[5]

SECTION	QUESTIONS	YOUR ANSWERS
Abstract	Are there any unfamiliar or jargon terms used in the abstract? If so, what do they mean? What is the study about? Who participated in the study? What was the main research method used in the study?	

(continued)

SECTION	QUESTIONS	YOUR ANSWERS
Introduction	Why was this research conducted?	
	What are the main theories that are important in this research?	
	Are there any major differences of opinion about this research area, and if so, what are they?	
	What do we already know about this topic?	
	What do we not know about this topic?	
	What is the author's research question or hypothesis?	
Method	What did participants do from the time they started the study to when they completed the study?	
	What was the main technique used in this study?	
	Why did the researchers set the study up in this way?	
Results	How did the researchers quantify the responses they got?	
	Did the groups or treatment conditions produce different patterns of results? If so, what were the patterns?	
	Did the results support the researchers' hypotheses or predictions?	
	Were you surprised by the results?	
Discussion	Can you summarize the study's findings and why they are important? Can you explain why the results came out the way they did?	
	Did the Discussion section answer questions raised in the Introduction?	
	What are the practical applications of the study's results?	
	Do current theories need to change based on the results of the study?	
	Do you agree with the authors' interpretation of the results?	
	What is the single most important thing this study tells us about behavior and/or the mind?	
References	Are references included?	

Readings and Assignments in the Demir et al. Book

Module 1:

Chapter 1, *An introduction to empirical research articles in psychology.*

Assignment:

"Your best friend Chelsea comes to you for advice, knowing that you are taking a psychology course. In one of her classes, her instructor asked the students to find a peer-reviewed article about happiness. Chelsea found a two-page article on happiness in *O, The Oprah Magazine* and asked you if it is a peer-reviewed article. First answer her question, and then explain what counts as a peer-review article and briefly summarize the process involved."

> *Motivation: Scaffolding.* This article explains why peer-reviewed journal articles are different from other things students might read about psychology, and breaks down the structure of a typical article (literature review, method, results, discussion, and so forth). This provides context and scaffolding for the articles that students read in later modules.

Module 2:

Chapter 5, *Biological psychology: Exercise and the brain.*

Assignment:

"As your first job after college, you are hired to design and coordinate activities for the residents of a local nursing home. Your supervisor has asked you to plan a six-month schedule of events for the residents, and her only directive to you is 'to include some type of physical exercise for the residents' in your schedule. You know that many of the residents suffer from memory deficits, and you would like to plan some physical activities that might help them improve their memory. According to the research presented in this article, not all types of physical exercise increase the volume of the hippocampus or are associated with improved memory. Plan a six-month calendar of activities to present to your supervisor, including a variety of activities intended to help improve residents' memory. List these activities, and include a brief explanation of why you chose the ones you did and any other reasoning that you used to formulate your plan."

Module 3:

Chapter 2, *Cognitive psychology: Do college students know how to study effectively?*

Assignment:

"You've learned that a good friend from high school is having some difficulty coping with the academic demands of college. Your friend puts in plenty of time studying and is highly motivated, but just seems to 'blank out' on exams. Write an e-mail to your friend giving advice on how to study better, based on applied memory research. Be sure to include the following concepts AND explain them in your own words: testing effect, illusions of competence, and rereading. Also, include at least one other memory-related concept of your choosing."

Module 4:

Chapter 7, *Social psychology: Gratitude and psychosocial well-being.*

Assignment:

"Imagine the following scenario: You have just been hired as a consultant for a documentary at a national news media station. The station is working on a documentary that claims that what individuals experience in their lives is based on random occurrences, and they should focus on what they want to do with their lives rather than trying to understand why these events happened. Prepare a brief report for your boss that includes two suggestions about how individuals might benefit from displaying grateful thinking in their lives as opposed to accepting occurrences as random."

Module 5:

Chapter 12, *Health psychology: Social networks and physical health.*

Assignment:

"Imagine that two older family members have recently suffered heart attacks. One family member lives alone and has few visitors or close friends or family members. The other lives with his spouse and visits his children and grandchildren regularly. Based on the information presented in this article, what predictions might you make for the recovery or long-term health of your family members? Write an e-mail message to your family physician explaining any concerns you may have about your family members, focusing on the relationship between social networks and health."

Discussion Assignments

Discussion assignments accomplish several different things in this class. First, they provide an opportunity for you to get to know and learn from other students. They also let you see the diversity of different viewpoints on psychological issues, while en-

> *Thinking: Use Discussion to Build Thinking Skills.* Students may not realize it, but discussion posts can be a substantive learning exercise, especially when they get guidance about what and how to post.

couraging you to explore psychology as it relates to your own life. Lastly, discussions encourage you to think about material in ways that make it more memorable and easier to comprehend.

Research shows that students who participate in discussions earn better grades in online courses. It's important, therefore, that you participate frequently and put thought into what you post. Research also tells us that communicating online creates some concerns that we wouldn't normally have in a face-to-face discussion. Online, what you say tends to come across as more negative or critical than it would in a regular conversation, even when you're just trying to joke around. It's also easy to treat someone more harshly than you would normally, due to the lack of nonverbal signals, expressions, and so forth. Therefore, in this class, I want you to make a special effort to make sure that you treat each other with RESPECT and KINDNESS in your online communications. Feel free to disagree with one another (and with me), but be sure that you are criticizing the idea and not the person. I reserve the right to delete posts that I find insulting, disparaging toward particular groups of people, or otherwise damaging to our online community.

Discussion assignments work like this: Each week, there will be three different kinds of discussion. Within each type, there are a choice of several different discussion threads you can participate in. You're required to participate in at least ONE from each of the three types. Participation means posting at least one substantive response of your own, and replying to at least two other people. This is the minimum requirement, but you're welcome to participate in as many threads as often as you'd like.

Discussion Types (participate in each one each week):

1. Personalize It! This kind of discussion asks you to relate the week's material to your own life, using experiences you've had or your own opinions. Remember, share only what you feel comfortable sharing, and you'll have a choice of topics so you need not get involved in a discussion you're uncomfortable with. Post your own experiences, and respond to at least two other students' posts: Have you had a similar experience? Are there any supportive comments you can offer? What do you think these experiences mean?

Memory: Steer Students into Deep Processing. One of the "deepest" forms of processing is self-reference—how information fits into the context of one's own self-concept and past experiences.

Example: One day, researchers may be able to erase painful memories, like they did in the movie *Eternal Sunshine of the Spotless Mind.* If you could erase your worst memory, would you choose to do so? Why or why not? What does this tell us about memory in general?

Memory: Base New Knowledge on Old Knowledge. The assignment asks students to elaborate on what they learned so far and draw links between it and the current material being learned.

Thinking: Use Analogies (the Right Way). This discussion primes students to draw analogies among different concepts in the course, which would likely be more effective than passively viewing analogies that the instructor generates. Because student-generated analogies can contain errors, it's important for the instructor to participate in a discussion like this to correct any misconceptions.

---

2. Relate Old to New. This kind of discussion asks you to explore and explain the linkages between what we already learned in the course thus far and the week's new material.

Each week, I'll assign one person to moderate and guide the discussion, and one person to summarize the discussion at the end. I'll subdivide the class into different assigned groups so that the groups aren't too large.

> *Thinking: Use Discussion to Build Thinking Skills.* This is one technique for promoting more-meaningful engagement in peer-to-peer discussions.

Example: This week, we are studying *learning.* Each person in the group should post an explanation linking some concept in learning to an earlier concept we've covered in the class. Be sure that you identify all the concepts using correct terminology. Then, respond to at least two classmate's posts: Do you see the connections that they do? Is there anything you could add to their explanations? Do you have questions about anything they said, or are there points that are unclear?

3. **Psychology in the Media.** This kind of discussion asks you to link course material to the wider culture as portrayed in the media. This will include threads on classic media, fictional series and movies, and current events.

Memory: Base New Knowledge on Old Knowledge. Most college-age students have extensive knowledge about at least some aspects of popular media, and thus this can form a basis for encoding new course material.

Motivation: Intrinsic Interest. Similarly, most college students have extensive interest in popular media; this interest can become a "hook" to draw them further into course concepts, such as visual perception, that aren't intrinsically interesting to most people.

Example: From *Star Wars* to *The Lord of the Rings* to *The Dark Knight Rises,* movie special effects just keep getting better. Describe one or more of your favorite effects, offer some ideas about how the effect was created, and then tell us why you think the effect fooled the visual system so well. Be sure to incorporate concepts from the Sensation and Perception chapter.

MiniQuest Assignments

The purpose of MiniQuests is to give you a variety of different ways to practice thinking skills as they relate to psychology, and to apply the material in new ways that appeal to you. Each module will have a set of different MiniQuests for you to choose from. **Pick one**, then read the directions carefully. Each MiniQuest is unique, so be sure you understand what you need to do before starting, and be sure to allow plenty of time to work on it.

> *Motivation: Games and "Gamification."* Here I've borrowed from some of the language of multiplayer games to describe small, diverse assignments that students can pick and choose from. An open-ended assignment format like this is one way to incorporate a variety of activities such as simulations, role-playing exercises, case studies, analogies, and more.

Example MiniQuests

Sniffy the Virtual Rat. "Sniffy" is

a program you can run on your computer to simulate what it is like to train a rodent using operant conditioning principles. Running Sniffy is fun and intuitive once you get started, but there are several steps to the assignment.

Step One: Review Important Concepts in Operant Learning. This exercise

requires you to understand the following concepts having to do

> *Multimedia: Simulations.* Sniffy provides a realistic replication of important aspects of operant conditioning (learning from rewards and punishment). It also provides a few useful things a real rodent can't, such as a graphic illustration of what is going on in Sniffy's mind as he goes through the learning process (the so-called "mind window").

with learning: reinforcement, operant conditioning, shaping. Please go over these concepts to be sure that you understand them.

Step Two: Download Sniffy the Virtual Rat. Go to the following web site: http://www.wadsworth.com/psychology_d/templates /student_resources/0534633609_sniffy2/sniffy/download.htm.

There are two links to the demo version of the program, one for Windows and one for Macintosh. Click on whichever one is appropriate for your computer.

Step Three: Familiarize Yourself with the Sniffy Program. On the same page where you download the demo, click on and run the Tutorials labeled Overview and Project 2.

Step Four: Exercises. Locate Exercises 22 and 23; read the instructions and complete the exercises.

Step Five: Written Report. Write up an approximately 500-word essay reflecting and reporting on your experiences with Sniffy. Be sure to cover the following:

- About how long did it take you to "magazine-train" Sniffy?

- Is there anything surprising you notice about the training processes?

- What strategies seemed particularly successful when shaping Sniffy to press the bar?

- How high are the different bars in the Operant Associations "mind window" at the beginning and end of training?

Playing with Neurons. The way that neurons communicate is complex, but in some ways it resembles processes in the everyday world. In this assignment, make up a game that would teach people about some aspect of neural processing. It's up to you how to configure your game, but in your assignment, turn in at least a 500-word essay describing the game. In your essay, be sure to cover at least the following:

Motivation: Games and "Gamification." One way to introduce games is to have students generate them.

Thinking: Use Analogies (the Right Way). This is another example of student-generated analogy. For example, students might draw analogies between people racing to do "the Wave" and how messages are transmitted from one neuron to the next. The source analogy would be well known, as students would use concrete concepts from everyday life.

- What are the main concept or concepts the game is supposed to illustrate? (Be sure to use correct terminology)
- How is the game played?
- What are the rules?
- Are there any variations, special equipment needed, or other important details?

Learn Lucid Dreaming. As we learned about in the section on sleep, lucid dreaming is the state of being aware that one is dreaming and being able to consciously control one's dreams. **Be sure to start this MiniQuest at least one week before it is due to allow adequate time to complete the process**. Lucid dreaming is a learnable skill, and can be promoted by a number of different techniques. This MiniQuest asks you to learn more about lucid dreaming research, then to try lucid dreaming techniques yourself; lastly, you'll document and reflect on what happened during this experience.

Motivation: Intrinsic Interest; Memory: Involve Emotions (Carefully). Most people are intrinsically very intrigued by dreams and what they mean. In contemporary psychology, however, there isn't much emphasis on dreams as important phenomena. One exception is the lucid-dreaming phenomenon described here. Dreams are also emotionally charged for most people, and embarking on the effort to change and redirect dreams is a surprising, emotionally charged experience.

Step One: Learn more about lucid dreaming. Read the following research article about lucid dreaming, being sure to apply the reading techniques you've been learning about in the Demir et al. book. Fill out a reading matrix for this article. Find one web site about lucid dreaming. Does it seem to say the same things that the article authors said?

Thinking: Assign Students to Practice the Thinking Skills You Want. This MiniQuest requires further practice of the critical-reading skills that are a major objective of the course.

Step Two: Using the sources you read, create a multiday plan for learning how to lucid dream.

Step Three: Carry out the plan, fine-tuning as you go, if necessary. Keep a daily journal to record what happens as you go.

Step Four: Turn in a written report consisting of the following:

- Your reading matrix for the article you read
- A link and description of the web site you found
- Your written plan
- Description of what happened when you carried out the plan. (You don't have to include any personal notes or descriptions of your actual dreams.)

Repeatable Quizzes

The purpose of the repeatable quizzes is to help you learn and remember the concepts presented in the textbook chapters. Unlike most quizzes and tests you've encountered before, these are intended as learning activities in and of themselves. Research shows that quizzing is a particularly effective way to learn information quickly, thus these quizzes are set up to encourage you to test yourself early and often as you read each chapter.

> *Memory: Include Frequent Tests and Test-Like Activities.* Learning management systems make it feasible to generate and auto-grade infinitely many attempts, given a big enough bank of reusable questions. Given what we know about the testing effect, quizzing is one of the best ways to promote learning using technology.

The quizzes work like this: There is one repeatable quiz for each assigned chapter. You can take the quiz as many times as you like, and **only the highest grade counts**. There are fifteen questions per quiz attempt, and you get thirty minutes each time. Each attempt will consist of questions randomly selected from a large database of questions, so you usually won't see the same question more than once. You'll see your score immediately after you click Submit on the quiz.

> *Memory: The Testing Effect.* There are different ways to handle scoring and feedback, based on your own preferences, concerns about test bank security, and so on. Because the testing effect holds up even when students get no feedback, you can delay or even refrain from giving students the right answers when scoring quizzes, and still reap benefits from testing.

Because the quizzes are repeatable and only the highest one counts, there's no risk associated with making lots of tries, even if you haven't finished the chapter yet or aren't sure you have mastered it. Each try lets you practice the material, so even if you've gotten a perfect score already, it still benefits you to keep doing attempts up to the deadline. Also, I sometimes choose questions from the quizzes to put on the module exams, so the more attempts you do, the better chance you'll get to preview a question on the upcoming module exam.

> *Motivation: Games and "Gamification."* Note that setting the quizzes up like this encourages students to approach them with a "game-like" mindset, in which there are opportunities to overcome early failures and in which failure can be a useful experience.

Module Exams

The purpose of the module exams is to encourage you to revisit and integrate across the three chapters within each module. Each module exam covers material from the textbook chapters and online lectures; well before the exam is due, I'll post a list of learning objectives that can serve as your study guide. The format is half multiple choice and half short answer. The style and scope of the questions are the same as the questions on the repeatable quizzes and online lectures, so these two activities are particularly useful study opportunities for module exams.

Introductory Module

The introductory module is a collection of activities designed to familiarize you with the setup of the course and the way the different online tools work, and to introduce you to your classmates. It is due the first week of class, and I suggest you start working on it on Day 1. Here are the different parts of the assignment:

> *Motivation: "Early and Often" Assessment Philosophy.* Even a small orientation assignment can set up online students in a positive pattern of frequently logging in, and set a tone of high expectations.

Discussion. Participate in the class getting-to-know-you discussion thread. Tell us a little about yourself, then complete the sentence: "When

> *Motivation: Procrastination.* Be clear about how often you want students to log in.

you think of me, picture . . . ." Contribute at least one original post and reply to at least two of your classmates' posts.

Syllabus Quiz. This is a multiple-choice quiz that covers information in the syllabus, including how often you are expected to log in. You can attempt the quiz twice and keep only your highest score.

Using Course Technology. This part consists of a few specific tasks I'd like you to do so that you'll be familiar with the online aspects of the course. These include:

> *Attention: Assess Cognitive Load.* Even "digital native" students often struggle with the technical aspects of online learning, and this drains off cognitive resources needed for learning. A quick "walk-through" at the beginning of class can help ensure that students are focused on course concepts, not the technology.

1. Send me an e-mail using the Message function within the course. In this e-mail, explain how students can get assistance with any technical problems they might run into, and be sure to include the university tech support phone number.

2. Contribute to the "Study Tips" wiki. (This will give you practice for the Critical Thinking wiki assignment.) Find the page that I've created and make at least one entry on the page. Link at least one online resource (web page, video, or other media) to your entry. Comment on at least two other students' entries.

3. Submit work using the Assignments tool. Locate the research application assignment and read over it carefully. Then, go back to Assignments and submit a 250- to 400-word explanation summarizing the main points of the research application assignment. Be sure to talk about how the reading matrix part works.

4. Complete the "Managing Your Mind" online lecture. This is a short module with interactive demonstrations and explanations of how to maximize learning by respecting the way attention and memory work. In particular, you'll learn how multitasking during learning actually costs you time and effort, rather than saving it.

Attention: Discourage Divided Attention. This module explicitly teaches students about the limitations of attention, the relationship between memory and attention, and the costs of dividing attention. Most people, students included, have a highly unrealistic concept of their own attentional capacity, something this module would deliberately target. This is especially relevant in an online context, given the abundant opportunities for distraction.

Notes

Acknowledgments

Index

Notes

PREFACE

1. A. W. Chickering and S. C. Ehrmann (1996), Implementing the seven principles: Technology as lever, in *The Seven Principles: TLT Ideas and Resources* (retrieved from http://www.tltgroup.org/programs/seven.html).

2. A. W. Chickering and Z. F. Gamson (1987, March), Seven principles for good practice in undergraduate education, *AAHE Bulletin*, 3–7.

1. IS ONLINE LEARNING HERE TO STAY?

1. I. E. Allen, J. Seaman, and C. Sloan (2011), *Going the distance: Online education in the United States, 2011* (Research Report No. 978-0-9840-2881-8; retrieved from http://www.babson.edu/Academics/centers/blank-center/global -research/Documents/going-the-distance.pdf).

2. D. Youngberg (2012, August 13), Why online education won't replace college—yet, *Chronicle of Higher Education* (retrieved from http://www.chronicle .com).

3. S. Thrun (2012, October), Democratizing higher education (keynote address presented at the International Conference on Online Learning, Orlando, FL).

4. D. G. Oblinger, J. M. Wilson, and C. Thille (2013), The digital revolution: Online innovations that strengthen completion and quality (plenary session presented at the annual meeting of the Association of American Colleges and Universities, Atlanta).

5. W. G. Bowen (2013), *Higher Education in the Digital Age* (Amazon Kindle version).

6. Learned Luddites (2013, October 12), *Economist*, 41; S. Kolowich (2013, May 2), Why professors at San Jose State won't use a Harvard professor's

MOOC, *Chronicle of Higher Education* (retrieved from http://www.chronicle .com).

7. S. Kolowich (2013, May 6), Faculty backlash grows against online partnerships, *Chronicle of Higher Education* (retrieved from http://www.chronicle .com); S. Kolowich (2013, August 1), California puts MOOC bill on ice, *Chronicle of Higher Education* (retrieved from http://www.chronicle.com).

8. S. Kolowich (2013, August 1), California puts MOOC bill on ice, *Chronicle of Higher Education* (retrieved from http://www.chronicle.com).

9. S. Kolowich (2013, February 4), Georgia Tech and Coursera try to recover from MOOC stumble, *Chronicle of Higher Education* (retrieved from http://www.chronicle.com).

10. R. Wellen (2013), Open access, megajournals, and MOOCs: On the political economy of academic unbundling, *SageOpen* 3(4), doi:10.1177 /2158244013507271.

11. I. E. Allen and J. Seaman (2013, November), Tracking MOOCs: Who, what, when, and why? (paper presented at the Annual Sloan Consortium International Conference on Online Learning, Orlando, FL).

12. D. Koller (2013, November), The online revolution: Learning without limits (keynote address presented at the Annual Sloan Consortium International Conference on Online Learning, Orlando, FL).

13. A. Agarwal (2013, November), Reinventing education (keynote address presented at the Annual Sloan Consortium International Conference on Online Learning, Orlando, FL).

14. F. Donoghue (2012, September 13), Online learning: Final concerns (blog post, retrieved from http://chronicle.com/blogs/innovations/online -learning-final-concerns/29947).

15. S. C. Ehrmann (1995), Asking the right questions, *Change: The Magazine of Higher Learning* 27(2): 20–27.

16. Ibid.; C. Twigg (2005), Increasing success for underserved students: Redesigning introductory courses (monograph, retrieved from http://www.then cat.org/Monographs/IncSuccess.pdf).

17. T. Walsh (2011), *Unlocking the Gates: How and Why Leading Universities Are Opening Up Access to Their Courses* (Amazon Kindle version).

18. J. Klor de Alva (2010, October 31), For profit learning is cheaper and other myths, *Chronicle of Higher Education* (retrieved from http://www.chronicle .com).

19. M. Parry (2011, August 28), Online venture energizes vulnerable college, *Chronicle of Higher Education* (retrieved from http://www.chronicle .com).

20. See, e.g., D. G. Oblinger and J. L. Oblinger (2005), Is it age or IT: First steps toward educating the net generation, in *Educating the Net Generation*, ed. D. G. Oblinger and J. L. Oblinger (EDUCAUSE); and M. Prensky (2001), Digital natives, digital immigrants, *On the Horizon* 9(5) (retrieved from http://www .marcprensky.com/writing/Prensky%20- %20Digital%20Natives,%20Digital %20Immigrants%20-%20Part1.pdf).

21. A. Koutropoulos (2011), Digital natives: Ten years after, *Journal of Online Learning & Teaching* 7(4): 525–538; S. Lohnes and C. Kinzer (2007), Questioning assumptions about students' expectations about technology in college

classrooms, *Innovate: Journal of Online Education* 3(5) (retrieved from http://www.innovateonline.info/).

22. A. Koutropoulos (2011), Digital natives: Ten years after, *Journal of Online Learning & Teaching* 7(4): 525–538.

23. T. Kidd (2005), Key aspects affecting students' perception regarding the instructional quality of online and web based courses, *International Journal of Instructional Technology & Distance Learning* 10(2) (retrieved from http://www.itdl.org/Journal/Oct_05/).

24. Home page, *Online Learning Mag* (2013) (retrieved from http://online learningmag.com).

25. J. Jones (2012, August 5), You've got mail: And better things to do, *Chronicle of Higher Education* (retrieved from http://chronicle.com/).

26. L. T. Benjamin (2002), Lecturing, in *The Teaching of Psychology: Essays in Honor of Wilbert J. McKeachie and Charles L. Brewer*, ed. S. F. Davis and W. Buskist, 57–67 (Mahwah, NJ: Lawrence Erlbaum Associates).

27. S. Kosslyn (2011), *Better PowerPoint: Quick Fixes Based on How Your Audience Thinks* (Amazon Kindle version).

28. E. R. Tufte (2003), Power corrupts—PowerPoint corrupts absolutely, *Research Technology Management* 46(6): 62.

29. D. A. Bligh (2000), *What's the Use of Lectures?* (San Francisco: Jossey-Bass); K. Wilson and J. H. Korn (2007), Attention during lectures: Beyond ten minutes, *Teaching of Psychology* 34(2): 85–89.

30. E. Mazur (1991, January/February), Can we teach computers to teach? *Computers in Physics*, 31–38.

31. See, e.g., C. Wieman and K. Perkins (2005), Transforming physics education, *Physics Today* 56(11) (retrieved from http://www.physicstoday.org/vol-58/iss-11/p36.shtml).

32. S. C. Ehrmann (1995), Asking the right questions: What does research tell us about technology and higher learning? in *Flashlight Evaluation Handbook* (retrieved from http://www.tltgroup.org/flashlightP.htm).

33. For a detailed description of the Math Emporium and its cost impacts see J. D. Toma (2010), *Building Organizational Capacity: Strategic Management in Higher Education* (Baltimore: Johns Hopkins University Press).

34. National Center for Academic Transformation (2005), *Impact on Students: Virginia Tech* (retrieved from http://www.thencat.org/PCR/R1/VT/VT_FR1.htm).

35. National Center for Academic Transformation (2005), *Impact on Students: University of Idaho* (retrieved from http://www.thencat.org/PCR/R2/UId/UId_FR1.htm).

36. C. Twigg (2003, September/October), Improving quality and reducing costs: New models for online learning, *EDUCAUSE Review* (retrieved from https://net.educause.edu/ir/library/pdf/erm0352.pdf).

37. National Center for Academic Transformation (2005), *Impact on Students: The University of Tennessee, Knoxville* (retrieved from http://www.thencat.org/PCR/R2/UTK/UTK_FR1.htm).

38. National Center for Academic Transformation (2005), *Impact on Students: Florida Gulf Coast University* (retrieved from http://www.thencat.org/PCR/R3/FGCU/FGCU_FR1.htm).

39. C. Twigg (2005), Increasing success for underserved students: Redesigning introductory courses (monograph, retrieved from http://www.thencat .org/Monographs/IncSuccess.pdf).

40. K. L. Dickson, M. D. Miller, and D. Wirtz (2009), Introduction to Psychology redesign: Student success and active student involvement through technology and team-teaching (unpublished grant proposal, Department of Psychology, Northern Arizona University, Flagstaff).

41. For full details of the redesign plan and impacts see NCAT's report at http://www.thencat.org/States/AZ/Abstracts/NAU%20Psychology_Abstract .htm.

2. ONLINE LEARNING: DOES IT WORK?

1. I. Allen and J. Seaman (2012), Conflicted: Faculty and online education, 2012 (retrieved from http://www.eric.ed.gov/contentdelivery/servlet/ERICServ let?accno=ED535214); J. Seaman (2012, October), Sloan-C online learning report: Will the real online learning please stand up? (paper presented at the Annual Sloan Consortium International Conference on Online Learning, Orlando, FL).

2. A. W. Chickering and S. C. Ehrmann (1996), Implementing the seven principles: Technology as lever, in *The Seven Principles: TLT Ideas and Resources* (retrieved from http://www.tltgroup.org/programs/seven.html).

3. P. Babcock and M. Marks (2011), The falling time cost of college: Evidence from half a century of time use data, *Review of Economics & Statistics* 93(2): 467–478.

4. R. Arum and J. Roksa (2011), *Academically Adrift: Limited Learning on College Campuses* (Chicago: University of Chicago Press).

5. A. W. Chickering and S. C. Ehrmann (1996), Implementing the seven principles: Technology as lever, in *The Seven Principles: TLT Ideas and Resources* (retrieved from http://www.tltgroup.org/programs/seven.html).

6. J. V. Boettcher (2011), *Ten Best Practices for Teaching Online: Quick Guide for New Online Faculty* (retrieved from http://www.designingforlearning.info /services/writing/ecoach/tenbest.html).

7. A. W. Chickering and Z. F. Gamson (1987), Seven principles for good practice in undergraduate education, *AAHE Bulletin*, 3–7.

8. See, e.g., E. Mazur (1991) Can we teach computers to teach? *Computers in Physics*, January/February 1991, 31–38; C. Wieman and K. Perkins (2005), Transforming physics education, *Physics Today* 56(11) (retrieved from http:// www.physicstoday.org/vol-58/iss-11/p36.shtml).

9. C. Twigg (1999), Improving learning and reducing costs: Redesigning large-enrollment courses (monograph, retrieved from http://www.thencat.org /Monographs/ImpLearn.html); N. Dabbagh and B. Bannan-Ritland (2005), *Online Learning: Concepts, Strategies, and Application* (Upper Saddle River, NJ: Pearson Education Inc.).

10. J. D. Bransford, A. L. Brown, and R. C. Cocking (2000), *How People Learn: Brain, Mind, Experience, and School* (Washington, DC: National Academies Press).

11. S. A. Ambrose, M. W. Bridges, M. DiPietro, M. C. Lovett, and M. K. Norman (2010), *How Learning Works: Seven Research-Based Principles for Smart Teaching* (Amazon Kindle version).

12. See, e.g., J. V. Boettcher (2011), *Ten Best Practices for Teaching Online: Quick Guide for New Online Faculty* (retrieved from http://www.designingfor learning.info/services/writing/ecoach/tenbest.html); Center for Teaching and Learning, University of Maryland University College (n.d.), *Best Practices for Online Teaching* (retrieved from http://www.umuc.edu/facultydevelopment upload/bestpractices.pdf).

13. M. D. Dickey (2005), Engaging by design: How engagement strategies in popular computer and video games can inform instructional design, *Educational Technology Research and Development* 53(2): 67–83.

14. See, e.g., A. H. Almala (2006), Applying the principles of constructivism to a quality e-learning environment, *Distance Learning . . . for Educators, Trainers, and Leaders* 3(1): 33–40; S. Hrastinski (2008), Asynchronous and synchronous e-learning, *EDUCAUSE Quarterly* 31(4): 51–55; C. Wei, N. Chen, and Kinshuk (2012), A model for social presence in online classrooms, *Educational Technology Research and Development* 60(3): 529–545.

15. D. M. Finnegan (2006), E-learning success: Readability versus reading skill, *International Journal of Instructional Technology and Distance Learning* 10 (retrieved from http://www.itdl.org/Journal/Oct_06/article04.htm).

16. Ibid.

17. B. P. Woodfine, M. Nunes, and D. J. Wright (2008), Text-based synchronous e-learning and dyslexia: Not necessarily the perfect match! *Computers & Education* 50(3): 703–717.

18. J. A. Short, E. Williams, and B. Christie (1976), *The Social Psychology of Telecommunication* (London: John Wiley); C. Tu and M. McIsaac (2002), The relationship of social presence and interaction in online classes, *American Journal of Distance Education* 16(3): 131–150, doi:10.1207/S15389286AJDE1603_2; C. Wei, N. Chen, and Kinshuk (2012), A model for social presence in online classrooms, *Educational Technology Research and Development* 60(3): 529–545.

19. C. Wei, N. Chen, and Kinshuk (2012), A model for social presence in online classrooms, *Educational Technology Research and Development* 60(3): 529–545.

20. T. Kidd (2005), Key aspects affecting students' perception regarding the instructional quality of online and web based courses, *International Journal of Instructional Technology & Distance Learning* 10(2) (retrieved from http:// www.itdl.org/Journal/Oct_05/).

21. U.S. Department of Education, Office of Planning, Evaluation, and Policy Development (2010), *Evaluation of Evidence-Based Practices in Online Learning: A Meta-analysis and Review of Online Learning Studies* (Washington, DC: Government Printing Office).

22. M. Shachar and Y. Neumann (2010), Twenty years of research on the academic performance differences between traditional and distance learning: Summative meta-analysis and trend examination, *Journal of Online Learning and Teaching* 6(2) (retrieved from http://jolt.merlot.org/vol6no2/shachar_0610 .htm).

23. W. G. Bowen, M. M. Chingos, K. A. Lack, and T. I. Nygren (2012), Interactive learning at public universities: Evidence from randomized trials (retrieved from ITHAKA S+R web site: http://www.sr.ithaka.org).

24. See, e.g., D. Youngberg (2012, August 13), Why online education won't replace college—yet, *Chronicle of Higher Education* (retrieved from http://chronicle.com/); K. Parker, A. Lenhart, and K. Moore (2011), The digital revolution and higher education: College presidents, public differ on value of online learning (retrieved from Pew Internet & American Life Project web site, http://www.pewsocialtrends.org/files/2011/08/online-learning.pdf).

25. D. Stuber-McEwen, P. Wiseley, and S. Hoggatt (2009), Point, click, and cheat: Frequency and type of academic dishonesty in the virtual classroom, *Online Journal of Distance Learning Administration* 12(3) (retrieved from http://www.westga.edu/~distance/ojdla/fall123/stuber123.html).

26. D. F. Crown and M. S. Spiller (1998), Learning from the literature on collegiate cheating: A review of the empirical literature. *Journal of Business Ethics* 17(6): 683–700; K. Kennedy, S. Nowak, R. Raghuraman, J. Thomas, and S. F. Davis (2000), Academic dishonesty and distance learning: Student and faculty views, *College Student Journal* 34(2): 309–314; D. Youngberg (2012, August 13), Why online education won't replace college—yet, *Chronicle of Higher Education* (retrieved from http://chronicle.com/); J. R. Young (2012, June 3), Online classes see cheating go high-tech, *Chronicle of Higher Education* (retrieved from http://chronicle.com/).

27. D. Berrett (2012, August 21), An academic ghostwriter, the "shadow scholar," comes clean, *Chronicle of Higher Education* (retrieved from http://chronicle.com/).

28. D. Bartram (2009), The international test commission guidelines on computer-based and Internet-delivered testing, *Industrial and Organizational Psychology* 2:11–13.

29. G. G. Smith, D. Ferguson, and M. Caris (2003), The Web versus the classroom: Instructor experiences in discussion-based and mathematics-based disciplines, *Journal of Educational Computing Research* 29:29–59; R. Roach (2001, June 7), Safeguarding against online cheating, *Black Issues in Higher Education* 92.

30. C. Nowell and D. Laufer (1997), Undergraduate student cheating in the fields of business and economics, *Journal of Economic Education* 28(1): 3–12; O. R. Harmon and J. Lambrinos (2008), Are online exams an invitation to cheat? *Journal of Economic Education* 39(2): 116–125, doi:10.3200/JECE.39.2.116–125.

31. T. C. Grijalva, C. Nowell, and J. Kerkvliet (2006), Academic honesty and online courses, *College Student Journal* 40(1): 180–185; J. Kerkvliet (1994), Cheating by economics students: A comparison of survey results, *Journal of Economic Education* 25(2): 121–133.

32. L. Hart and L. Morgan (2010), Academic integrity in an online registered nurse to baccalaureate nursing program, *Journal of Continuing Education in Nursing* 41(11): 498–505, doi:10.3928/00220124-20100701-03; D. Stuber-McEwen, P. Wiseley, and S. Hoggatt (2009), Point, click, and cheat: Frequency and type of academic dishonesty in the virtual classroom, *Online Journal of Distance Learning Administration* 12(3) (retrieved from http://www.westga.edu/~distance/ojdla/fall123/stuber123.html); G. Watson and J. Sottile (2012),

Cheating in the digital age: Do students cheat more in online courses? *Online Journal of Distance Learning Administration* 13(1).

33. T. C. Grijalva, C. Nowell, and J. Kerkvliet (2006), Academic honesty and online courses, *College Student Journal* 40(1): 180–185.

34. O. R. Harmon and J. Lambrinos (2008), Are online exams an invitation to cheat? *Journal of Economic Education* 39(2): 116–125, doi:10.3200/JECE.39.2.116–125; M. M. Lanier (2006), Academic integrity and distance learning, *Journal of Criminal Justice Education* 17(2): 244–261, doi:10.1080/10511250600866166.

35. K. Kennedy, S. Nowak, R. Raghuraman, J. Thomas, and S. F. Davis (2000), Academic dishonesty and distance learning: Student and faculty views, *College Student Journal* 34(2): 309–314; G. Watson and J. Sottile (2012), Cheating in the digital age: Do students cheat more in online courses? *Online Journal of Distance Learning Administration* 13(1).

36. J. Lang (2013), *Cheating Lessons: Learning from Academic Dishonesty* (Amazon Kindle version).

37. M. D. Miller (2009), What the science of cognition tells us about instructional technology, *Change: The Magazine of Higher Learning* 41:71–74.

38. C. G. King, R. W. Guyette, and C. Piotrowski (2009), Online exams and cheating: An empirical analysis of business students' views, *Journal of Educators Online* 6(1) (Retrieved from http://files.eric.ed.gov/fulltext/EJ904058.pdf).

39. D. L. R. Jones (2011), Academic dishonesty: Are more students cheating? *Business Communication Quarterly* 74(2): 141–150, doi:10.1177/1080569911404059; C. G. King, R. W. Guyette, and C. Piotrowski (2009), Online exams and cheating: An empirical analysis of business students' views, *Journal of Educators Online* 6(1) (Retrieved from http://files.eric.ed.gov/fulltext/EJ904058.pdf).

40. J. Baron and S. M. Crooks (2005), Academic integrity in web based distance education, *TechTrends* 49(2): 40–45.

41. A. M. Krsak (2007), Curbing academic dishonesty in online courses. *TCC* 2007 Proceedings, 159–170 (retrieved from http://etec.hawaii.edu/proceedings /2007/krsak.pdf).

42. D. L. R. Jones (2011), Academic dishonesty: Are more students cheating? *Business Communication Quarterly* 74(2): 141–150, doi:10.1177/1080569911404059.

43. A. M. Krsak (2007), Curbing academic dishonesty in online courses. *TCC* 2007 Proceedings, 159–170 (retrieved from http://etec.hawaii.edu/proceedings /2007/krsak.pdf).

44. D. Koller (2013, November), The online revolution: Learning without limits (keynote address presented at the Annual Sloan Consortium International Conference on Online Learning, Orlando, FL).

45. B. S. Bloom (1956), *Taxonomy of Educational Objectives, Handbook I: The Cognitive Domain* (New York: David McKay Co.).

46. L. W. Anderson, D. R. Krathwohl, P. W. Airasian, K. A. Cruikshank, R. E. Mayer, P. R. Pintrich, J. Raths, and M. C. Wittrock (2000), *A Taxonomy for Learning, Teaching, and Assessing: A Revision of Bloom's Taxonomy of Educational Objectives* (New York: Pearson, Allyn & Bacon).

47. For a concise summary of what these terms mean and how they interact with different types of knowledge see Center for Excellence in Learning and Teaching, *A Model of Learning Objectives Based on a Taxonomy for Learning, Teaching, and Assessing: A Revision of Bloom's Taxonomy of Educational Objectives*

(retrieved from http://www.cde.ca.gov/sp/el/er/documents/bloomtaxonomy. pdf).

48. R. Schoenfeld-Tacher, S. McConnell, and M. Graham (2001), Do no harm: A comparison of the effects of on-line vs. traditional delivery media on a science course, *Journal of Science Education and Technology* 10(3): 257–265.

49. Z. Szabo and J. Schwart (2011), Learning methods for teacher education: The use of discussions to improve critical thinking, *Technology, Pedagogy and Education* 20(1): 79–94, doi:10.1080/1475949X.2010.534866.

50. C. Xin and A. Feenberg (2006), Pedagogy in cyberspace: The dynamics of online discourse, *Journal of Distance Education* 21(2): 1–25.

51. S. Carlson (2001, September 28), Distance education is harder on women than on men, study finds, *Chronicle of Higher Education* (retrieved from http://chronicle.com/).

52. L. Neff, M. D. Miller, S. Pieper, and G. Michalicek (2011), Moodle student experiences: A case study (unpublished manuscript, E-Learning Center, Northern Arizona University, Flagstaff).

3. THE PSYCHOLOGY OF COMPUTING

1. B. de Souza, A. da Silva, A. Roazzi, and S. da Silva Carrilho (2012), Putting the cognitive mediation networks theory to the test: Evaluation of a framework for understanding the digital age, *Computers in Human Behavior* 28(6): 2320–2330, doi:10.1016/j.chb.2012.07.002.

2. J. Wilkins (1997), Protecting our children from Internet smut: Moral duty or moral panic? *Humanist* 57(5): 4.

3. E. Ellerman (2006), The Internet in context, in *Psychology and the Internet: Intrapersonal, Interpersonal, and Transpersonal Implications*, 2nd ed., ed. J. Gackenbach, 11–33 (Waltham, MA: Academic Press).

4. R. S. Fortner (2005), *Radio, Morality, and Culture: Britain, Canada, and the United States, 1919–1945* (Google e-book).

5. E. Ellerman (2006), The Internet in context, in *Psychology and the Internet: Intrapersonal, Interpersonal, and Transpersonal Implications*, 2nd ed., ed. J. Gackenbach, 11–33 (Waltham, MA: Academic Press).

6. P. F. Lazarsfeld (1940), *Radio and the Printed Page: An Introduction to the Study of Radio and Its Role in the Communication of Ideas* (Rahway, NJ: Quinn & Boden) (retrieved from https://archive.org/details/radiotheprintedpoolazarich).

7. A. L. Eisenberg (1936), as cited in E. Wartella and N. Jennings (2000), Children and computers: New technology—old concerns, *Children and Computer Technology* 10(2) (retrieved from http://www.princeton.edu/futureofchildren/publications/journals/article/index.xml?journalid=45&articleid=201&sectionid=1310&submit).

8. N. Carr (2008, July/August), Is Google making us stupid? *The Atlantic* (retrieved from http://www.theatlantic.com).

9. N. Carr (2010), *The Shallows: What the Internet Is Doing to Our Brains* (Amazon Kindle version).

10. Ofcom (2011, August 4), A nation addicted to smartphones (retrieved from http://media.ofcom.org.uk/2011/08/04/a-nation-addicted-to-smartphones/).

11. S. Pinker (2010, June 10), Mind over mass media, *New York Times* (retrieved from htttp//www.nytimes.com).

12. J. Nielsen (2006), F-shaped pattern for reading web content (retrieved from http://www.nngroup.com/articles/f-shaped-pattern-reading -web-content/).

13. G. W. Small, T. D. Moody, P. Siddarth, and S. Y. Bookheimer (2009), Your brain on Google: Patterns of cerebral activation during Internet searching, *American Journal of Geriatric Psychiatry* 17(2): 116–126.

14. G. Small and G. Vorgan (2008), Meet your iBrain, *Scientific American Mind* 19(5): 42–49.

15. G. W. Small, T. D. Moody, P. Siddarth, and S. Y. Bookheimer (2009), Your brain on Google: Patterns of cerebral activation during Internet searching, *American Journal of Geriatric Psychiatry* 17(2): 116–126.

16. See, e.g., D. L. Strayer and F. A. Drews (2007), Cell-phone-induced driver distraction, *Current Directions in Psychological Science* 16(3): 128–131, doi:10.1111/j.1467-8721.2007.00489.x.

17. D. K. Duncan, A. R. Hoekstra, and B. R. Wilcox (2012), Digital devices, distraction, and student performance: Does in-class cell phone use reduce learning? *Astronomy Education Review* 11(1): 010108-1–010108-4, doi: 10.3847 /AER2012011; R. Junco (2012), In-class multitasking and academic performance, *Computers in Human Behavior* 28(6): 2236–2243, doi:10.1016/j.chb .2012.06.031; R. Junco and S. R. Cotten (2011), Perceived academic effects of instant messaging use, *Computers & Education* 56(2): 370–378; R. Junco and S. R. Cotten (2012), No A 4 U: The relationship between multitasking and academic performance, *Computers & Education* 59(2): 505–514.

18. H. Pashler, S. K. Kang, and R. Y. Ip (2013), Does multitasking impair studying? Depends on timing, *Applied Cognitive Psychology* 27(5): 593–599.

19. F. Sana, T. Weston, and N. J. Cepeda (2013), Laptop multitasking hinders classroom learning for both users and nearby peers, *Computers & Education* 62:24–31, doi:10.1016/j.compedu.2012.10.003.

20. E. Ophir, C. Nass, and A. D. Wagner (2009), Cognitive control in media multitaskers, *Proceedings of the National Academy of Sciences* 106:15583–15587.

21. See also K. H. Lui and A. N. Wong (2012), Does media multitasking always hurt? A positive correlation between multitasking and multisensory integration, *Psychonomic Bulletin & Review* 19(4): 647–653.

22. For an excellent discussion of limitations to our subjective awareness of attention and individual differences see C. Chabris and D. Simon (2010), *The Invisible Gorilla: And Other Ways Our Intuitions Deceive Us* (New York: Crown).

23. I learned this demonstration from Saundra Ciccarelli of Florida Gulf State College.

24. M. Prensky (2001a), Digital natives, digital immigrants, *On the Horizon* 9(5): 1–6 (retrieved from http://www.marcprensky.com/writing/Prensky%20 -%20Digital%20Natives,%20Digital%20Immigrants%20-%20Part1.pdf); M. Prensky (2001b), Digital natives, digital immigrants: Do they really think

different? *On the Horizon* 9(6): 1–6 (retrieved from http://www.marcprensky .com/writing/Prensky%20- %20Digital%20Natives,%20Digital%20Immigrants %20-%20Part2.pdf); M. Prensky (2006), Listen to the natives, *Educational Leadership* 63(4): 8–13.

25. D. Oblinger and J. Oblinger (2005), Is it age or IT: First steps toward understanding the net generation, in *Educating the Net Generation*, ed. D. Oblinger and J. Oblinger, 1–20 (retrieved from http://net.educause.edu/ir /library/pdf/pub7101.pdf).

26. Ibid.

27. Ibid.

28. G. Small and G. Vorgan (2008), Meet your iBrain, *Scientific American Mind* 19(5): 42–49.

29. M. Bullen (2012, April 20), The new net generation myth (blog post, retrieved from http://netgennonsense.blogspot.com/2012/04/new-net-generation -myth.html).

30. M. Bullen, T. Morgan, and A. Qayyum (2011), Digital learners in higher education: Generation is not the issue, *Canadian Journal of Learning and Technology* 37(1): 1–24.

31. Ibid.

32. Ibid.; S. Bennett, K. Maton, and L. Kervin (2008), The "digital natives" debate: A critical review of the evidence, *British Journal of Educational Technology* 39(5): 775–786.

33. Ibid.; C. C. Jones and G. G. Healing (2010), Net generation students: Agency and choice and the new technologies, *Journal of Computer Assisted Learning* 26(5): 344–356, doi:10.1111/j.1365-2729.2010.00370.x; A. Koutropoulos (2011), Digital natives: Ten years after, *Journal of Online Learning and Teaching* 7(4): 525–538.

34. S. Lohnes and C. Kinzer (2007), Questioning assumptions about students' expectations for technology in college classrooms, *Innovate: Journal of Online Education* 3(5).

35. S. Ransdell, B. Kent, S. Gaillard-Kenney, and J. Long (2011), Digital immigrants fare better than digital natives due to social reliance, *British Journal of Educational Technology* 42(6):931–938, doi:10.1111/j.1467-8535.2010.01137.x.

36. See, e.g., D. DiSalva (2010, January/February), Are social networks messing with your head? *Scientific American Mind* 20:48–55.

37. See, e.g., S. Scribner (2013, January 11), My breakup with Facebook, *Salon* (retrieved from http://www.salon.com).

38. See, e.g., http://ravelry.com, a multi-million-user space geared toward yarn crafters.

39. J. A. Bargh and K. A. McKenna (2004), The Internet and social life, *Annual Review of Psychology* 55:573–590, doi:10.1146/annurev.psych.55.090902.141922.

40. Ibid.; for a contrasting view of the impact of Internet use on relationships with friends and family see N. H. Nie and L. Erbring (2000), Internet and society: A preliminary report, *IT & Society* 1(1): 275–283.

41. K. A. McKenna, A. S. Green, and M. J. Gleason (2002), Relationship formation on the Internet: What's the big attraction? *Journal of Social Issues* 58(1): 9–31, doi:10.1111/1540-4560.00246.

42. S. M. Bergman, M. E. Fearrington, S. W. Davenport, and J. Z. Bergman (2011), Millennials, narcissism, and social networking: What narcissists do on social networking sites and why, *Personality and Individual Differences* 50(5): 706–711, doi:10.1016/j.paid.2010.12.022; L. E. Buffardi and W. Campbell (2008), Narcissism and social networking web sites, *Personality and Social Psychology Bulletin* 34(10): 1303–1314, doi:10.1177/0146167208320061.

43. L. E. Buffardi and W. Campbell (2008), Narcissism and social networking web sites, *Personality and Social Psychology Bulletin* 34(10): 1303–1314, doi:10.1177/0146167208320061.

44. C. J. Carpenter (2012), Narcissism on Facebook: Self-promotional and anti-social behavior, *Personality and Individual Differences* 52(4): 482–486, doi:10.1016/j.paid.2011.11.011.

45. J. Paul, H. M. Baker, and J. Cochran (2012), Effect of online social networking on student academic performance, *Computers in Human Behavior* 28(6): 2117–2127, doi:10.1016/j.chb.2012.06.016.

46. R. Junco and S. R. Cotten (2012), No A 4 U: The relationship between multitasking and academic performance, *Computers & Education* 59(2): 505–514.

47. M. A. Jenkins-Guarnieri, S. L. Wright, and B. D. Johnson (2013), The interrelationships among attachment style, personality traits, interpersonal competency, and Facebook use, *Psychology of Popular Media Culture* 2(2): 117–131, doi:10.1037/a0030946.

48. A. Nadkarni and S. G. Hofmann (2012), Why do people use Facebook? *Personality and Individual Differences* 52(3): 243–249, doi:10.1016/j.paid.2011.11.007; G. Seidman (2013), Self-presentation and belonging on Facebook: How personality influences social media use and motivations, *Personality and Individual Differences* 54(3): 402–407, doi:10.1016/j.paid.2012.10.009; K. M. Sheldon, N. Abad, and C. Hinsch (2011), A two-process view of Facebook use and relatedness need-satisfaction: Disconnection drives use, and connection rewards it, *Journal of Personality and Social Psychology* 100(4): 766–775, doi:10.1037/a0022407.

49. S. Lohnes and C. Kinzer (2007), Questioning assumptions about students' expectations for technology in college classrooms, *Innovate: Journal of Online Education* 3(5).

50. Ibid.

51. See https://www.facebook.com/help/groups/groups-for-schools for complete details on how to use this Facebook feature.

52. See, e.g., B. Dahl (2012), Can I safely use Facebook with students for class interaction? *Magna 20 Minute Mentor* (retrieved from http://www.magnapubsadmin.com/uploads/bdo712facebookpps.pdf).

53. J. A. Bargh and K. A. McKenna (2004), The Internet and social life, *Annual Review of Psychology* 55:573–590, doi:10.1146/annurev.psych.55.090902.141922.

54. A. W. Chickering and S. C. Ehrmann (1996), Implementing the seven principles: Technology as lever, in *The Seven Principles: TLT Ideas and Resources* (retrieved from http://www.tltgroup.org/programs/seven.html).

55. K. Byron and D. C. Baldridge (2005), Toward a model of nonverbal cues and emotion in email, *Academy of Management Annual Meeting Proceedings*, B1–B6, doi:10.5465/AMBPP.2005.18781269.

56. J. B. Walthier and K. P. D'Addario (2001), The impacts of emoticons on message interpretation in computer-mediated communication, *Social Science Computer Review* 19(3): 324–347, doi:10.1177/0894439301019003007.

57. K. Byron (2008), Carrying too heavy a load? The communication and miscommunication of emotion by email, *Academy of Management Review* 33(2): 309–327; J. B. Walthier and K. P. D'Addario (2001), The impacts of emoticons on message interpretation in computer-mediated communication, *Social Science Computer Review* 19(3): 324–347, doi:10.1177/0894439301019003007.

58. M. Alonzo and M. Aiken (2004), Flaming in electronic communication, *Decision Support Systems* 36(3): 205–213, doi:10.1016/S0167-9236(02)00190-2.

59. L. L. Festinger, A. A. Pepitone, and T. T. Newcomb (1952), Some consequences of de-individuation in a group, *Journal of Abnormal and Social Psychology* 47(2): 382–389, doi:10.1037/h0057906.

60. A. N. Joinson (2007), Disinhibition and the Internet, in *Psychology and the Internet: Intrapersonal, Interpersonal, and Transpersonal Implications*, 2nd ed., ed. J. Gackenbach, 75–92 (Waltham, MA: Academic Press).

61. A. N. Joinson (2001), Self-disclosure in computer-mediated communication: The role of self-awareness and visual anonymity, *European Journal of Social Psychology* 31:177–192.

62. Ibid.

63. N. Lapidot-Lefler and A. Barak (2012), Effects of anonymity, invisibility, and lack of eye-contact on toxic online disinhibition, *Computers in Human Behavior* 28:434–443, doi:10.1016/j.chb.2011.10.014.

64. M. D. Dickey (2005), Three-dimensional virtual worlds and distance learning: Two case studies of Active Worlds as a medium for distance education, *British Journal of Educational Technology* 36(3): 439–451.

65. A. N. Joinson (2001), Self-disclosure in computer-mediated communication: The role of self-awareness and visual anonymity, *European Journal of Social Psychology* 31:177–192.

66. R. S. Nickerson (2012), Technology and cognition amplification, in *Intelligence and Technology: The Impact of Tools on the Nature and Development of Human Abilities*, ed. R. J. Sternberg and D. D. Preiss, 3–27 (New York: Routledge).

4. ATTENTION

1. J. R. Stroop (1935), Studies of interference in serial verbal reactions, *Journal of Experimental Psychology* 18(6): 643–662, doi:10.1037/h0054651.

2. R. Ptak (2012), The frontoparietal attention network of the human brain: Action, saliency, and a priority map of the environment, *Neuroscientist* 18(5): 502–515, doi:10.1177/1073858411409051.

3. B. O. Olatunji, C. N. Sawchuk, T. C. Lee, J. M. Lohr, and D. F. Tolin (2008), Information processing biases in spider phobia: Application of the Stroop and "white noise" paradigm, *Journal of Behavior Therapy and Experimental Psychiatry* 39(2): 187–200, doi:10.1016/j.jbtep.2007.03.002.

4. A. Mack and I. Rock (1998), *Inattentional Blindness* (Cambridge, MA: MIT Press).

5. A. Mack (2003), Inattentional blindness: Looking without seeing, *Current Directions in Psychological Science* 12(5): 180–184, doi:10.1111/1467-8721 .0125.

6. C. Chabris and D. Simon (2010), *The Invisible Gorilla: And Other Ways Our Intuitions Deceive Us* (New York: Crown).

7. E. Spelke, W. Hirst, and U. Neisser (1976), Skills of divided attention, *Cognition* 4(3): 215–230, doi:10.1016/0010-0277(76)90018-4.

8. See, e.g., A. Mack and I. Rock (1998), *Inattentional Blindness* (Cambridge, MA: MIT Press); D. G. MacKay (1987), *The Organization of Perception and Action: A Theory for Language and Other Cognitive Skills* (Berlin: Springer-Verlag).

9. B. Bridgeman and D. Staggs (1982), Plasticity in human blindsight, *Vision Research* 22(9): 1199–1203, doi:10.1016/0042-6989(82)90085-2.

10. J. L. Woehrle and J. P. Magliano (2012), Time flies faster if a person has a high working-memory capacity, *Acta Psychologica* 139(2): 314–319, doi:10.1016/j. actpsy.2011.12.006.

11. J. C. Davis and M. C. Smith (1972), Memory for unattended input, *Journal of Experimental Psychology* 96(2): 380–388, doi:10.1037/h0033628.

12. N. Moray (1959), Attention in dichotic listening: Affective cues and the influence of instructions, *Quarterly Journal of Experimental Psychology* 11:56–60, doi:10.1080/17470215908416289.

13. D. G. MacKay (1973), Aspects of the theory of comprehension, memory and attention, *Quarterly Journal of Experimental Psychology* 25(1): 22–40, doi:10.1080/14640747308400320.

14. D. L. Strayer and F. A. Drews (2007), Cell-phone-induced driver distraction, *Current Directions in Psychological Science* 16(3): 128–131, doi:10.1111/j.1467-8721.2007.00489.x.

15. J. O'Regan, R. A. Rensink, and J. J. Clark (1999), Change-blindness as a result of 'mudsplashes,' *Nature* 398(6722), doi:10.1038/17953; R. A. Rensink, J. O'Regan, and J. J. Clark (2000), On the failure to detect changes in scenes across brief interruptions, *Visual Cognition* 7(1–3): 127–145, doi:10.1080 /135062800394720; D. J. Simons and D. T. Levin (1997), Change blindness, *Trends in Cognitive Sciences* 1(7): 261–267, doi:10.1016/S1364-6613(97)01080-2.

16. D. T. Levin, N. Momen, S. Drivdahl, and D. J. Simons (2000), Change blindness blindness: The metacognitive error of overestimating change-detection ability, *Visual Cognition* 7(1–3): 397–412, doi:10.1080/135062800394865.

17. R. A. Rensink, J. O'Regan, and J. J. Clark (2000), On the failure to detect changes in scenes across brief interruptions, *Visual Cognition* 7(1–3): 127–145, doi:10.1080/135062800394720.

18. See, e.g., J. S. Johnson, J. P. Spencer, S. J. Luck, and G. Schöner (2009), A dynamic neural field model of visual working memory and change detection, *Psychological Science* 20(5): 568–577, doi:10.1111/j.1467-9280.2009.02329.x.

19. J. Jonides, R. L. Lewis, D. Nee, C. A. Lustig, M. G. Berman, and K. Moore (2008), The mind and brain of short-term memory, *Annual Review of Psychology* 59:193–224, doi:10.1146/annurev.psych.59.103006.093615; R. W. Engle (2002), Working memory capacity as executive attention, *Current Directions in Psychological Science* 11(1): 19–23, doi:10.1111/1467-8721.00160; N. Unsworth

and R. W. Engle (2007), The nature of individual differences in working memory capacity: Active maintenance in primary memory and controlled search from secondary memory, *Psychological Review* 114(1): 104–132, doi:10.1037/0033-295X.114.1.104; A. L. Gilchrist and N. Cowan (2011), Can the focus of attention accommodate multiple, separate items? *Journal of Experimental Psychology: Learning, Memory, and Cognition* 37(6): 1484–1502, doi:10.1037/a0024352; N. Cowan (2011), The focus of attention as observed in visual working memory tasks: Making sense of competing claims, *Neuropsychologia* 49(6): 1401–1406, doi:10.1016/j.neuropsychologia.2011.01.035; N. Cowan, E. M. Elliott, J. Saults, C. C. Morey, S. Mattox, A. Hismjatullina, and A. A. Conway (2005), On the capacity of attention: Its estimation and its role in working memory and cognitive aptitudes, *Cognitive Psychology* 51(1): 42–100, doi:10.1016/j.cogpsych.2004.12.001; K. Oberauer (2002), Access to information in working memory: Exploring the focus of attention, *Journal of Experimental Psychology: Learning, Memory, and Cognition* 28(3): 411–421, doi:10.1037/0278-7393.28.3.411.

20. A. L. Gilchrist and N. Cowan (2011), Can the focus of attention accommodate multiple, separate items? *Journal of Experimental Psychology: Learning, Memory, and Cognition* 37(6): 1484–1502, doi:10.1037/a0024352; K. Oberauer (2002), Access to information in working memory: Exploring the focus of attention, *Journal of Experimental Psychology: Learning, Memory, and Cognition* 28(3): 411–421, doi:10.1037/0278-7393.28.3.411.

21. See, e.g., N. Unsworth and R. W. Engle (2007), The nature of individual differences in working memory capacity: Active maintenance in primary memory and controlled search from secondary memory, *Psychological Review* 114(1): 104–132, doi:10.1037/0033-295X.114.1.104.

22. M. H. Ashcraft (2002), Math anxiety: Personal, educational, and cognitive consequences, *Current Directions in Psychological Science* 11(5): 181–185, doi:10.1111/1467-8721.00196; M. H. Ashcraft and J. A. Krause (2007), Working memory, math performance, and math anxiety, *Psychonomic Bulletin & Review* 14(2): 243–248, doi:10.3758/BF03194059.

23. For one review see A. De La Fuente, S. Xia, C. Branch, and X. Li (2013), A review of attention-deficit/hyperactivity disorder from the perspective of brain networks, *Frontiers in Human Neuroscience* 7(192), doi:10.3389/fnhum.2013.00192.

24. See, e.g., R. Martinussen, J. Hayden, S. Hogg-Johnson, and R. Tannock (2005), A meta-analysis of working memory impairments in children with attention-deficit/hyperactivity disorder, *Journal of the American Academy of Child & Adolescent Psychiatry* 44(4): 377–384, doi:10.1097/01.chi.0000153228.72591.73.

25. B. Bolea, M. Adamou, S. Young, et al. (2012, June), ADHD matures: Time for practitioners to do the same? *Journal of Psychopharmacology* 26(6): 766–770 (serial online, available from PsycINFO, Ipswich, MA; accessed January 1, 2014).

26. D. D. Tomasi, N. D. Volkow, G. J. Wang, R. R. Wang, F. F. Telang, E. C. Caparelli, C. Wong, M. Jayne, and J. S. Fowler (2011), Methylphenidate enhances brain activation and deactivation responses to visual attention and

working memory tasks in healthy controls, *Neuroimage* 54(4): 3101–3110, doi:10.1016/j.neuroimage.2010.10.060.

27. M. J. Sciutto and M. Eisenberg (2007), Evaluating the evidence for and against the overdiagnosis of ADHD, *Journal of Attention Disorders* 11(2): 106–113, doi:10.1177/1087054707300094.

28. M. H. Duncan (1979), Attention deficit disorder (ADD) 1980: Unnecessary mistakes in diagnosis and treatment of learning and behavior problems of the MBD/hyperactive syndrome, *Journal of Clinical Child Psychology* 8(3): 180–182, doi:10.1080/15374417909532915.

29. L. Castle, R. E. Aubert, R. R. Verbrugge, M. Khalid, and R. S. Epstein (2007), Trends in medication treatment for ADHD, *Journal of Attention Disorders* 10(4): 335–342, doi:10.1177/1087054707299597.

30. M. J. Sciutto and M. Eisenberg (2007), Evaluating the evidence for and against the overdiagnosis of ADHD, *Journal of Attention Disorders* 11(2): 106–113, doi:10.1177/1087054707300094.

31. K. K. Szpunar, N.Y. Khan, and D. L. Schacter (2013), Interpolated memory tests reduce mind wandering and improve learning of online lectures, *PNAS, Proceedings of the National Academy of Sciences of the United States of America* 110(16): 6313–6317.

32. D. G. MacKay (1987), *The Organization of Perception and Action: A Theory for Language and Other Cognitive Skills* (Berlin: Springer-Verlag).

33. Table excerpted from M. D. Miller, E. Brauer, and J. Shaber (2011), Getting to Carnegie Hall: Novel timed homework practice to develop basic circuit analysis skills (paper presented by E. Brauer, Annual Conference and Exposition, American Society for Engineering Education).

34. M. D. Miller, E. Brauer, and J. Shaber (2011), Getting to Carnegie Hall: Novel timed homework practice to develop basic circuit analysis skills (paper presented by E. Brauer, Annual Conference and Exposition, American Society for Engineering Education).

35. See, e.g., F. Paas, A. Renkl, and J. Sweller (2003), Cognitive load theory and instructional design: Recent developments, *Educational Psychologist* 38(1): 1–4, doi:10.1207/S15326985EP3801_1; L. Sweller (1988), Cognitive load during problem solving: Effects on learning, *Cognitive Science* 12(2): 257–285, doi:10.1207/s15516709cog1202_4.

36. A. Wong, N. Marcus, P. Ayres, L. Smith, G. A. Cooper, F. Paas, and J. Sweller (2009), Instructional animations can be superior to statics when learning human motor skills, *Computers in Human Behavior* 25(2): 339–347.

37. S. Agostinho, S. Tindall-Ford, and K. Roodenrys (2013), Adaptive diagrams: Handing control over to the learner to manage split-attention online, *Computers & Education* 64:52–62.

38. G. R. Morrison and G. J. Anglin (2005), Research on cognitive load theory: Application to e-learning, *Educational Technology Research and Development* 53(3): 94–104, doi:10.1007/BF02504801.

39. Ibid.

40. T. de Jong (2010), Cognitive load theory, educational research, and instructional design: Some food for thought, *Instructional Science: An International Journal of the Learning Sciences* 38(2): 105–134.

41. Ibid.; G. R. Morrison and G. J. Anglin (2005), Research on cognitive load theory: Application to e-learning, *Educational Technology Research and Development* 53(3): 94–104, doi:10.1007/BF02504801.

42. T. de Jong (2010), Cognitive load theory, educational research, and instructional design: Some food for thought, *Instructional Science: An International Journal of the Learning Sciences* 38(2): 105–134.

43. S. Agostinho, S. Tindall-Ford, and K. Roodenrys (2013), Adaptive diagrams: Handing control over to the learner to manage split-attention online, *Computers & Education* 64:52–62.

44. T. Clarke, P. Ayres, and J. Sweller (2005), The impact of sequencing and prior knowledge on learning mathematics through spreadsheet applications, *Educational Technology Research and Development* 53(3): 15–24, doi:10.1007/BF02504794.

45. M. D. Miller and M. E. Rader (2010), Two heads are better than one: Collaborative development of an online course content template, *Journal of Online Learning and Teaching* 6:246–255.

46. R. Wiseman (2012, November 21), Colour changing card trick (video file, retrieved from http://www.youtube.com/watch?v=v3iPrBrGSJM).

47. An example module on attention and learning that I authored can be downloaded from https://nau.academia.edu/MichelleMiller.

48. M. G. Berman, J. Jonides, and S. Kaplan (2008), The cognitive benefits of interacting with nature, *Psychological Science* (Wiley-Blackwell) 19(12): 1207–1212, doi:10.1111/j.1467-9280.2008.02225.x.

49. D. Valtchanov, K. R. Barton, and C. Ellard (2010), Restorative effects of virtual nature settings, *Cyberpsychology, Behavior & Social Networking* 13(5): 503–512, doi:10.1089/cyber.2009.0308.

5. MEMORY

1. J. Lang (2011, December 14), Teaching and human memory, part 2, *Chronicle of Higher Education* (retrieved from http://chronicle.com/).

2. R. S. Nickerson and M. Adams (1979), Long-term memory for a common object, *Cognitive Psychology* 11(3): 287–307.

3. M. Rinck (1999), Memory for everyday objects: Where are the digits on numerical keypads? *Applied Cognitive Psychology* 13(4): 329–350.

4. R. C. Atkinson and R. M. Shiffrin (1971), The control of short-term memory, *Scientific American* 225(2): 82–90, doi:10.1038/scientificamericano 871-82; R. M. Shiffrin and R. C. Atkinson (1969), Storage and retrieval processes in long-term memory, *Psychological Review* 76(2): 179–193, doi:10.1037/h0027277.

5. J. S. Nairne (2002), Remembering over the short-term: The case against the standard model, *Annual Review of Psychology* 53(1): 53–81, doi:10.1146/annurev.psych.53.100901.135131.

6. A. D. Baddeley (1986), *Working Memory* (Oxford: Clarendon Press); A. D. Baddeley, N. Thomson, and M. Buchanan (1975), Word length and the structure of short-term memory, *Journal of Verbal Learning & Verbal Behavior*

14(6): 575–589, doi:10.1016/S0022-5371(75)80045-4; G. J. Hitch and A. D. Baddeley (1976), Verbal reasoning and working memory, *Quarterly Journal of Experimental Psychology* 28(4): 603–621, doi:10.1080/14640747608400587.

7. N. Cowan (2011), The focus of attention as observed in visual working memory tasks: Making sense of competing claims, *Neuropsychologia* 49(6): 1401–1406, doi:10.1016/j.neuropsychologia.2011.01.035; N. Cowan, E. M. Elliott, J. Saults, C. C. Morey, S. Mattox, A. Hismjatullina, and A. A. Conway (2005), On the capacity of attention: Its estimation and its role in working memory and cognitive aptitudes, *Cognitive Psychology* 51(1): 42–100, doi:10.1016/j.cogpsych .2004.12.001; R. W. Engle (2002), Working memory capacity as executive attention, *Current Directions in Psychological Science* 11(1): 19–23, doi:10.1111/1467 -8721.00160; K. Oberauer (2002), Access to information in working memory: Exploring the focus of attention, *Journal of Experimental Psychology: Learning, Memory, and Cognition* 28(3): 411–421, doi:10.1037/0278-7393.28.3.411; J. A. Lewis-Peacock, A. T. Drysdale, K. Oberauer, and B. R. Postle (2012), Neural evidence for a distinction between short-term memory and the focus of attention, *Journal of Cognitive Neuroscience* 24(1): 61–79, doi:10.1162/ jocn_a_00140.

8. N. Cowan (2010), The magical mystery four: How is working memory capacity limited, and why? *Current Directions in Psychological Science* 19(1): 51–57, doi:10.1177/0963721409359277.

9. N. Cowan, E. M. Elliott, J. Saults, C. C. Morey, S. Mattox, A. Hismjatullina, and A. A. Conway (2005), On the capacity of attention: Its estimation and its role in working memory and cognitive aptitudes, *Cognitive Psychology* 51(1): 42–100, doi:10.1016/j.cogpsych.2004.12.001.

10. R. C. Martin and C. Romani (1994), Verbal working memory and sentence comprehension: A multiple-components view, *Neuropsychology* 8(4): 506–523, doi:10.1037/0894-4105.8.4.506; C. Romani and R. Martin (1999), A deficit in the short-term retention of lexical-semantic information: Forgetting words but remembering a story, *Journal of Experimental Psychology: General* 128(1): 56–77, doi:10.1037/0096-3445.128.1.56.

11. J. S. Nairne, personal communication, 2000.

12. A. Paivio and K. Csapo (1973), Picture superiority in free recall: Imagery or dual coding? *Cognitive Psychology* 5(2): 176–206, doi:10.1016 /0010-0285(73)90032-7.

13. J. Foer (2011), *Moonwalking with Einstein: The Art and Science of Remembering Everything* (Amazon Kindle version).

14. F. I. Craik and R. S. Lockhart (1972), Levels of processing: A framework for memory research, *Journal of Verbal Learning & Verbal Behavior* 11(6): 671–684, doi:10.1016/S0022-5371(72)80001-X.

15. K. Dickson, M. S. Devoley, and M. D. Miller (2006), Effect of study guide exercises on multiple-choice exam performance in introductory psychology, *Teaching of Psychology* 33(1): 40–42; K. Dickson, M. D. Miller, and M. S. Devoley (2005), Effect of textbook study guides on student performance in Introductory Psychology, *Teaching of Psychology* 32(1): 34–39.

16. E. A. Kensinger (2009), How emotion affects older adults' memories for event details, *Memory* 17(2): 208–219, doi:10.1080/09658210802221425; K. S.

LaBar and R. Cabeza (2006), Cognitive neuroscience of emotional memory, *Nature Reviews Neuroscience* 7(1): 54–64, doi:10.1038/nrn1825.

17. D. G. MacKay, M. Shafto, J. K. Taylor, D. E. Marian, L. Abrams, and J. R. Dyer (2004), Relations between emotion, memory, and attention: Evidence from taboo Stroop, lexical decision, and immediate memory tasks, *Memory & Cognition* 32(3): 474–488, doi:10.3758/BF03195840; S. Porter and K. A. Peace (2007), The scars of memory: A prospective, longitudinal investigation of the consistency of traumatic and positive emotional memories in adulthood, *Psychological Science* (Wiley-Blackwell) 18(5): 435–441, doi:10.1111 /j.1467-9280.2007.01918.x; D. C. Rubin (2005), A basic-systems approach to autobiographical memory, *Current Directions in Psychological Science* 14(2): 79–83, doi:10.1111/j.0963-7214.2005.00339.x.

18. T. Canli, H. Sivers, S. L. Whitfield, I. H. Gotlib, and J. E. Gabrieli (2002), Amygdala response to happy faces as a function of extraversion, *Science* 296(5576), doi:10.1126/science.1068749.

19. G. B. Maddox, M. Naveh-Benjamin, S. Old, and A. Kilb (2012), The role of attention in the associative binding of emotionally arousing words, *Psychonomic Bulletin & Review* 19(6): 1128–1134, doi:10.3758/s13423-012-0315-x.

20. J. S. Nairne, S. R. Thompson, and J. S. Pandeirada (2007), Adaptive memory: Survival processing enhances retention, *Journal of Experimental Psychology, Learning, Memory & Cognition* 33(2): 263–273, doi:10.1037/0278-7393.33.2.263.

21. J. S. Nairne and J. S. Pandeirada (2010), Adaptive memory: Ancestral priorities and the mnemonic value of survival processing, *Cognitive Psychology* 61(1): 1–22, doi:10.1016/j.cogpsych.2010.01.005.

22. J. S. Nairne and J. S. Pandeirada (2010), Adaptive memory: Nature's criterion and the functionalist agenda, *American Journal of Psychology* 123(4): 381–390.

23. The starting list of twenty greatest players was adapted from www.in sidehoops.com.

24. This diagramming scheme and the system for eliciting the expert knowledge is loosely based on M. T. Chi and R. D. Koeske (1983), Network representation of a child's dinosaur knowledge, *Developmental Psychology* 19(1): 29–39, doi:10.1037/0012-1649.19.1.29.

25. See also W. G. Chase and H. A. Simon (1973), Perception in chess, *Cognitive Psychology* 4(1): 55–81, doi:10.1016/0010-0285(73)90004-2.

26. J. D. Bransford, A. L. Brown, and R. C. Cocking (2000), *How People Learn: Brain, Mind, Experience, and School* (Washington, DC: National Academies Press).

27. See also S. A. Ambrose, M. W. Bridges, M. DiPietro, M. C. Lovett, and M. K. Norman (2010), *How Learning Works: Seven Research-Based Principles for Smart Teaching* (Amazon Kindle version).

28. J. D. Karpicke and J. R. Blunt (2011), Retrieval practice produces more learning than elaborate studying with concept mapping, *Science* 331(6018): 772–775, doi:10.1126/science.1199327; J. D. Karpicke and H. Roediger (2007), Repeated retrieval during learning is the key to long-term retention, *Journal of Memory and Language* 57(2): 151–162, doi:10.1016/j.jml.2006.09.004; J. D. Karpicke and H. Roediger (2008), The critical importance of retrieval for learning, *Science* 319(5865): 966–968, doi:10.1126/science.1152408; M. A. Mc-

Daniel, H. Roediger, and K. B. McDermott (2007), Generalizing test-enhanced learning from the laboratory to the classroom, *Psychonomic Bulletin & Review* 14(2): 200–206, doi:10.3758/BF03194052.

29. J. D. Karpicke, A. C. Butler, and H. Roediger (2009), Metacognitive strategies in student learning: Do students practise retrieval when they study on their own? *Memory* 17(4): 471–479, doi:10.1080/09658210802647009.

30. G. Johnson (2008), Online study tools: College student preference versus impact on achievement, *Computers in Human Behavior* 24(3): 930–939, doi:10.1016/j.chb.2007.02.012.

31. For a review see N. J. Cepeda, H. Pashler, E. Vul, J. T. Wixted, and D. Rohrer (2006), Distributed practice in verbal recall tasks: A review and quantitative synthesis, *Psychological Bulletin* 132(3): 354–380, doi:10.1037/0033-2909.132.3.354.

32. G. Xue, L. Mei, C. Chen, Z. Lu, R. Poldrack, and Q. Dong (2011), Spaced learning enhances subsequent recognition memory by reducing neural repetition suppression, *Journal of Cognitive Neuroscience* 23(7): 1624–1633, doi:10.1162/jocn.2010.21532.

33. P. C. Brown, H. L. Roediger III, and M. A. McDaniel (2014), *Make it Stick: The Science of Successful Learning* (Cambridge, MA: The Belknap Press of Harvard University Press).

34. Ibid.

35. M. S. Birnbaum, N. Kornell, E. Bjork, and R. A. Bjork (2013), Why interleaving enhances inductive learning: The roles of discrimination and retrieval, *Memory & Cognition* 41(3): 392–402, doi:10.3758/s13421-012-0272-7; N. Kornell and R. A. Bjork (2008), Learning concepts and categories: Is spacing the "enemy of induction"? *Psychological Science* (Wiley-Blackwell) 19(6): 585–592, doi:10.1111/j.1467-9280.2008.02127.x.

36. D. Rohrer (2012), Interleaving helps students distinguish among similar concepts, *Educational Psychology Review* 24:355–367.

37. N. Kornell and R. A. Bjork (2008), Learning concepts and categories: Is spacing the "enemy of induction"? *Psychological Science* (Wiley-Blackwell) 19(6): 585–592, doi:10.1111/j.1467-9280.2008.02127.x.

38. R. A. Bjork (1994), Memory and metamemory considerations in the training of human beings, in, *Metacognition: Knowing about Knowing*, ed. J. Metcalfe and A. P. Shimamura, 185–205 (Cambridge, MA: MIT Press).

39. Salamy (2009, January 22), Snake phobia treatment (video file, retrieved from http://www.medclip.com/index.php?page=videos&section=view&vid_id=103291).

40. TED India (2010, January), Kiran Sethi: Kids, take charge (video file, retrieved from http://www.ted.com/talks/kiran_bir_sethi_teaches_kids_to_take_charge.html).

41. TED (2008, March), Jill Bolte Taylor: My stroke of insight (video file, retrieved from http://www.ted.com/talks/jill_bolte_taylor_s_powerful_stroke_of_insight.html).

42. For a more extensive list of video-sharing assignment ideas see P. Sherer and T. Shea (2011), Using online video to support student learning and engagement, *College Teaching* 59(2): 56–59.

43. For an example of this kind of assignment see the student wiki for my Teaching Practicum course, http://psy665.wikispaces.com.

44. N. Hara, C. Bonk, and C. Angeli (2000), Content analysis of online discussion in an applied educational psychology course, *Instructional Science* 28(2): 115–152, doi:10.1023/A:1003764722829.

45. This "mystery process" description is adapted from the experimental materials in J. D. Bransford and M. K. Johnson (1972), Contextual prerequisites for understanding: Some investigations of comprehension and recall, *Journal of Verbal Learning and Verbal Behavior* 11(6): 717–726.

46. J. E. Opfer, R. H. Nehm, and M. Ha (2012), Cognitive foundations for science assessment design: Knowing what students know about evolution, *Journal of Research in Science Teaching* 49(6): 744–777, doi:10.1002/tea.21028.

47. M. Lovett, O. Meyer, and C. Thille (2008), The Open Learning Initiative: Measuring the effectiveness of the OLI statistics course in accelerating student learning, *Journal of Interactive Media in Education* 2008(1): 1–16.

6. THINKING

1. J. Peppler, J. Dannhausen, and K. M. Willock (2007, April/May), Not your grandma's nursing education, *NSNA Imprint*, 47–52.

2. D. Kahneman and A. Tversky (1973), On the psychology of prediction, *Psychological Review* 80:237–251.

3. P. C. Wason (1966), Reasoning, in *New Horizons in Psychology*, ed. B. M. Foss, 135–151 (Harmondsworth, UK: Penguin).

4. P. W. Cheng and K. J. Holyoak (1985), Pragmatic reasoning schemas, *Cognitive Psychology* 17:391–416; further illustrations of Wason task variations with explanations can be found at http://www.cep.ucsb.edu/socex/wason.htm #The%20general%20structure.

5. A. Newell and H. A. Simon (1972), *Human Problem Solving* (Oxford: Prentice-Hall).

6. J. Metcalfe and D. Wiebe (1987), Intuition in insight and noninsight problem solving, *Memory & Cognition* 15:238–246.

7. T. M. Amabile (1983), The social psychology of creativity: A componential conceptualization, *Journal of Personality and Social Psychology* 45(2): 357–376, doi:10.1037/0022-3514.45.2.357; T. I. Lubart (1999), Creativity across cultures, in *Handbook of Creativity*, ed. R. J. Sternberg, 339–350 (New York: Cambridge University Press); R. E. Mayer (1989), Cognitive views of creativity: Creative teaching for creative learning, *Contemporary Educational Psychology* 14(3): 203–211, doi:10.1016/0361-476X(89)90010-6.

8. T. M. Amabile (1979), Effects of external evaluation on artistic creativity, *Journal of Personality and Social Psychology* 37(2): 221–233, doi:10.1037/0022-3514.37.2.221.

9. B. A. Hennessey and T. M. Amabile (2010), Creativity, *Annual Review of Psychology*, 61:569–598, doi:10.1146/annurev.psych.093008.100416.

10. A. Ruscio and T. M. Amabile (1999), Effects of instructional style on problem-solving creativity, *Creativity Research Journal* 12(4): 251.

11. B. A. Hennessey and T. M. Amabile (2010), Creativity, *Annual Review of Psychology* 61:569–598, doi:10.1146/annurev.psych.093008.100416.

12. K. J. Holyoak and P. Thagard (1995), *Mental Leaps: Analogy in Creative Thought* (Cambridge, MA: MIT Press); K. J. Holyoak and P. Thagard (1997), The analogical mind, *American Psychologist* 52:35–44.

13. J. Haglund and F. Jeppsson (2012), Using self-generated analogies in teaching of thermodynamics, *Journal of Research in Science Teaching* 49(7): 898–921, doi:10.1002/tea.21025.

14. This analogy is credited to Robert Stake and is widely repeated within education circles. For an example, see http://teachingthroughthearts.blogspot .com/2011/07/formative-assessment-when-cook-tastes.html.

15. B. A. Spellman and K. J. Holyoak (1992), If Saddam is Hitler then who is George Bush? Analogical mapping between systems of social roles, *Journal of Personality & Social Psychology* 62(6): 913–933.

16. L. E. Richland and I. M. McDonough (2010), Learning by analogy: Discriminating between potential analogs, *Contemporary Educational Psychology* 35(1): 28–43, doi:10.1016/j.cedpsych.2009.09.001.

17. M. L. Gick and K. J. Holyoak (1980), Analogical problem solving, *Cognitive Psychology* 12(3): 306–355, doi:10.1016/0010-0285(80)90013-4.

18. Ibid.; M. L. Gick and K. J. Holyoak (1983), Schema induction and analogical transfer, *Cognitive Psychology* 15(1): 1–38, doi:10.1016/0010-0285(83)90002-6.

19. L. E. Richland and I. M. McDonough (2010), Learning by analogy: Discriminating between potential analogs, *Contemporary Educational Psychology* 35(1): 28–43, doi:10.1016/j.cedpsych.2009.09.001.

20. K. J. Holyoak and P. Thagard (1997), The analogical mind, *American Psychologist* 52:35–44.

21. L. E. Richland and I. M. McDonough (2010), Learning by analogy: Discriminating between potential analogs, *Contemporary Educational Psychology* 35(1): 28–43, doi:10.1016/j.cedpsych.2009.09.001.

22. L. E. Richland, J. W. Stigler, and K. J. Holyoak (2012), Teaching the conceptual structure of mathematics, *Educational Psychologist* 47(3): 189–203, doi:10.1080/00461520.2012.667065.

23. J. Haglund and F. Jeppsson (2012), Using self-generated analogies in teaching of thermodynamics, *Journal of Research in Science Teaching* 49(7): 898–921, doi:10.1002/tea.21025.

24. K. A. Ericsson (2003), Exceptional memorizers: Made, not born, *Trends in Cognitive Sciences* 7(6): 233–235, doi:10.1016/S1364-6613(03)00103-7; M. Kim (2012), Theoretically grounded guidelines for assessing learning progress: Cognitive changes in ill-structured complex problem-solving contexts, *Educational Technology Research & Development* 60(4): 601–622, doi:10.1007 /s11423-012-9247-4.

25. See, e.g., M. Chi and R. Koeske (1983), Network representations of a child's dinosaur knowledge, *Developmental Psychology* 19:29–39.

26. J. D. Bransford, A. L. Brown, and R. C. Cocking (2000), *How People Learn: Brain, Mind, Experience, and School* (Washington, DC: National Academies Press); D. Z. Hambrick, J. C. Libarkin, H. L. Petcovic, K. M. Baker, J. Elkins, C. N. Callahan, and N. D. LaDue (2012), A test of the

circumvention-of-limits hypothesis in scientific problem solving: The case of geological bedrock mapping, *Journal of Experimental Psychology: General* 141(3): 397–403.

27. D. Z. Hambrick, J. C. Libarkin, H. L. Petcovic, K. M. Baker, J. Elkins, C. N. Callahan, and N. D. LaDue (2012), A test of the circumvention-of-limits hypothesis in scientific problem solving: The case of geological bedrock mapping, *Journal of Experimental Psychology: General* 141(3): 397–403, doi:10.1037/a0025927.

28. J. W. Pellegrino and M. L. Hilton (2012), *Education for Life and Work: Developing Transferable Knowledge and Skills in the 21st Century* (Washington, DC: National Academies Press).

29. J. D. Bransford, A. L. Brown, and R. C. Cocking (2000), *How People Learn: Brain, Mind, Experience, and School* (Washington, DC: National Academies Press); J. W. Pellegrino and M. L. Hilton (2012), *Education for Life and Work: Developing Transferable Knowledge and Skills in the 21st Century* (Washington, DC: National Academies Press).

30. J. D. Bransford, A. L. Brown, and R. C. Cocking (2000), *How People Learn: Brain, Mind, Experience, and School* (Washington, DC: National Academies Press).

31. Ibid.

32. J. W. Pellegrino and M. L. Hilton (2012), *Education for Life and Work: Developing Transferable Knowledge and Skills in the 21st Century* (Washington, DC: National Academies Press).

33. J. D. Bransford, A. L. Brown, and R. C. Cocking (2000), *How People Learn: Brain, Mind, Experience, and School* (Washington, DC: National Academies Press).

34. Ibid.

35. Ibid.; D. F. Halpern (1998), Teaching critical thinking for transfer across domains: Dispositions, skills, structure training, and metacognitive monitoring, *American Psychologist* 53(4): 449–455.

36. S. K. Carpenter (2012), Testing enhances the transfer of learning, *Current Directions in Psychological Science* (Sage Publications Inc.), 21(5): 279–283, doi:10.1177/0963721412452728.

37. A. C. Butler, N. Godbole, and E. J. Marsh (2013), Explanation feedback is better than correct answer feedback for promoting transfer of learning, *Journal of Educational Psychology* 105(2): 290–298, doi:10.1037/a0031026; R. Moreno and R. E. Mayer (2005), Role of guidance, reflection, and interactivity in an agent-based multimedia game, *Journal of Educational Psychology* 97(1), 117–128, doi:10.1037/0022-0663.97.1.117.

38. C. P. Dwyer, M. J. Hogan, and I. Stewart (2012), An evaluation of argument mapping as a method of enhancing critical thinking performance in e-learning environments, *Metacognition and Learning* 7(3): 219–244, doi:10.1007/s11409-012-9092-1.

39. D. F. Halpern (1998), Teaching critical thinking for transfer across domains: Dispositions, skills, structure training, and metacognitive monitoring, *American Psychologist* 53(4): 449–455; D. F. Halpern, K. Millis, A. C. Graesser, H. Butler, C. Forsyth, and Z. Cai (2012), Operation ARA: A computerized

learning game that teaches critical thinking and scientific reasoning, *Thinking Skills and Creativity* 7(2), 93–100, doi:10.1016/j.tsc.2012.03.00.

40. D. F. Halpern, K. Millis, A. C. Graesser, H. Butler, C. Forsyth, and Z. Cai (2012), Operation ARA: A computerized learning game that teaches critical thinking and scientific reasoning, *Thinking Skills and Creativity* 7(2), 93–100, doi:10.1016/j.tsc.2012.03.00.

41. S. O. Lilienfeld, R. Ammirati, and K. Landfield (2009), Giving debiasing away: Can psychological research on correcting cognitive errors promote human welfare? *Perspectives on Psychological Science* 4(4): 390–398, doi:10.1111/j.1745-6924.2009.01144.x.

42. H. A. Butler (2012), Halpern critical thinking assessment predicts real-world outcomes of critical thinking, *Applied Cognitive Psychology* 26(5): 721–729, doi:10.1002/acp.2851.

43. D. F. Halpern (1999, Winter), Teaching for critical thinking: Helping college students develop the skills and dispositions of a critical thinker, *New Directions for Teaching and Learning*, 69–74.

44. S. O. Lilienfeld (2005), The 10 commandments of helping students distinguish science from pseudoscience in psychology, *APS Observer* 18 (retrieved from http://www.psychologicalscience.org).

45. Ibid.

46. D. F. Halpern (1999, Winter), Teaching for critical thinking: Helping college students develop the skills and dispositions of a critical thinker, *New Directions for Teaching and Learning*, 69–74.

47. S. O. Lilienfeld (2005), The 10 commandments of helping students distinguish science from pseudoscience in psychology, *APS Observer* 18 (retrieved from http://www.psychologicalscience.org).

48. D. F. Halpern (1998), Teaching critical thinking for transfer across domains: Dispositions, skills, structure training, and metacognitive monitoring, *American Psychologist* 53(4): 449–455.

49. Ibid.

50. T. Van Gelder (2007), The rationale for Rationale, *Law, Probability & Risk* 6(1–4): 23–42, doi:10.1093/lpr/mgm032.

51. C. P. Dwyer, M. J. Hogan, and I. Stewart (2012), An evaluation of argument mapping as a method of enhancing critical thinking performance in e-learning environments, *Metacognition and Learning* 7(3): 219–244, doi:10.1007/s11409-012-9092-1.

52. A. Jeong and W. Lee (2012), Developing causal understanding with causal maps: The impact of total links, temporal flow, and lateral position of outcome nodes, *Educational Technology Research & Development* 60(2): 325–340, doi:10.1007/s11423-011-9227-0; for additional explanation and a demonstration see https://sites.google.com/site/causalmaps/.

53. A. Mendenhall and T. E. Johnson (2010), Fostering the development of critical thinking skills, and reading comprehension of undergraduates using a Web 2.0 tool coupled with a learning system, *Interactive Learning Environments* 18(3): 263–276, doi:10.1080/10494820.2010.500537.

54. T. Van Gelder (2007), The rationale for Rationale, *Law, Probability & Risk* 6(1–4): 23–42, doi:10.1093/lpr/mgm032.

55. J. W. Pellegrino and M. L. Hilton (2012), *Education for Life and Work: Developing Transferable Knowledge and Skills in the 21st Century* (Washington, DC: National Academies Press).

56. For a review see C. E. Hmelo-Silver (2004), Problem-based learning: What and how do students learn? *Educational Psychology Review* 16(3): 235–266.

57. Ibid.

58. S. Şendağ and H. H. Ferhan Odabaşı (2009), Effects of an online problem based learning course on content knowledge acquisition and critical thinking skills, *Computers & Education* 53(1): 132–141, doi:10.1016/j.compedu .2009.01.008.

59. V. P. Dennen (2000), Task structuring for on-line problem based learning: A case study, *Educational Technology & Society* 3(3): 329–336.

60. S. Şendağ and H. H. Ferhan Odabaşı (2009), Effects of an online problem based learning course on content knowledge acquisition and critical thinking skills, *Computers & Education* 53(1): 132–141, doi:10.1016/j.compedu .2009.01.008.

61. V. P. Dennen (2000), Task structuring for on-line problem based learning: A case study, *Educational Technology & Society* 3(3): 329–336.

62. See http://cft.vanderbilt.edu/teaching-guides/teaching-activities/case -studies/.

63. S. L. Brooke (2006), Using the case method to teach online classes: Promoting Socratic dialogue and critical thinking skills, *International Journal of Teaching and Learning in Higher Education* 18(2): 142–149.

64. Ibid.

65. Ibid.

66. E. Miles (2009), Inside the body: Fluid pressures and processes (animation, retrieved from http://www.merlot.org/merlot/viewMaterial.htm ?id=417242).

67. G. Burruss (2005), Analogy for testing statistical significance (tutorial, retrieved from http://www.merlot.org/merlot/viewMaterial.htm?id=82914).

68. L. E. Richland and I. M. McDonough (2010), Learning by analogy: Discriminating between potential analogs, *Contemporary Educational Psychology* 35(1): 28–43, doi:10.1016/j.cedpsych.2009.09.001.

69. L. Neff, M. D. Miller, S. Pieper, and G. Michalicek, Moodle student experiences: A case study (unpublished manuscript, E-Learning Center, Northern Arizona University, Flagstaff).

70. Z. Szabo and J. Schwartz (2011), Learning methods for teacher education: The use of online discussions to improve critical thinking, *Technology, Pedagogy and Education* 20(1): 79–94.

71. Ibid.

72. L. S. Neff (n.d.), Designing effective online discussions (slide show, retrieved from http://www2.nau.edu/d-elearn/events/viewFile.php?ID=91).

73. R. Holliman and E. Scanlon (2006), Investigating cooperation and collaboration in near synchronous computer mediated conferences, *Computers & Education* 46(3): 322–335, doi:10.1016/j.compedu.2005.11.002.

74. Ibid.

75. Y. Hsieh and C. Tsai (2012), The effect of moderator's facilitative strategies on online synchronous discussions, *Computers in Human Behavior* 28(5): 1708–1716, doi:10.1016/j.chb.2012.04.010.

76. Ibid.

77. Ibid.

7. INCORPORATING MULTIMEDIA EFFECTIVELY

1. To view this vignette see http://www.ctcfl.ox.ac.uk/Chinese/lessons/3/speaking.htm.

2. U.S. Department of Education, Office of Planning, Evaluation and Policy Development (2010), Evaluation of evidence-based practices in online learning: A meta-analysis and review of online learning studies (retrieved from http://www2.ed.gov/rschstat/eval/tech/evidence-based-practices/finalreport.pdf).

3. C. L. Yue, E. Bjork, and R. A. Bjork (2013), Reducing verbal redundancy in multimedia learning: An undesired desirable difficulty? *Journal of Educational Psychology* 105(2): 266–277, doi:10.1037/a0031971.

4. C. Riener and D. Willingham (2010, September/October), The myth of learning styles, *Change: The Magazine of Higher Learning* (retrieved from http://www.changemag.org).

5. Visual learners convert words to pictures in the brain and vice versa. *Science Daily* (2009, March 28) (retrieved from http://www.sciencedaily.com/releases/2009/03/090325091834.htm).

6. J. Geake (2008), Neuromythologies in education, *Educational Research* 50(2): 123–133, doi:10.1080/00131880802082518.

7. D. M. Kraemer, L. M. Rosenberg, and S. L. Thompson-Schill (2009), The neural correlates of visual and verbal cognitive styles, *Journal of Neuroscience* 29(12): 3792–3798, doi:10.1523/JNEUROSCI.4635-08.2009.

8. V. Gyselinck, E. Jamet, and V. Dubois (2008), The role of working memory components in multimedia comprehension, *Applied Cognitive Psychology* 22(3): 353–374, doi:10.1002/acp.1411.

9. H. Pashler, M. McDaniel, D. Rohrer, and R. Bjork (2008), Learning styles: Concepts and evidence, *Psychological Science in the Public Interest* 9:105–119.

10. G. P. Krätzig and K. D. Arbuthnott (2006), Perceptual learning style and learning proficiency: A test of the hypothesis, *Journal of Educational Psychology* 98(1): 238–246, doi:10.1037/0022-0663.98.1.238.

11. C. Riener and D. Willingham (2010, September/October), The myth of learning styles, *Change: The Magazine of Higher Learning* (retrieved from http://www.changemag.org).

12. R. E. Mayer (2009), *Multimedia Learning*, 2nd ed. (New York: Cambridge University Press).

13. C. L. Yue, E. Bjork, and R. A. Bjork (2013), Reducing verbal redundancy in multimedia learning: An undesired desirable difficulty? *Journal of Educational Psychology* 105(2): 266–277, doi:10.1037/a0031971.

14. R. E. Mayer (2009), *Multimedia Learning*, 2nd ed. (New York: Cambridge University Press).

15. E. van Genuchten, K. Scheiter, and A. Schüler (2012), Examining learning from text and pictures for different task types: Does the multimedia effect differ for conceptual, causal, and procedural tasks? *Computers in Human Behavior* 28(6): 2209–2218, doi:10.1016/j.chb.2012.06.028.

16. E. Sung and R. E. Mayer (2012), When graphics improve liking but not learning from online lessons, *Computers in Human Behavior* 28: 1618–1625.

17. R. E. Mayer, M. Hegarty, S. Mayer, and J. Campbell (2005), When static media promote active learning: Annotated illustrations versus narrated animations in multimedia instruction, *Journal of Experimental Psychology: Applied* 11(4): 256–265; N. Narayanan and M. M. Hegarty (2002), Multimedia design for communication of dynamic information, *International Journal of Human-Computer Studies* 57(4), 279–315, doi:10.1006/ijhc.2002 .1019; C. Wieman and K. Perkins (2005, November), Transforming physics education, *Physics Today Online* (retrieved from http://www.physicstoday .org).

18. To view the animation see https://commons.wikimedia.org/wiki/File :CDC_Overweight_and_Obesity_map3.gif.

19. To view the animation see http://openmultimedia.ie.edu/OpenProducts /decision_making/decision_making/index.html.

20. A. Wong, W. Leahy, N. Marcus, and J. Sweller (2012), Cognitive load theory, the transient information effect and e-learning, *Learning and Instruction* 22(6): 449–457; A. Wong, N. Marcus, P. Ayres, L. Smith, G. A. Cooper, F. Paas, and J. Sweller (2009), Instructional animations can be superior to statics when learning human motor skills, *Computers in Human Behavior* 25(2): 339–347, doi:10.1016/j.chb.2008.12.012.

21. R. E. Mayer, M. Hegarty, S. Mayer, and J. Campbell (2005), When static media promote active learning: Annotated illustrations versus narrated animations in multimedia instruction, *Journal of Experimental Psychology: Applied* 11(4): 256–265.

22. For an example see http://techcrunch.com/2011/09/13/jiffpad-creates -personalized-medical-diagrams-via-ipad/.

23. C. E. Wieman, W. K. Adams, P. P. Loeblein, and K. K. Perkins (2010), Teaching physics using PhET simulations, *Physics Teacher* 48(4): 225–227.

24. Ibid.

25. A. T. Stull, M. Hegarty, and R. E. Mayer (2009), Getting a handle on learning anatomy with interactive three-dimensional graphics, *Journal of Educational Psychology* 101(4): 803–816.

26. For more details on PHeT's process see http://phet.colorado.edu /publications/phet_design_process.pdf.

27. N. D. Finkelstein, W. K. Adams, C. J. Keller, P. B. Kohl, K. K. Perkins, N. S. Podolefsky, S. Reid, and R. R. LeMaster (2005), When learning about the real world is better done virtually: A study of substituting computer simulations for laboratory equipment, *Physical Review Special Topics—Physics Education Research* 1(1), 010103-1—010103-8.

28. To view Packet Tracer see http://www.cisco.com/web/learning/ne tacad/course_catalog/PacketTracer.html; for an empirical study using Packet Tracer see M. C. Mayrath, P. K. Nihalani, and D. H. Robinson (2011), Varying tutorial modality and interface restriction to maximize transfer in a complex simulation environment, *Journal of Educational Psychology* 103(2): 257–268.

29. For examples of how Sniffy looks in use see http://wadsworth.cengage .com/psychology_d/special_features/sniffy.html or http://www.youtube.com /watch?v=7h8L96WHXn4.

30. N. Coombs (2010), *Making Online Teaching Accessible: Inclusive Course Design for Students with Disabilities* (Amazon Kindle version).

8. MOTIVATING STUDENTS

1. R. M. Ryan and E. L. Deci (2000), Self-determination theory and the facilitation of intrinsic motivation, social development, and well-being, *American Psychologist* 55(1): 68–78.

2. E. L. Deci (1971), Effects of externally mediated rewards on intrinsic motivation, *Journal of Personality and Social Psychology* 18(1): 105–115.

3. M. Vansteenkiste, W. Lens, and E. L. Deci (2006), Intrinsic versus extrinsic goal contents in self-determination theory: Another look at the quality of academic motivation, *Educational Psychologist* 41(1): 19–31, doi:10.1207 /s15326985ep4101_4.

4. M. V. Covington (2000), Intrinsic versus extrinsic motivation in schools: A reconciliation, *Current Directions in Psychological Science* 9(1): 22–25; R. M. Ryan and E. L. Deci (2000), Self-determination theory and the facilitation of intrinsic motivation, social development, and well-being, *American Psychologist* 55(1): 68–78; M. Vansteenkiste, W. Lens, and E. L. Deci (2006), Intrinsic versus extrinsic goal contents in self-determination theory: Another look at the quality of academic motivation, *Educational Psychologist* 41(1): 19–31, doi:10.1207 /s15326985ep4101_4.

5. R. M. Ryan and E. L. Deci (2000), Self-determination theory and the facilitation of intrinsic motivation, social development, and well-being, *American Psychologist* 55(1): 68–78.

6. M. V. Covington (2000), Intrinsic versus extrinsic motivation in schools: A reconciliation, *Current Directions in Psychological Science* 9(1): 22–25.

7. D. C. McClelland and A. M. Liberman (1949), The effect of need for achievement on recognition of need-related words, *Journal of Personality* 18:236–251, doi:10.1111/j.1467-6494.1949.tb01243.x.

8. A. R. Cohen, E. Stotland, and D. M. Wolfe (1955), An experimental investigation of need for cognition, *Journal of Abnormal and Social Psychology* 51(2): 291–294, doi:10.1037/h0042761; J. T. Cacioppo and R. E. Petty (1982), The need for cognition, *Journal of Personality and Social Psychology* 42(1): 116–131, doi:10.1037/0022-3514.42.1.116.

9. P. J. Hustinx, H. Kuyper, M. C. van der Werf, and P. Dijkstra (2009), Achievement motivation revisited: New longitudinal data to demonstrate its

predictive power, *Educational Psychology* 29(5): 561–582, doi:10.1080/014434
10903132128.

10. A. Bandura (1977), Self-efficacy: Toward a unifying theory of behavioral change, *Psychological Review* 84(2): 191–215.

11. M. Muraven and R. F. Baumeister (2000), Self-regulation and depletion of limited resources: Does self-control resemble a muscle? *Psychological Bulletin* 126(2): 247.

12. Ibid.

13. Ibid.

14. D. T. Neal, W. Wood, and A. Drolet (2013), How do people adhere to goals when willpower is low? The profits (and pitfalls) of strong habits, *Journal of Personality & Social Psychology* 104(6): 959–975, doi:10.1037/a0032626.

15. R. A. Bartsch, K. A. Case, and H. Meerman (2012), Increasing academic self-efficacy in statistics with a live vicarious experience presentation, *Teaching of Psychology* 39(2): 133–136, doi:10.1177/0098628312437699; P. R. Pintrich (2003), A motivational science perspective on the role of student motivation in learning and teaching contexts, *Journal of Educational Psychology* 95(4): 667–686, doi:10.1037/0022-0663.95.4.667.

16. A. Bandura (1986), *Social Foundations of Thought and Action: A Social Cognitive Theory* (Englewood Cliffs, NJ: Prentice-Hall); M. Bong and E. M. Skaalvik (2003), Academic self-concept and self-efficacy: How different are they really? *Educational Psychology Review* 15(1): 1–40.

17. R. A. Bartsch, K. A. Case, and H. Meerman (2012), Increasing academic self-efficacy in statistics with a live vicarious experience presentation, *Teaching of Psychology* 39(2): 133–136, doi:10.1177/0098628312437699.

18. P. R. Pintrich (2003), A motivational science perspective on the role of student motivation in learning and teaching contexts, *Journal of Educational Psychology* 95(4): 667–686, doi:10.1037/0022-0663.95.4.667.

19. Ibid.

20. M. V. Covington (2000), Intrinsic versus extrinsic motivation in schools: A reconciliation, *Current Directions in Psychological Science* 9(1): 22–25.

21. M. Vansteenkiste, W. Lens, and E. L. Deci (2006), Intrinsic versus extrinsic goal contents in self-determination theory: Another look at the quality of academic motivation, *Educational Psychologist* 41(1): 19–31, doi:10.1207/s15326985ep4101_4.

22. K. De Castella, D. Byrne, and M. Covington (2013), Unmotivated or motivated to fail? A cross-cultural study of achievement motivation, fear of failure, and student disengagement, *Journal of Educational Psychology* 105(3): 861–880, doi:10.1037/a0032464.

23. Ibid.

24. C. S. Dweck (2006), *Mindset: The New Psychology of Success* (New York: Random House).

25. F. Cury, D. da Fonseca, A. J. Elliot, and A. C. Moller (2006), The social model of achievement motivation and the 2 × 2 achievement goal framework, *Journal of Personality & Social Psychology* 90(4): 666–679, doi:10.1037/0022-3514.90.4.666.

26. C. S. Dweck (2007), The perils and promises of praise, *Educational Leadership* 65(2): 34–39.

27. Ibid.

28. A. Rattan, C. Good, and C. S. Dweck (2012), "It's OK—not everyone can be good at math": Instructors with an entity theory comfort (and demotivate) students, *Journal of Experimental Social Psychology* 48(3): 731–737, doi:10.1016/j.jesp.2011.12.012.

29. C. S. Dweck (2007), The perils and promises of praise, *Educational Leadership* 65(2): 34–39.

30. J. Aronson, C. B. Fried, and C. Good (2002), Reducing the effects of stereotype threat on African American college students by shaping theories of intelligence, *Journal of Experimental Social Psychology* 38(2): 113.

31. A. R. Artino (2008), Promoting academic motivation and self-regulation: Practical guidelines for online instructors, *Techtrends: Linking Research & Practice to Improve Learning* 52(3): 37–45, doi:10.1007/s11528-008-0153-x.

32. A. R. Artino and J. M. Stephens (2009), Academic motivation and self-regulation: A comparative analysis of undergraduate and graduate students learning online, *Internet & Higher Education* 12(3/4): 146–151, doi:10.1016/j.iheduc.2009.02.001.

33. I. E. Allen, J. Seaman, and C. Sloan (2007), *Online Nation: Five Years of Growth in Online Learning* (retrieved from http://sloanconsortium.org/publications/survey/online_nation).

34. G. C. Elvers, D. J. Polzella, and K. Graetz (2003), Procrastination in online courses: Performance and attitudinal differences, *Teaching of Psychology* 30(2): 159–162.

35. Ibid.

36. N. Michinov, S. Brunot, O. Le Bohec, J. Juhel, and M. Delaval (2011), Procrastination, participation, and performance in online learning environments, *Computers & Education* 56(1): 243–252, doi:10.1016/j.compedu.2010.07.025.

37. D. H. Schunk and B. J. Zimmerman (1997), Social origins of self-regulatory competence, *Educational Psychologist* 32(4): 195.

38. A. R. Artino (2008), Promoting academic motivation and self-regulation: Practical guidelines for online instructors, *Techtrends: Linking Research & Practice to Improve Learning* 52(3): 37–45, doi:10.1007/s11528-008-0153-x.

39. Ibid.

40. P. R. Pintrich, D. A. Smith, T. Garcia, and W. J. McKeachie (1993), Reliability and predictive validity of the Motivated Strategies for Learning Questionnaire (MSLQ), *Educational and Psychological Measurement* 53(3): 801–813, doi:10.1177/0013164493053003024.

41. A. R. Artino (2008), Promoting academic motivation and self-regulation: Practical guidelines for online instructors, *Techtrends: Linking Research & Practice to Improve Learning* 52(3): 37–45, doi:10.1007/s11528-008-0153-x; J. L. Whipp and S. Chiarelli (2004), Self-regulation in a web-based course: A case study, *Educational Technology Research and Development* 52(4): 5–22, doi:10.1007/BF02504714.

42. A. R. Artino (2008), Promoting academic motivation and self-regulation: Practical guidelines for online instructors, *Techtrends: Linking Research & Practice to Improve Learning* 52(3): 37–45, doi:10.1007/s11528-008-0153-x.

43. M. D. Miller and B. Scarnati (2013), Developing faculty capacity to support student success: The First Year Learning Initiative (talk presented at the Annual Sloan Consortium International Conference on Online Learning, Orlando, FL).

44. J. McGonigal (2011), *Reality Is Broken: Why Games Make Us Better and How They Can Change the World* (Amazon Kindle version).

45. M. D. Dickey (2005), Engaging by design: How engagement strategies in popular computer and video games can inform instructional design, *Educational Technology Research & Development* 53(2): 67–83, doi:10.1007/BF02504866; M. Dickey (2006), Game design narrative for learning: Appropriating adventure game design narrative devices and techniques for the design of interactive learning environments, *Educational Technology Research & Development* 54(3): 245–263, doi:10.1007/s11423-006-8806-y.

46. K. M. Kapp (2012), *The Gamification of Learning and Instruction: Game-Based Methods and Strategies for Training and Education* (Amazon Kindle version).

47. Ibid.

48. M. Csikszentmihalyi (1997), *Finding Flow: The Psychology of Engagement with Everyday Life* (New York: Basic Books).

49. J. McGonigal (2011), *Reality Is Broken: Why Games Make Us Better and How They Can Change the World* (Amazon Kindle version).

50. K. M. Kapp (2012), *The Gamification of Learning and Instruction: Game-Based Methods and Strategies for Training and Education* (Amazon Kindle version).

51. Ibid.

52. J. McGonigal (2011), *Reality Is Broken: Why Games Make Us Better and How They Can Change the World* (Amazon Kindle version).

53. Ibid.

54. K. M. Kapp (2012), *The Gamification of Learning and Instruction: Game-Based Methods and Strategies for Training and Education* (Amazon Kindle version).

55. Ibid.

9. PUTTING IT ALL TOGETHER

1. R. Goldstein (2010), Major developments in undergraduate psychology, *APS Observer* 23:23–26; M. Hebl, C. Brewer, and L. Benjamin (2000), *Handbook for Teaching Introductory Psychology*, vol. 2 (Mahwah, NJ: Lawrence Erlbaum Associates).

2. M. D. Miller and M. E. Rader (2010), Two heads are better than one: Collaborative development of an online course content template, *Journal of Online Learning and Teaching* 6:246–255.

3. M. Demir, M. Birkett, K. Dickson, and M. Miller, eds. (2012), *Psychological Science in Action: Applying Psychology to Everyday Issues* (San Diego: Cognella).

4. American Psychological Association (2007), *APA Guidelines for the Undergraduate Psychology Major* (Washington, DC: APA) (retrieved from www .apa.org/ed/resources.html).

5. Adapted from M. Demir, M. Birkett, K. Dickson, and M. Miller, eds. (2012), *Psychological Science in Action: Applying Psychology to Everyday Issues* (San Diego: Cognella).

Acknowledgments

THIS BOOK SPRINGS from my experiences as a cognitive psychologist immersed in scholarship on the mind, brain, and learning. It is built on the work of many brilliant researchers and theorists: Robert Bjork, John Bransford, Susan Ambrose, Mark McDaniel, H. L. Roediger, Nelson Cowan, Jeffrey Karpicke, Harold Pashler, Richard Mayer, Randi Martin, James Nairne, Daniel Simon, Keith Holyoak, Doug Rohrer, Mark Ashcraft, Alan Baddeley, and John Anderson, just to name a few who have influenced me the most. It is an honor to translate their work for an audience of non-psychologists, and I hope I have done an adequate job of conveying the power of their discoveries.

My academic life began with Donald G. MacKay, my mentor and graduate adviser. He took an eager but scattered college student and patiently turned me into a trained scientist—while never forgetting the sense of wonder and fun that brought us to this field in the first place. Don once told me that research is essentially play behavior, and this science-as-play philosophy has given me the courage to keep going where curiosity takes me, even when the routes are unconventional.

When author James Lang publicly praised one of my "translational" works in the *Chronicle of Higher Education* in 2011, it was one of the proudest moments of my career—and one of the most fateful, as it led directly to the creation of this book. Lang is part of a new wave of authors and researchers pushing for fundamental transformation in how we think about college teaching. I truly hope that this book further advances that important conversation.

Elizabeth Knoll, my editor at Harvard University Press, championed this book at every step of its creation, and without her leadership, it would simply not exist. I'm also grateful to Elizabeth for recruiting a set of insightful, kind, and incredibly knowledgeable reviewers, whose feedback was indispensable for improving the manuscript. Elizabeth's encouragement carried me—a first-timer at book writing—through more episodes of self-doubt and confusion than I can count. Through her thoughtful and rigorous editing of this and many other books, she has made an immense contribution to the scholarly literature on teaching and learning.

This book also wouldn't exist but for the support of my husband, J. Richard McDonald. Besides being supremely effective on the home front, Rick is an accomplished professional in the field of instructional technology—and thus he is my most important sounding board for ideas on how technology can complement learning. The concepts in this book took shape through many a conversation over dinner, laundry, coffee, and road trips. Rick also contributed research assistance to several chapters, and graciously served as the subject of the "expert knowledge" demonstration featured in Chapter 5. Having this kind of intellectual partnership built into the very foundation of one's life is a rare gift, and I am grateful for it every day.

I enjoy robust support at my university "home" as well. Northern Arizona University is a fertile environment for people who devote their lives to teaching and learning, and I have benefited from the passion, patience, and generosity of countless NAU faculty, staff, and administrators. First and foremost, I owe thanks to Linda Shadiow, who recently retired as the director of faculty development at NAU. It was Linda who encouraged me to take some of the essays I'd been writing for my graduate students and turn them into publications—a crucial first step toward writing this book. Linda's office also administers the President's Distinguished Teaching Fellows program, which has offered me both the opportunity to collaborate with NAU's best teachers and financial support for research and dissemination.

NAU's University College, and especially its dean, Karen Pugliesi, have also provided essential support for my work. Karen believed in the book from the very beginning, cheering me on as I cleared each hurdle in the race to publication and providing me with the time, space, and institutional affirmation that I needed to get the project done. I'm also grateful to the former dean of NAU's College of Social and Behavioral Sciences, Michael Stevenson, for pushing me to prioritize writing this book when I felt pulled to pieces by competing demands. And the NAU E-Learning Center, led by director Don Carter, has been a treasure trove of innovation, ideas, and support for exploring new frontiers in teaching with technology.

Collaborations with faculty colleagues have also been a source of strength throughout my time at NAU. Blase Scarnati, the cocreator of NAU's First Year Learning Initiative, has sparked my creativity in ways I couldn't have imagined and —through FYLI—has challenged me to explore new ways to promote powerful, learner-centered pedagogies and course designs. Elizabeth Brauer of NAU's Department of Electrical and Computer Engineering is one of the most forward-thinking educators I know; she has shown me exactly how cognitive principles can enhance a challenging, well-designed course. K. Laurie Dickson, who is now NAU's vice provost for curriculum and assessment, spearheaded the first scholarship of teaching and learning projects I ever worked on, opening up a whole new realm in which I could apply my training as a cognitive psychologist. With Blase, Liz, and Laurie, I've brainstormed, visioned, number-crunched, problem-solved, written and rewritten—some of the hardest work of my life, but also the most fun.

I come by writing honestly, being the daughter of a journalist and a textbook author who surrounded me with their love of the craft. My late father, Tommy Miller, once told me to "cherish the words"— and although he didn't get to see these particular words on paper, they are very much his legacy. And my mom, Darla Miller, has been an inexhaustible source of not just motherly but also professional encouragement—offering advice, reading feedback, helping me get past all the inevitable setbacks, and much more than I can say.

Index